The Computational Analysis of English

A Corpus-Based Approach

Edited by
Roger Garside
Geoffrey Leech
Geoffrey Sampson

LONGMAN

London and New York

Longman Group UK Limited,
Longman House, Burnt Mill, Harlow,
Essex CM20 2JE, England
and Associated Companies throughout the world.

Published in the United States of America
by Longman Inc., New York

First published 1987

British Library Cataloguing in Publication Data

The computational analysis of English: a
   corpus-based approach.
   1. English language – Data processing
   2. English language – Grammar – Theory,
   etc.
   I. Garside, Roger   II. Leech, Geoffrey
   III. Sampson, Geoffrey
   428'.028'5   PE1074.5

ISBN 0-582-29149-6

Library of Congress Cataloging in Publication Data

The Computational analysis of English.

   Bibliography: p.
   Includes index.
   1. English language – Data processing.   I. Garside,
Roger. II. Leech, Geoffrey. III. Sampson, Geoffrey.
PE1074.5.C66 1987   420'.28'5   86-33738
ISBN 0-582-29149-6

Printed and bound in Great Britain at the Bath Press, Avon.

Contents

Foreword		**v**
Notational conventions and abbreviations		**ix**
List of contributors		**xii**
Chapter 1	General introduction *Geoffrey Leech*	1
Chapter 2	Probabilistic models of analysis *Geoffrey Sampson*	16
Chapter 3	The CLAWS word-tagging system *Roger Garside*	30
Chapter 4	Tag selection using probabilistic methods *Ian Marshall*	42
Chapter 5	Constituent-likelihood grammar *Eric Atwell*	57
Chapter 6	The UCREL probabilistic parsing system *Roger Garside and Fanny Leech*	66
Chapter 7	The grammatical database and parsing scheme *Geoffrey Sampson*	82
Chapter 8	Text input and pre-processing: Dealing with ' the orthographic form of texts *Barbara Booth*	97
Chapter 9	Syntax versus orthography: Problems in the automatic parsing of idioms *Susan Blackwell*	110
Chapter 10	Dealing with ill-formed English text *Eric Atwell and Stephen Elliott*	120

Chapter 11   Automatic intonation assignment   139
                  Gerry Knowles and Lita Lawrence

Chapter 12   Towards a distributional lexicon   149
                  Andrew Beale

Appendix A   Sources of material   163
                  Roger Garside

Appendix B   Alternative grammatical coding systems   165
                  Geoffrey Sampson

References   184
Index   191

Foreword

1. Why this book?

This book describes a programme of research undertaken in the Unit for Computer Research on the English Language (UCREL) at the University of Lancaster from 1979 to 1986. UCREL is a research unit shared by the Departments of Computing and of Linguistics and Modern English Language. All the contributors to the book have participated in this research programme, which includes work at the University of Leeds as well as at the University of Lancaster.

It is distinctive of this research programme that it bases natural language processing (in this case the processing of English) on the analysis of a large corpus of naturally-occurring text. Another distinctive feature, not unconnected with the first, is the application of probabilistic methods to the computational analysis of language.

Neither of these features is unique to the UCREL research programme. The use of computer corpora has evolved over the past twenty-five years out of the pioneering work of Francis and Kučera in compiling the Brown University Corpus of American English (see pp. 4–9 and references on pp. 186–7). Our UCREL research has been so far largely based on the Lancaster-Oslo/Bergen Corpus (LOB Corpus) of British English texts, compiled so as to be a close match to the Brown Corpus.[†]

Equally, probabilistic methods, after long years of neglect, have recently begun to be taken seriously in natural language processing, particularly in the area of speech analysis, where important research has occurred at Carnegie-Mellon University (see e.g. Erman and Lesser 1980; Lowerre and Reddy 1980) and at the IBM Thomas J. Watson Research Center (see Bahl *et al*. 1983; Jelinek 1986).

[†] Other computer corpus-based research on English has been carried out in various European centres, notably at Lund (see Svartvik, Eeg-Olofsson, Forsheden *et al*. 1982), at Amsterdam and Nijmegen (see Aarts and Meijs 1984), at Birmingham (see Sinclair 1982; Renouf 1984), and at Oslo and Bergen. The Universities of Oslo and Bergen have acted as centres of information, dissemination, and co-ordination of computer corpus research under the organizational umbrella of ICAME (the International Computer Archive of Modern English). *ICAME Journal* (formerly *ICAME News*) provides an information source and research forum for the small but growing international community of scholars working in this field.

Nevertheless, we consider that the UCREL research reported here is in many ways a unique contribution, particularly in the area of grammatical analysis by computer, and that it opens up promising areas of research development and application which are of potential interest to a wide readership, including those researching or studying in the areas of linguistics (especially computational linguistics), computer science, information science, and the present-day English language. It is to students and researchers in these areas that this book is primarily addressed.

2.   The design and scope of the book

The book's design and scope can best be explained by a chapter-by-chapter outline of its contents.

Chapter 1 is a general introduction, explaining the rationale of the corpus-based approach, and describing the context of previous and current work in which the work of UCREL takes place.

Chapter 2 explains the role of probabilistic models and methods, contrasting these with the non-probabilistic models and methods more usually adopted in computational linguistics.

Chapters 3 and 4 deal with the implementation of these ideas in the grammatical word-tagging system known as CLAWS, which has been used in providing a version of the LOB Corpus in which every word is associated with its appropriate grammatical category.

Chapters 5 and 6 show how the techniques of CLAWS can be generalized to grammar as a whole, and can be extended to the syntactic analysis (i.e. parsing) of the LOB Corpus.

If the syntactic analysis of a large corpus of unrestricted English is to be undertaken, it is necessary to have an agreed parsing scheme, against which the computer's chosen parse of any given sentence is to be judged correct or incorrect. The parsing scheme used for the LOB Corpus is outlined in Chapter 7.

Chapter 8 describes an enhanced version of CLAWS (CLAWS2) which is designed to accept any English text in normal orthographic form. This chapter focuses on the problems of orthographic decoding (e.g. the interpretation of capital letters and of full-stops) which the new system has to handle.

Chapter 9 deals with another problematic area which cannot be ignored in the processing of a large unrestricted corpus: the treatment of grammatically idiosyncratic sequences which we term "idioms", although they only partially correspond to idioms in the normal sense.

The last three chapters deal with subsidiary research projects which are not an essential part of the main LOB corpus analysis programme, but which illustrate how its basic methodology can be extended into related areas.

Chapter 10 deals with the task of adapting the CLAWS system to the detection of errors in texts. The chapter's main purpose is to show how probabilistic techniques can be applied to the general area of text critiquing, and especially to the identification of errors in spelling.

Chapter 11 illustrates another field of practical application: speech synthesis. Although corpora of written texts, such as the LOB Corpus, are more readily obtainable in machine-readable form, corpora of spoken texts, such as a small corpus now being compiled at Lancaster, are an important resource for research in speech processing, and once again the methodology of probabilistic grammatical analysis is applicable.

Chapter 12 turns to a third area of extended application: the compilation of a distributional lexicon, i.e. a lexicon which contains information about the frequency of lexical and grammatical co-occurrences. Such a lexical database is intended eventually to serve as a yardstick against which to evaluate computer-generated texts, to see how nearly they approximate to "natural, idiomatic" English.

Among the values which we hope this book will have for many readers are detailed descriptions of: (a) program algorithms; and (b) systems of classification and anlaysis for English. In neither area, however, do we provide the depth of information which researchers would need if they were to attempt to replicate our methods. To have done so would have been to add prohibitively to the length of the book: it should be borne in mind, in particular, that any adequate natural language processing system requires both a lexicon and a grammar – and that both of these, if completeness is aimed at, are data structures of immense size. In practice, then, we have tried to achieve a reasonable compromise between generality of explanation and exhaustiveness of detail.

Two Appendices provide additional documentation. Appendix A gives details of how to obtain copies, for further research, of those corpora and computer programs which are publicly available. Appendix B gives a detailed comparison of different word-classification systems (tagsets) employed in UCREL research and in related projects. This second Appendix will be useful in providing explanations of symbols occurring in various chapters, especially chapters 3, 4, 6, 8 and 9.

3. Acknowledgements

The work of the UCREL team rests on a long history (from the beginnings of the LOB Corpus in 1970) of human effort which includes that of contributors to this book, but also includes assistance, often vital and time-consuming, provided by others. The list of those who deserve acknowledgement is therefore long. It includes Rosemary Leonard, for indispensable work on the LOB Corpus in its earlier stages, and Stig Johansson, Knut Hofland, and Jostein Hauge (of the Universities of Oslo and Bergen) for taking on the onerous task of completing the Corpus in Norway. Stig Johansson, Knut Hofland, and Mette-Cathrine Jahr also merit our gratitude for their important Norwegian contribution to the joint research project which developed CLAWS and the tagged LOB Corpus. Another essential contribution was that generously provided by Nelson Francis and Henry Kučera, of Brown University, in allowing us to make use of the results of their own research on the Brown Corpus.

Without funding resources, the UCREL programme could not have survived or made progress. We acknowledge gratefully the financial support of the following: in the compilation of the LOB Corpus, Longman Group Ltd and the British Academy; for the grammatical tagging of the LOB Corpus, the Social Science Research Council (now the ESRC) (Research Grant HR 7081/1); for collaborative research at Oslo and Bergen, the Norwegian Research Council for Science and the Humanities; for further research on the tagging and parsing of the LOB Corpus, the Science and Engineering Research Council (Research Grant GR/C/47700); for textual error detecting as described in Chapter 10, International Computers Ltd. Those of us at Lancaster gratefully acknowledge the support of the IBM (UK) Scientific Centre, and the Humanities Research Committee of the University of Lancaster, for the speech synthesis project described in Chapter 11; in this project, we have particularly valued the help and collaboration of Geoffrey Kaye, Briony Williams, and Peter Alderson, all of the IBM (UK) Scientific Centre, Winchester. Those of us at Leeds, likewise, are grateful to the RSRE Speech Research Unit, Malvern, for sponsorship of research on parsing by simulated annealing discussed in Chapters 2 and 5. Chapters 3, 4 and 6 are based in part on earlier publications. For permission to use the republished material in Chapter 3, we thank Slatkine Reprints; for permission to use that in Chapter 4, we thank the journal *Computers and the Humanities*; and for permission to use that in Chapter 6, we thank the Association for Computational Linguistics.

R.G.G. University of Lancaster
G.N.L. University of Lancaster
G.R.S. University of Leeds
July 1986

Notational conventions and abbreviations

The research discussed in this book frequently involves close attention to details of English orthography and typography. This inevitably makes the book itself somewhat complex typographically. The conventions we have used are as follows.

Forms quoted as examples of English, whether taken from the LOB Corpus, from other sources, or (in a few cases) invented, are printed in *italics*. Often a quoted example will include indications of its structural analysis, as decided by a linguist or output by an automatic parser: roman type is used to distinguish such elements from the material which occurs on the original printed page. For instance, a roman square bracket represents a constituent boundary, while an italic bracket represents a punctuation mark found in the text under analysis (which may or may not occur at a grammatical constituent boundary).

The grammatical category of a constituent is marked by a label in roman type (drawn from a class of labels discussed in Chapter 7) immediately *following* the roman opening square bracket marking the beginning of the constituent. It is not usually necessary to repeat the label at the corresponding closing bracket (since nesting structure shows which closing brackets pair with which opening brackets); but if a closing bracket is labelled, in order to clarify a complex example, then the label appears immediately *before* the closing bracket. (In other words, category labels are always written inside the brackets they label.)

When quoted examples include structural analysis, only as much of this is shown as is needed to make the point at issue. Low-level constituents are often ignored.

Examples quoted from the LOB Corpus are followed by reference numbers in round brackets, for instance "(G24 63)". These identify the location of the example within the Corpus. The element before the space in such a reference identifies one of the 500 texts in the Corpus (in this case, the 24th text within Category G); the element after the space identifies a line or lines within that text. (Line numbers refer to the "horizontal" version of the Corpus, which is arranged like an ordinary written document with many words per line, as opposed to the "vertical" version in which each line contains a single word only.) The composition of the LOB Corpus is explained in Chapter 1. Detailed information about the individual texts corresponding to the various text numbers is given in Johansson *et al.* (1978); for instance, text G24 is a passage from Walter O. Bentley, *The Cars in My Life* (Hutchinson).

The LOB Corpus contains many special coding conventions (again, see Johansson *et al.* 1978 for details). Some of these stem from limitations of computer character-sets, which were more restrictive in the years when the Corpus was being assembled than they are today: thus the pound sign is represented in the Corpus as asterisk followed by plus sign, *+; a Spanish tilde is represented as *?4 following the letter on which it appears. Other codes were introduced in order to identify linguistic features which are not regularly marked explicitly in ordinary orthography: for instance, abbreviations (whether or not ending in stops) are preceded in the Corpus by the symbol-sequence \0. Some codes represent typographical shifts: *4 means "begin bold face". And, in the "vertical" version of the Corpus (see above), which includes one word per line, there are special symbols associated with the fact that continuous character-sequences are sometimes divided into more than one "word": an enclitic such as the *n't* of *don't* is treated as a separate word and placed on a line of its own, but the fact that it is written continuously with the preceding root is marked by a greater-than sign: >*n't*.

In quoting examples from the Corpus we have normally translated these various special codes back into the ordinary orthographic forms they represent, so that *+ is replaced by £, \0 is omitted, and so on. But occasionally the LOB coding convention is relevant to the point under discussion, and in such cases we quote the form as it appears in the Corpus.

Since the italic v. roman distinction is used to represent the distinction between quoted text and structural analysis, it cannot be used to mark the typographical distinction between roman and italics in an original text. A few examples quoted in this book do contain roman/italic contrasts in the original, but in no case do these contrasts seem significant in relation to the context in which they are quoted. Rather than burdening the reader with further notational complexities, we have suppressed the distinction in these cases and printed the whole in italics. (The distinction is of course preserved in the LOB Corpus itself.)

When examples of a linguistic problem are drawn from authentic texts such as those in the LOB Corpus, they frequently contain irrelevant wording which is best omitted for the sake of clarity of exposition. The normal indication of ellipsis is a series of three stops ...; but this punctuation mark can also occur as part of the text being quoted, and the italic v. roman contrast is incapable of distinguishing these cases. Therefore we have borrowed a convention from the programming language Pascal, and use *two* stops .. in order to indicate an omission within a quoted sequence, or to indicate that a sentence begins earlier than or continues beyond the material quoted. The two-stop symbol does not occur as a standard English punctuation mark; the three-stop symbol, on the other hand, always represents punctuation appearing in the original text.

Finally, the following acronyms and abbreviations are frequently used:

AI: artificial intelligence

Brown Corpus: the Brown University Standard Corpus of Present-Day American English (see Francis and Kučera 1964)

CL: computational linguistics

CLAWS: Constituent-Likelihood Automatic Word-tagging System

CLAWS1, CLAWS2:   where necessary we distinguish the earlier version of CLAWS, CLAWS1, from the later version, CLAWS2

IC: immediate constituent (Wells 1947)

ICAME: the International Computer Archive of Modern English, University of Bergen

IT: information technology

KWIC: Key Word In Context, a type of computer-generated concordance which displays, for each token of a given word-type in a corpus, a line centred on that word and showing a few preceding and following words

LOB Corpus: the Lancaster-Oslo/Bergen Corpus of British English

MT: machine translation

NL: natural language

UCREL: Unit for Computer Research on the English Language, University of Lancaster

w.i.c.:   word-initial capital.

List of Contributors

Eric Atwell is a Lecturer in Computer Studies, University of Leeds

Andrew Beale is a Research Associate in the Department of Linguistics and Modern English Language, University of Lancaster

Susan Blackwell is a Research Associate in the Department of Computing, University of Lancaster

Barbara Booth is a Research Associate in the Department of Computing, University of Lancaster

Stephen Elliott is a Research Associate in the Department of Linguistics and Modern English Language, University of Lancaster

Roger Garside is a Lecturer in the Department of Computing, University of Lancaster

Gerry Knowles is a Lecturer in the Department of Linguistics and Modern English Language, University of Lancaster

Lita Lawrence is a Research Associate in the Department of Linguistics and Modern English Language, University of Lancaster

Fanny Leech is Information Officer in the Department of Computing, University of Lancaster

Geoffrey Leech is Professor of Linguistics and Modern English Language, University of Lancaster

Ian Marshall is a Lecturer in the Department of Mathematics, Computing and Statistics, Leicester Polytechnic

Geoffrey Sampson is Professor of Linguistics, University of Leeds

CHAPTER 1

General introduction

Geoffrey Leech

1. The corpus-based approach

The progress of science is often pictured as a continuing process of divergence and specialization, the result of which is increasing lack of communication between those working in different fields. But the most exciting and creative developments are often those which go in the other direction, uniting diverse disciplines in a common enterprise. Such a convergence took place in the 1950s and 1960s, when the new "science" of *artificial intelligence* (AI) was born out of a common effort by computer scientists, psychologists, logicians and others to see if they could teach computers to "think" and behave (in certain respects) like human beings.

In this book we shall present another example of convergence of specialisms – this time, in an effort to teach computers (in certain respects) to be capable of understanding and processing human language. Since we shall confine our attention to one human language – English – the relevant specialisms are computer science, English language, and the interdisciplinary field of *computational linguistics* (CL). This merger of different disciplines or subdisciplines has seemed an extremely promising development to its participants, including the contributors to this volume, who adopt a *corpus-based* paradigm within computational linguistics.

We feel that this approach deserves a larger audience, both because of its intrinsic interest, and because of the future value of the results of this research.

There is a problem, in such a situation, of being unable to rely on a ready-made readership. Those who read this book may come from a variety of backgrounds – including, let us say, computer science, linguistics (including computational linguistics), cognitive science, and applied language studies. We shall try to avoid the dangers of including material which is either too elementary or too difficult for any group of readers. This involves compromises, but perhaps, if we are successful, the result will be that the book will reach out to a new kind of readership.

The methods associated with computational linguistics over the past 15 years have been deeply influenced by the outlook of researchers in AI. But the parallel between AI and the research we are going to describe should not be pressed too far. In fact, if this book achieves its purpose, there will be less inclination in the future than there has been in the past to assume that the paradigm of AI is the only one to be successfully applied to natural language processing.[†]

The AI approach is based on the assumption that computers, in order to process natural language, must be able to draw on an extensive resource of knowledge about the world to which the natural language makes reference, and must also have an ability to reason, i.e. to draw inferences on the basis of that knowledge. It is fairly well established that human minds, when they process language, do indeed rely on cognitive capabilities of these kinds, and the natural conclusion, for those who believe that "artificial intelligence" should copy human intelligence, is that computers should copy human intelligence as closely as possible in the processing of natural language, just as in other operations which simulate human mental behaviour.

We can see that this *knowledge-based* and *inference-based* approach is plausible not only for natural language processing but also for other fields where the goal is to provide machines with human-like capabilities: e.g. in motor skills (robotics), or in sensory perception (for example, vision). In cases of this kind, research in cognitive psychology has tended to confirm the view (contrary to the once strongly-held tenets of behaviourism) that the human mind interprets stimuli from its environment, and initiates responses to its environment, by drawing on rich mental structures and complex reasoning processes. However, whereas in fields such as inferencing, robotics, and sensory perception probabilistic information has been assumed to be important, the dominant view in computational linguistics has been that probabilistic information and quantitative methods in general have little or no part in the way human beings process language. This has meant that the AI paradigm, for purposes of natural language processing, has been interpreted in a particularly inflexible way.

In contrast, the methods adopted in our investigations, and in some others to which we shall make reference, rely heavily on probabilities. To obtain the necessary frequency data, we have to analyse a large enough body of naturally occurring texts in English (or in some other language) so that realistic predictions can be made on the basis of observed frequencies. There is therefore an important reliance, in this probabilistic approach, on machine-readable collections of text, i.e. on *machine-readable corpora*. Hence the approach which contrasts with the AI-based approach comes to be called *corpus-based*.

The contrast between the AI-based approach and the corpus-based approach needs some elaboration, and this is a major theme of Geoffrey Sampson's Chapter 2 below. But one observation may be made at this stage; that natural language processing offers a particularly difficult challenge to the AI-based approach. Let us for a moment assume, in accordance with the AI approach, that language cannot be successfully analysed without a knowledge resource which enables all relevant references to, and

---

[†] The term *natural language processing* is commonly applied, these days, to research designed to enable computers to analyse or generate textual material in a human language such as English. The term "natural language" (NL) has been preferred to "human language" in computer science, perhaps because of the opposition which has been recognized, both in logic and in computing, between the *natural languages* which human beings acquire in infancy and the *artificial languages* which are developed through research (including *computer languages*).

facts about, the world outside the computer to be represented in some kind of data resource within the computer. (This is the machine's equivalent of man's "knowledge of the world".) It is clear that the store of machine knowledge required to process natural language is greater than that required for other fields of man–machine interaction. Apart from language, the richest vehicle for incoming information from the computer's environment (if it is to simulate human information processing) is vision. But a visual input device needs knowledge which is only a part of the knowledge that may be needed to process natural language: i.e. knowledge regarding visible concrete objects in the computer's immediate environment. The knowledge needed to process any incoming message in a natural language such as English must include much more than this (e.g. knowledge of abstractions, of relations between past, present, and future events) and is of barely imaginable complexity. Hence, in practice, all natural language processing performed according to the AI paradigm must operate on the basis of a relatively impoverished (and in practice severely limited) knowledge resource. For the foreseeable future, AI-based natural language processing will be *domain-limited*; i.e. it will operate only with discourse relating to a restricted subject matter or purpose. (Well-known successful examples of such domain-limited systems are LUNAR (see Woods 1977), METEO (Thouin 1982) and the Linguistic String Parser (Sager 1981), dealing respectively with the geology of lunar rocks, weather forecasts, and scientific and technical reports.

On the other hand, the corpus-based approach to natural language processing makes no claim to being able to interpret language in an entirely human-like manner. (But note Sampson's argument, Chapter 2, pp. 22, 26, that human language processing may in some ways be more like this approach than like the orthodox AI-based approach.) The assumption of the corpus-based approach, on the contrary, is that if we analyse quantitatively a sufficiently large amount of language data, we will be able to compensate for the computer's lack of sophisticated knowledge and powers of inference, at least to a considerable extent. The strength of the corpus-based approach is that, through probabilistic predictions, it is able to deal with any kind of English language text which is presented to it: it is eminently robust. Its weakness is that the very reliance on probability admits the possibility of error. The probabilistic system makes the best "guess" available to it, based on textual material that has been analysed in the past.

This combination of strength and weakness is the exact opposite of the AI-based system, which assumes (if the knowledge relative to a given set of utterances can be replicated in the computer) that 100% successful processing is possible, but which falls short of the ability to deal with uncensored, unrestricted text.

We would argue that the two approaches are complementary: they are, we suggest, digging the same tunnel from opposite ends, and at some future time may meet somewhere in the middle. By this we mean that while future research within the AI-based paradigm must be in the direction of broadening the domain of discourse, future research within the corpus-based paradigm must be in the direction of increasing the degree of accuracy and the analytic depth of present-day systems: in so far as these complementary research programmes are successful, they will tend to eliminate the differences between the results of the two types of methodology. In fact, the two methodologies will probably contribute to one another's success.

This argument supports the claim that the corpus-based approach deserves more attention than it has received up to now. The claim is not that the AI-based approach should be *displaced* by the corpus-based approach, but that both approaches should receive adequate support. In terms of currently practical applications, the AI-based approach is the one which best suits *natural language front ends* (such as *question-and-answer systems* for databases), and some other tasks (e.g. some types of *machine translation*) where accuracy is at a premium and where the domain can be highly restricted. On the other hand, the corpus-based approach is more suitable for *man—machine interface* research where the goal is to produce computer systems which will accept any input in a given natural language. These research goals include *speech recognition* (decoding spoken language); *text-to-speech systems* (converting written input into spoken output); *optical character recognition* ("reading" printed or written texts); *text critiquing* (evaluating a machine-readable text in terms of correctness, stylistic acceptability, etc.); and various information processing tasks which do not require 100% accuracy, but require economical analysis of large quantities of varied textual data.

2.   Machine-readable corpora of English texts

To explain the background to corpus-based research, it will be necessary to look back twenty-five years to the days of relatively primitive computer technology.

The first well-known computer corpus to be compiled was the *Brown Corpus* (officially known as the Brown University Standard Corpus of Present-day American English), consisting of just over a million text-words of written American English taken from texts published in 1961. (Fuller details of the composition of this and of other corpora are given below.) The Corpus became available for academic research in 1964: it was "published" in the form of magnetic tape, and accompanied by a Manual of Information (Francis and Kučera 1964). The main aim of the devisers of the Corpus (W. Nelson Francis and Henry Kučera) was to contribute to linguistic research. The importance of a corpus as an empirical basis for linguistic descriptions had been stressed by linguists in the years preceding the publication of the Brown Corpus (e.g. in Quirk 1960); Francis and Kučera's innovation was to see the advantages of making such a corpus machine-readable. But, particularly in the USA, the early 1960s were an inopportune time to be compiling such a corpus, since a dominant trend of linguistics in that period (and to some extent still today) rejects the value of a corpus as a database for linguistic research. Nevertheless, within a few years of the Brown Corpus's "publication", over 160 copies had been acquired by other academic institutions, and the Corpus had been found useful for research in many different fields – not only in linguistics, but in education, psychology, philosophy, stylistics, and technology, to mention but a few (see Francis 1980: 193; Johansson 1986a).

In 1970 a parallel project was begun at the University of Lancaster, with the aim of compiling a corpus of British English which as far as practicable would match the Brown Corpus in terms of its composition. Owing to many difficulties, the project's completion was delayed; indeed, it would not have been completed at all if it had not been for timely and generous help from Norway: Stig Johansson (University of Oslo), with Jostein Hauge and Knut Hofland (of the Norwegian Computing Centre for the Humanities, Bergen), was able to finish in 1978 the compilation of the corpus, which has since become known as the LOB Corpus (or in full, the Lancaster/Oslo-Bergen Corpus of British English). Like the Brown Corpus, the LOB Corpus is available for use in academic research, and has been widely distributed in the form of magnetic tape.

Any reader who is used to the inputting of text in large quantities by the use of new technologies (especially optical character readers) will no doubt be mystified by the length of time it took us to complete the rather moderate-sized LOB Corpus, consisting of a little over a million words. In fact, the Lancaster experience was a particularly bad example of the difficulties which beset the creators of computer corpora in the 1960s and 1970s, and to some extent even now. It will be useful to list and explain the major difficulties, as in part they account for the fact that computer corpora still belong to an underfunded, underdocumented and underresearched area. For example, there is as yet no bibliographical register of computer corpora, and it is often only by hearsay, or by reading the footnotes of research reports, that one finds out about some of the large, though largely ill-organized, resources of machine-readable modern English text that exist in the world.[†]

The main difficulties have been these:

(a)   Up to the later 1970s, the only reliable source of machine-readable text was manual input (by keyboard). The facilities on mainframe computers for proofreading, editing, etc. of large quantities of text were primitive.

(b)   The problem of copyright bedevilled, and continues to bedevil, the input and storage of text in a computer. As a result, some computer corpora in private use are unobtainable; others can be used only for restricted purposes; others are available for academic research but cannot be made use of elsewhere, e.g. in commercial contexts.

(c)   Funding has, until recently, been difficult to obtain, on the grounds that before a computer corpus has been developed, it is difficult to justify the amount of time and effort which goes into its preparation. The research value of a corpus can generally be seen only in retrospect.

Of these three difficulties, the first one is now largely a matter of past history, because of the availability of OCRs (optical character readers), and an explosive growth in the quantities of ready-made machine-readable text (through the

---

[†] Tribute should be paid, however, to the work of Stig Johansson and his colleagues in Oslo and Bergen in improving this situation since the founding of the International Computer Archive of Modern English (ICAME) in 1977. Johansson is secretary of ICAME, and the founder-editor of the *ICAME Journal*, an international organ of information obtainable from the Norwegian Computing Centre for the Humanities (see Appendix A).

development of computer typesetting and word processing technologies). Even so, the developing technologies of text processing have not overcome the difficulties of obtaining error-free texts, or of translating texts from the format in which they were obtained into a format suitable for research (often a cryptographic task of some subtlety).

Apart from the Brown and LOB Corpora, other well-known English language computer corpora include the London–Lund Corpus (consisting of *c.* 435 000 words of spoken British English text from the Survey of English Usage – see Svartvik and Quirk 1980, Svartvik, Eeg-Olofsson, Forsheden *et al.* 1982), and the Leuven Drama Corpus (consisting of about a million words of British English dramatic texts – see Geens *et al.* 1975). On a much larger scale are the Birmingham Collection of English Text (an ongoing compilation for lexicographic research, currently reported to contain more than 20 million words – see Renouf 1984), and the Oxford Text Archive, containing a whole library of texts of various languages and periods for humanities research (see Oxford 1983). On a still larger scale, research on speech recognition at IBM's Thomas J. Watson Research Center in New York is reported to be using a corpus of about 60 million words as just one of a number of English text corpora on which research is in progress. (The Mead Data Corporation, based in the USA, is rumoured to have a text bank of 5 billion words for on-line database information retrieval services!)

The concept of a finite "standard" corpus, such as the Brown Corpus and the LOB Corpus were designed to be, is already out of date. As John Sinclair (compiler of the Birmingham Collection) points out (Sinclair 1982), the problem of data-capture, for corpus-based research, is becoming a question of how to select, from the vast quantities of machine-readable text in existence, the right sample for a particular purpose. Even so, for the purposes of grammatical analysis (or parsing), which is the main kind of research reported in this book, it is advantageous and convenient to work with a manageable corpus containing a balanced cross-section of different English text types. For developing parsing programs, the need for very large quantities of up-to-date text is less important, for example, than it is for lexical research. For this reason, our research at Lancaster and Leeds continues to be based largely on the LOB Corpus, which also has the advantage of being a virtually error-free representation of the original texts in their printed form.

3.   The composition of the Brown and LOB Corpora

The Brown Corpus and the LOB Corpus contain almost equivalent numbers of text extracts of the same varieties. Since these corpora will be referred to frequently in the following chapters, it is useful to give a summary of their contents. The basic unit of content, for each corpus, is a text extract (described familiarly as a "text", although few of the extracts constitute a single complete text). Each text contains 2000 text-words (i.e. word-tokens), or just over: a text ends at the first sentence-break on or after the 2000th word.

Table 1: Composition of the Brown and LOB Corpora

Text category (genre)		Number of texts	
		Brown	LOB
A	Press: reportage	44	44
B	Press: editorial	27	27
C	Press: reviews	17	17
D	Religion	17	17
E	Skills and hobbies	36	38
F	Popular lore	48	44
G	Belles lettres, biography, memoirs, etc.	75	77
H	Miscellaneous (mainly government documents)	30	30
J	Learned (including science and technology)	80	80
K	General fiction	29	29
L	Mystery and detective fiction	24	24
M	Science fiction	6	6
N	Adventure and western fiction	29	29
P	Romance and love story	29	29
R	Humour	9	9
Total		500	500

Why were the contents of the Brown and LOB Corpora subdivided as indicated in Table 1? With regard to the LOB Corpus, the subdivision was simply a close imitation of that of the Brown Corpus, in order to facilitate comparisons between British and American English. As for the Brown Corpus itself, the general composition of the corpus was decided with the help of a panel of "corpus-wise" scholars, who laid down principles of selection according to "a combination of plan, practical necessity, and randomness" (Francis 1979):

(a)   Given the state of computer technology at the time, a million words was the most that could be reasonably aimed at with the funds available.

(b)   Given the figure of a million words, the whole range of varieties of English could not be included, and therefore a limitation to *printed prose* was accepted. (See Francis 1980: 194 on the notion of "edited prose".)

(c)   Nevertheless, within the area of printed prose, a widely representative range of text-types, including fiction and non-fiction, should be included.

Once the distribution of texts among categories had been decided, however, the actual selection of texts was determined by random sampling, to ensure that no subjective preferences entered into the actual choice of this or that text. (For details see Francis 1980: 195; Johansson *et al.* 1978: 7–9, 21–40.)

4. The analysis of corpora

A machine-readable corpus can be stored in various formats or versions, which may differ considerably in the kind and amount of information they give to the user. Most obviously and neutrally, a corpus can be stored in a "raw" orthographic form, that is with the texts in the same form as they would have on a normal written page, with words represented by strings of characters separated by spaces. The compilers of the Brown and LOB Corpora had as their aim the representation of the corpus texts in such a way as to preserve in the computer all linguistically-relevant information in the originals. This was rather like attempting to make a computational "photocopy" of the texts, except that certain (e.g. pictorial) material was omitted, and certain other information was recoded in a form suitable for the computer. (Details of the orthographic "coding" of the Brown and LOB Corpora are given in the respective users' manuals, Francis and Kučera 1964 and Johansson *et al.* 1978.) For certain purposes, this amount of information may be unnecessary; for example, for producing orthographically sorted word-frequency lists (e.g. those of Kučera and Francis 1967; Carroll *et al.* 1971; and Hofland and Johansson 1982), punctuation symbols are generally otiose. On the other hand, other types of information, not available in the original orthographical representation of the text, may be very important. For example, in lexicographical research, it may be considered essential to sort word-tokens according to their membership of lexemes or *lemmas: look, looks, looked*, and *looking* being grouped together as instances of the same verb lemma *LOOK*. This, however, cannot be done automatically on the basis of spelling alone. Not only does morphological irregularity cause problems, but the prevalence of homography (a particularly severe problem for English) means that we cannot assume that all word tokens of the same spelling belong to the same lemma: *look* and *looks*, for example, may belong either to *LOOK* (noun) or to *LOOK* (verb). Thus, to generate a *lemmatized* word frequency list from a computer corpus, we have either to sort word-tokens manually, or to program the computer with enough "grammatical knowledge" for this *disambiguation* to be performed automatically (see Ch. 12 below).

   Such problems arise particularly when we want to use a computer corpus for retrieval of grammatical information. For example, to find all instances of perfective verb phrases in the corpus, we need to be able to identify all instances of the auxiliary *HAVE* followed by a past participle; but the recognition of a past participle is not possible on the basis of orthography alone. Considerations like this have led to research projects with the objective of producing an annotated or pre-analysed version of a corpus. The Brown and LOB Corpora, for example, now exist not only in "raw" form, but in a *grammatically tagged* version, in which each word-token is accompanied by a label indicating its grammatical category, or part of speech. (See especially Chapters 3 and 4, and Appendix B, below.) Although in principle the word-by-word tagging can be done manually, by human intervention, in practice there are a number of advantages (especially speed and consistency) in developing computer programs or systems to perform the tagging as far as possible automatically.

   The grammatical tagging of the Brown Corpus was undertaken at Brown

University during the period 1970–78, with the aid of a program TAGGIT written by B. B. Greene and G. M. Rubin (Greene and Rubin 1971; Francis 1980). Further discussion of this program will be found on pp. 30 and 42ff below, and for the present we will merely note that it attained a success-rate of *c.* 77–78% in disambiguating grammatical homographs, the remaining *c.* 22–23% being disambiguated by hand. If this strikes the reader as an unremarkable achievement, it is worth bearing in mind that English is a notoriously ambiguous language with respect to homography – for example, in the eight-word sentence *Norman forced her to cut down on smoking* each word is grammatically ambiguous, so that about 3500 different word-class labellings of this sentence (in terms of the labels provided by the LOB tagset) are in theory possible. It is also worth recalling that the vocabulary of a corpus is large and unrestricted: the Brown Corpus and the LOB Corpus each contain *c.* 50 000 graphic word-types. In this light, the grammatical tagging of a corpus is a formidable task, and the Brown project is seen to be a considerable pioneering achievement.

The grammatical tagging of the LOB Corpus was undertaken during the years 1978–83 as a combined research effort by Lancaster, Oslo, and Bergen Universities. Through the generosity of the Brown University team, we were able to make use of the two products of their tagging project: (a) the tagged Corpus itself; and (b) the TAGGIT automatic tagging program. The result of this was the development of a new automatic tagging system CLAWS1, as described in more detail especially in Chapters 3 and 4 below. CLAWS1 employed a probabilistic method of disambiguation, choosing what it calculated to be the most likely tag in all cases of homography, even where the calculation resulted in a near-tie between two or more alternative tags. CLAWS1 made an error in 3% to 4% of word-tokens, and in these cases its output had to be manually corrected.[†]

Some of the results of the Brown grammatical tagging project were published in Francis and Kučera (1982). In particular, this book contained lemmatized word frequency lists of the Brown Corpus. Similar lists are in preparation for the tagged LOB Corpus, for which a lemmatized concordance is already available.

Grammatical tagging is one kind of corpus analysis, and it is a relatively simple kind, when one bears in mind the vastly more complex tasks humans perform in processing natural language. But it illustrates a general methodology which may be adapted to more abstract and sophisticated levels of analysis, such as syntactic analysis (*parsing*) and semantic analysis. Work on the analysis of the LOB Corpus has now progressed to the extent that we are engaged in the parsing of the whole Corpus, and have developed programs to perform this analysis by probabilistic disambiguation methods similar to those of CLAWS1 (see Chs. 5, 6 and 7 below). If we include

---

[†] The measurement of "success-rate", in the case of the LOB tagging project, meant subtracting from the total those words which were erroneously tagged, since, unlike TAGGIT, CLAWS1 always selects a preferred tag. Punctuation tags (which were always unambiguously tagged) were discounted in calculating the success rate. Before the tagged LOB Corpus was made available to the academic community, it went through three stages of proofreading and correction. The final stage of proofreading (undertaken by Stig Johansson) involved many thousands of changes designed to achieve linguistic consistency throughout the corpus.

word-tagging and syntactic analysis under "parsing" in a more general sense, then the central theme of this book may be said to be the development of *corpus-based parsing systems*.

Although I have focused in this section on analysis of the Brown and LOB Corpora, similar developments in automatic or computer-aided corpus analysis have taken place in other centres, for example at the Universities of Lund, Nijmegen, and Amsterdam (see Svartvik, Eeg-Olofsson, Forsheden, *et al.* 1982; Aarts and Meijs 1984; Meijs 1987).

5. State of the art in computer corpus research

All this research takes place on a long time scale, on which gradual improvement of computer systems is to be expected, rather than sudden and dramatic advances. The output from one project provides the input to another, more advanced one: for example, at Lancaster we are now developing a new word-tagging system, CLAWS2, in which use is being made of the results of the CLAWS1 project (see Ch. 8). If one takes the view (cf. Kuhn 1962) that science progresses by revolution, whereas technology progresses chiefly by evolution – that is, by gradual improvement of design in the light of feedback of information from past performance of the artefact – then our model of progress is technological rather than scientific. From this point of view, the products of the CLAWS1 project, like the products of the Brown tagging project, were twofold: (1) a newly analysed or annotated version of the corpus; and (2) a program, or analytic system. Both (1) and (2) now provide the input to CLAWS2, just as the Brown tagged corpus and TAGGIT provided an input to CLAWS1. The corpus (1) provides a frequency database for enhancing the probabilistic predictions of the analytic system; and the performance of the system itself, including examination of its errors, provides feedback for the development of an improved system of the next "generation".

Of course, the technological model of progress is not all a matter of gradual evolution. There may be sudden breakthroughs, e.g. when radically new design features are adopted, and we would claim that such a breakthrough took place when a probabilistic disambiguation model was adopted for CLAWS1.

The evolutionary model, at its most general, can be represented as in Figure 1 (in which the dashed box and arrows represent the feedback part of the system):

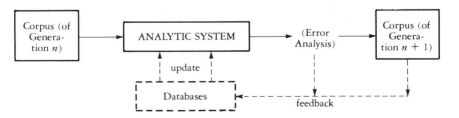

Figure

(Comparison may be drawn with the self-organizing principle employed in large-scale text analysis for probabilistic speech recognition systems – see Jelinek 1986.)

There is another sense in which progress in corpus-based research is gradual and evolutionary, a system of one generation standing on the shoulders of the preceding generation. This is in the step-by-step progress from less abstract to more abstract levels of analysis. Starting from the concept of an annotated corpus, we can envisage progressively enriched versions of the same corpus, in which representations of orthographic, then syntactic, then semantic, then pragmatic information sources are added. Likewise, we may think of successive stages in a transduction process whereby one level of text representation is replaced by another, more abstract representation of the same text, as in Figure 2:

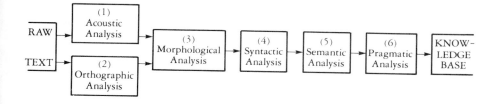

Figure 2 can be regarded as a model of computer text comprehension: an ultimate goal to which research in automatic corpus analysis is directing itself. Most work so far is being done in the area of grammatical analysis ((3) and (4)), but semantic analysis, especially with the limited goal of disambiguating word senses (*sense resolution*), is a prospect on the horizon.

The following are brief comments on the levels of analysis distinguished in Figure 2.

(1) **Orthographic analysis:** Certain disambiguations have to be carried out at the orthographic level. They include interpreting capitalization (for example, a word-initial capital (w.i.c.), as in *Brown*, can indicate the beginning of a sentence or the beginning of a proper noun). A full stop (.) can indicate the end of a sentence or the end of an abbreviation. See further Chapter 8.

(2) **Acoustic analysis:** In speech recognition research, this replaces orthographic analysis. It involves the analysis of acoustic parameters and segments in order to identify linguistically significant elements. (See Fallside and Woods 1985 for a survey of recent research in computer speech processing.)

(3) **Morphological analysis:** This normally applies to grammatical analysis in so far as it concerns the structure and classification of words. Grammatical tagging, as discussed above, involves a limited amount of morphological analysis (see Ch. 3, pp. 36–8); but, for English, morphological analysis plays a relatively small part in word-class assignment.

(4) **Syntactic analysis** (parsing) comprises the analysis of sentences into their constituents (words, phrases, clauses). In mainstream computational linguistics,

parsing comprises both *syntactic recognition* (a decision procedure assigning a sentence either to the set of grammatical sentences of the language or to its complement) and *syntactic analysis* (assignment of a constituent structure analysis to a grammatical sentence). In probabilistic grammar, syntactic recognition may be replaced by an evaluation procedure (see Ch. 11) for deciding how far a sentence or word sequence deviates from a norm of "natural" English. Such a procedure is more appropriate to corpus analysis than is a yes-or-no grammaticality decision, since the requirement of corpus analysis is a "total accountability" requirement that every corpus sentence be assigned an analysis, whether or not it is grammatical according to a formalized description of English.

(5)   **Semantic analysis** and (6) **pragmatic analysis** are both concerned with the assignment of an interpretation or meaning to a text or to a part of a text. The distinction between semantics (dealing with uncontextualized meaning) and pragmatics (dealing with contextualized meaning) is not universally accepted in linguistics, but is a useful division for the purposes of computer text comprehension. Semantic analysis is the assignment of a meaning to a text(-sentence) independently of the local knowledge-resources to which the computer system has access. Pragmatic analysis is the integration of the meaning (as determined by semantic analysis) into those knowledge-resources, including the identification of references, and the modification of beliefs.

Feedback is an important ingredient in the progress of computer systems towards more abstract levels of analysis, just as it is in their progress towards greater accuracy in single-level analysis. In the latter case, feedback is understood as the "ploughing back" of results of the analysis in the improvement of the analytic system; in the former, feedback is understood as the use of information derived from more abstract levels of analysis in analysis at less abstract levels. For example, to optimize a grammatical tagging system, it may be necessary to use information from higher-level parsing: the choice, let us say, between a past tense interpretation of the word *acquired* and its past participle interpretation may not be decidable without a full parse of the sentence in which it occurs. It is accepted that, at least on some occasions, human language interpretation requires the use of higher-level analysis in the disambiguation of a lower-level analysis, and there is no reason for supposing that, in this respect, the computer needs to employ a different method from that of the human interpreter. Therefore a longer-term goal is to run the different levels of computational analysis of natural language in parallel, rather than to implement them sequentially. Nevertheless, as a strategy for research and development, there is much to be said for the sequential approach, since the complexity of the whole task will become more manageable if it is broken down into separate stages. On this basis, we have so far treated grammatical tagging and parsing as two separate processes, the output of the one providing the input to the other. The effective integration of these processes is a subject for future research.

6.   Ancillary research objectives

As so far described, our corpus-based approach to natural language processing appears to be monolithic, and strongly focused on the goal of natural language analysis, especially parsing, rather than natural language generation. Before concluding this introductory survey, I shall point out how the approach lends itself to broader and more varied objectives than have so far appeared, and thus pave the way for the exploration of these objectives in the three final chapters.

(a)   Text critiquing

This term (cf. Winograd 1983: 26, 360) refers to the use of computers in evaluating and/or correcting natural language texts. The simplest example of a text critiquing device is the orthodox existing type of *spelling checker* which identifies as potential errors word-tokens which do not match with a stored lexicon (or wordlist). A significant step beyond this is a *spelling corrector* (cf. Yannakoudakis and Fawthrop 1983b) which is capable not only of identifying a potential error, but of proposing a likely correction (or a set of possible corrections, perhaps ordered in terms of likelihood). In a different direction, an advance in text critiquing will be a spelling checker which is capable of flagging as potential errors even word-tokens which correspond to "legal" English words, but which betray themselves as errors by their occurrence in an inappropriate context: e.g. *there* instead of *their*.

Chapter 10 below reports on progress in developing such a context-sensitive spelling checker, using probabilistic predictions about word-class sequences as a means of identifying words which are grammatically incongruent with their immediate context. The principle applied here is an extension of the principle employed in probabilistic disambiguation. In the latter case, the grammatically most likely sequence of word-class tags is chosen, and less likely sequences rejected. In the text-critiquing variant, the disambiguation is performed, and the resulting tag sequence is subjected to a test of "unlikelihood". Below a certain threshold of unlikelihood, it can be assumed that the word concerned is a "misfit" inappropriate to its environment, and can be flagged as a possible error. It is not yet clear how far such a test will succeed in pinpointing all and only spelling errors. It may well be that such errors will be indistinguishable, say, from stylistic infelicities or grammatical errors by non-native speakers. But this finding itself would be of some interest in suggesting how corpus-derived frequency data can be applied not only to spelling checking, but to the critiquing of texts in a broader sense.

(b)   Text synthesis

There is a close relation between text critiquing and text synthesis. Although text critiquing systems have so far been applied to human-generated text, their future value may be just as important in application to computer-generated text. If output from existing text-generating (e.g. machine translation) systems is anything to go by, future automatically-generated text is likely to contain stylistically unacceptable features, even if it achieves accurate expression of the required or intended message. Some kind of automatic style monitoring may therefore be desirable if computer text synthesis is to be acceptable to the human consumer.

Another project linking corpus-based research to text synthesis is reported in Chapter 11. If we divorce the term "text" from its habitual association with written language, we can reinterpret the task of *text-to-speech* systems as that of analysing an input written text, and synthesizing a corresponding spoken text. Like existing spelling checkers, existing text-to-speech systems tend to operate on a word-by-word basis. But this is clearly an inadequate basis for high-quality speech synthesis, which requires not only appropriate segmental phonology, but also appropriate prosodic features of stress, rhythm, and intonation. Such features cannot be adequately predicted from written text without additional information (of a grammatical, semantic, or even pragmatic nature) derived from larger-than-word units. Furthermore, information derived from the punctuation of the written input text makes an important contribution to the prediction of these prosodic features. Since the associations between features of written texts and corresponding prosodic features of spoken texts cannot be accurately determined on the basis of introspection, the project described in Chapter 11 involves the compilation of a corpus of spoken English and a corresponding written corpus. This is an example, therefore, of the direct application of corpus analysis to text synthesis.

(c)   Linguistic databases

As a final example of the breadth of application of corpus-based natural language processing, consider the subject of Chapter 12, namely a *distributional lexicon*. The account, in section 5 above, of the symbiotic relation between analysed corpus and analytic system failed to do justice to the role of the *linguistic database* as a crucial connexion between these two. Any system for processing of a large amount of NL text data must make use of a substantial linguistic database of one kind or another. For instance, the grammatical tagging system CLAWS1 uses a *lexicon* of approximately 7200 graphic word types (see pp. 35–6), listed alphabetically with their potential word-class tags. The UCREL parser incorporates a grammar which contains about 5000 production rules (see p. 77) with associated frequency weightings. Even a naive spelling checker contains a large lexicon of "legal" English words.

The performance of a natural language processing system depends to a large extent on the quality of the database(s) it uses. Equally, the enhancement of the system will depend heavily on the enhancement of the database(s). The enhancement of the database(s), in turn, depends to a greater or lesser extent on the data derived from an analysed corpus.

In principle, a linguistic database and a corpus can be regarded as independent. There exist lexical databases (such as the machine-readable versions of commercial

dictionaries – see p. 131) which have no direct relation to corpus data. Moreover;
such databases can be to some extent be improved by reference to non-corpus sources
such as the native speaker's knowledge of the language (even though they may
ultimately rely upon text databanks or "citation banks"). But if we are operating with
probabilistic systems, the frequency data derived from corpora are virtually
indispensable for system updating and enhancement. In the present context, then,
linguistic databases can be assumed to be corpus-dependent. The cycle of corpus-based
natural language processing research can be represented in the form of Figure 3:

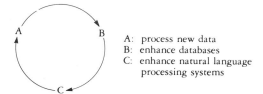

A: process new data
B: enhance databases
C: enhance natural language
    processing systems

Figure 3

    Phase C of the cycle is labelled "natural language processing" rather than simply
"natural language analysis" because once again the input of the database is not merely
to analysis but to synthesis. The distributional lexicon described in Chapter 12 is, in
fact, designed mainly as a tool for the "quality control" of synthesized text. Its aim is
to be a source of accessible frequency data not only in respect of grammatical tags, but
also for individual word forms and their collocations. Its potential value, as a database
for text-evaluation, is therefore less restricted than that of the text-critiquing system
described in Chapter 10, which makes use of word-class frequency data only.
However, the distributional lexicon, to be effective, will have to draw on a far larger
body of text than the LOB Corpus. At present the research is in its initial
experimental stages, and this is one of a number of areas where we must look to the
mid-term future for results of present developmental work.

CHAPTER 2

Probabilistic models of analysis

Geoffrey Sampson

1. Two schools of computational linguistics

The approach to automatic language analysis described in this book represents one of two fairly clearly differentiated schools of CL research. Of the two, ours is currently the minority tendency in terms of numbers of adherents and public "visibility" (though it is by no means restricted to the group of us who work at or in collaboration with Lancaster University's UCREL). This minoritarian status seems unlikely to last. If computational linguistics is to survive and develop as a worthwhile academic activity, its practitioners must adapt to the research styles represented here – and there are many signs that this is starting to happen.

The hallmarks of our approach are: (i) analytic techniques which depend on statistical properties of language structure rather than on absolute logical rules; and (ii) a focus on authentic data drawn from unrestricted domains of discourse rather than on invented examples. The two points are linked: the use of statistics is a consequence of the need for algorithms which are robust enough to cope with authentic rather than pre-selected linguistic material. Since the outside world has little use for CL unless it can handle authentic language, the future of the statistical approach seems assured.

2. The non-probabilistic approach

To clarify the contrast, let me sketch the alternative, majoritarian trend in CL. Adherents of this school are heavily influenced by concepts derived from cognitive psychology, and from branches of artificial intelligence which are cast largely in terms of deductive logic. They lay stress on the fact that human processing of language, in activities such as translation, or decoding of noise-distorted speech, crucially involves active understanding of the language processed; and they infer that any successful automatic language-processing system must make heavy use of complex grammatical rules, logical inferencing abilities, databases of real-world knowledge, and the like. This point of view has virtues and drawbacks. The obvious argument in its support is that, if humans use intelligence in processing language (as is certainly true), then the only way to get fully human-like performance in an automatic system will presumably be to simulate intelligence mechanically. Offsetting this, however, is the fact that – although computers may outperform humans in artificially-delimited domains such as playing draughts or chess – the task of simulating human intelligence as it is applied in an open-ended domain such as NL processing is far beyond the grasp of twentieth-century science. (Some would argue that mechanical simulation of creative, open-ended human thought-processes is a radically incoherent notion; but it is unnecessary for present purposes to take a position on this controversial philosophical thesis, since it is clear in any case that the task is a very long way from being achieved even if it is possible in principle.)

In consequence, CL research in practice tends to revolve round little "toy" subsets of artificially simple linguistic forms, in the hope that systems which succeed in dealing with these may eventually be expanded and linked together until they cover entire languages. To give a flavour of this research style, let me quote a few typical examples of the kinds of language dealt with by various CL systems discussed at the Inaugural Conference of the European Chapter of the Association for Computational Linguistics, held at Pisa in 1983 (having no wish to pillory individuals, I do not attribute the examples to their inventors):

> *Whatever is linguistic is interesting.*
> *A ticket was bought by every man.*
> *The man with the telescope and the umbrella kicked the ball.*
> *Hans bekommt von dieser Frau ein Buch.*
> *John and Bill went to Pisa. They delivered a paper.*
> *Maria é andata a Roma con Anna.*
> *Are you going to travel this summer? Yes, to Sicily.*

There was even a paper that argued that a parser ought to be robust enough to handle deviant sentences, and quoted as an example the sentence *Mary drove the car and John the truck*; if one is really fastidious about what counts as an English sentence, apparently this looks like a distortion of the "proper" sentence *Mary drove the car and John drove the truck*.

The grossly unrepresentative nature of such examples is palpable. Compare them with a like number of authentic sentences drawn using random techniques from the LOB Corpus:

- *Sing slightly flat.* (C04 109) – A straightforward sentence; but notice the slightly out-of-the-way use of an adjective as complement of a non-copular verb.
- *Mr. Baring, who whispered and wore* * *1pince-nez,* *0was seventy if he was a day.* (K22 22–3) – The symbols *1, *0 are LOB codes for beginning and end of italics; typographical shifts are often quite relevant for understanding the structure of written texts, though the CL literature rarely mentions them. Note

that an automatic parser must recognize that the configuration "full stop, space, capital" does not represent a sentence boundary in the case of *Mr. Baring*.

- *∗4Advice – Concentrate on the present.* (F12 46) – ∗4 means "begin bold face". Note contradictory cues about sentence-boundary (dash is usually sentence-internal, but capitalization of *Concentrate* suggests a new sentence); note also the indeterminacy of the logical relationship between the word before the dash and what follows.
- *Such events and such experiences merit a special designation.* (G69 174–5) – A straightforward sentence.
- *Say the power-drill makers, 75 per cent of major breakdowns can be traced to neglect of the carbon-brush gear.* (E03 47–8) – Note non-standard syntactic inversion in first clause.
- *The libation in honour of the deceased is found as a part of the most modern customs, as when some drops are poured out before a drink is taken: the toast.* (F19 64–6) – Here the sequence *as when* is moderately unusual; and again there is some vagueness about the logical relationship between the phrase *the toast* and what precedes the colon.
- *But he remained a stranger in a strange land.* (G15 24–5) – Unproblematic.

The LOB Corpus contains many sentences far more logically "messy" than any of these – even though that Corpus is by no means fully representative of the diversity of authentic English, since its contents are limited to written material which has undergone the disciplines of publication. Yet one could not fail to notice the difference in quality between even this group of authentic examples, and the invented examples quoted from the Pisa conference. Sometimes, CL researchers seem scarcely aware of the yawning gulf that separates their tiny languagettes from the complexity of real-life language. The literature of the subject does not often draw attention to the problem, because members of this school of thought take it for granted that ability to deal with authentic material is an unrealistic requirement. But it is an essential requirement for almost any system that is to do useful work. (There may be a few IT applications for which it is realistic to expect human users to adapt to the limitations of mechanical NL-processing systems, but this must surely be a marginal phenomenon.)

In the parsing domain, one correlate of the lack of interest in authenticity is that automatic parsers are based, explicitly or implicitly, on generative grammars – systems of rules which define the class of "all and only" the well-formed sentences of the language to be parsed. A wide range of such parsing systems are surveyed in works such as King (1983) and Sparck Jones and Wilks (1983). Researchers disagree on the formal nature of the grammatical rules needed – for instance, some argue that generalized phrase-structure grammar ("GPSG") is an adequate formalism while others hold that more powerful rules such as those embodied in augmented transition networks ("ATNs") are required; but it is widely accepted as axiomatic that a parser will operate by resting an input in some systematic manner against one after another of the structures provided by a grammar, until either one (or more) structure fits, or else the range of structures is exhausted (implying that the input is ill-formed and therefore unparsable). Some of these systems are strikingly successful in their own terms (one of the first in the field, W. A. Woods's ATN-based LUNAR question-answering system (e.g. Woods 1977), responded accurately to a remarkably high proportion of the questions submitted on its original field trial); and some of the systems are more sophisticated than others about the well-formed/ill-formed dichotomy (thus the parser described by Charniak (1983) in effect imposes a three-way classification on input strings, dividing them into fully well-formed, imperfect but nevertheless analysable, and unanalysable – a classification which might be seen as capturing the observation that native speakers understand things said by foreigners and small children which they would not say themselves). All of these systems quickly "fall over", however, when exposed to genuinely unselected, authentic input. Woods himself stressed how the percentage of successful responses by LUNAR fell as soon as the domain of users was broadened to include people whose inputs were less predictable than those of the participants at the original demonstration (Woods 1977: 559).

The reason for this fragility is that even the most complex generative grammar comes nowhere near in practice to incorporating the endless diversity of quirky linguistic phenomena that occur in authentic material. It is more than sixty years since Edward Sapir wrote that "All grammars leak" (Sapir 1921: 38), but the situation has not changed; cf. Jensen and Heidorn (1982: 2): "trying to write a grammar to describe explicitly all and only the sentences of a natural language is about as practical as trying to find the Holy Grail". Any generative grammar, whether in the form of a GPSG, a set of ATNs, or whatever, is by definition a system which distinguishes grammatical forms, to which the grammar assigns a structure, from ungrammatical and therefore unanalysable forms. Yet in real life it is scarcely possible – perhaps it is wholly impossible – to formulate a single grammatical rule that is not violated on occasion. What linguist would dispute that one of the solidly-established rules of standard English is the rule by which a reflexive pronoun in isolation may not act as subject of its clause? Despite the rule, I find in the subset of the LOB Corpus which I have parsed manually (cf. Ch. 7) the sequence:

> *Each side proceeds on the assumption that itself loves peace, but the other side consists of warmongers.* (G75 34–5)

– taken from a *New Statesman* article on nuclear war by Bertrand Russell. The construction "feels" moderately unusual; but it occurs, written by an author of great repute. It seems unlikely that the form represents a momentary lapse of attention by Russell (as it happens, the following sentence includes a second, parallel instance of the same construction, suggesting a careful rhetorical effect); but in a sense it is irrelevant how the form came to appear on the page – having appeared, it is easily understandable, and is available as a model which other English-speakers may imitate. (In context I doubt whether readers who were not professional linguists would even notice anything out of the ordinary in Russell's usage.) Comparable examples (not violations of this particular rule, but violations of rules which a linguist might take to be equally reliable) occur incessantly in authentic data. (Furthermore, authentic material contains not only frequent rule-violations but also very many and diverse constructions which are ignored by orthodox generative grammar as too "peripheral" to notice – this point is discussed at more length in Chapter 7.) A processing system which discards such phenomena as unanalysable is in practice close to useless.

One possible response to observations of this kind is to suppose that the particular generative grammars currently in use simply need revision to make them more accurate. The Russell example, for instance, might be accommodated by extending the rules governing reflexive pronouns so as to allow a reflexive as subject of a subordinate clause which is co-ordinated with a clause containing a contrasting subject; and other rule-violations would motivate other rule-revisions. I find it hard to imagine that in practice this revision process could ever be concluded. Like other rules concerning human behaviour, rules of grammar seem made to be broken. But notice that, even if it were possible ultimately to produce a wholly leak-free grammar, it is not clear that this would solve the problem at hand. Much of the difficulty of designing generative-grammar-based processing systems lies in the fact that, if a grammar is complex, it is hard to design an algorithm which succeeds in locating the consequences of the grammar for particular strings. If the activity of revising a generative grammar in response to recalcitrant authentic examples were ever to terminate in a perfectly leak-free grammar, that grammar would surely be massively more complicated than any extant grammar, and would thus pose correspondingly massive problems with respect to incorporation into a system of automatic analysis.

Accordingly, the idea of basing automatic language-processing on generative grammars of any category seems to me a dead end.

3. A probabilistic system: CLAWS

Despite the problems discussed in section 2, most of the CL research community remain strongly attached to the concept of a sharp distinction between "well-formed" and "ill-formed" word-sequences. Recently there has been a flurry of interest in parsing ill-formed input (see e.g. the Jensen and Heidorn and Charniak papers already quoted, and papers in the July–December 1983 special issue of the *American Journal of Computational Linguistics*); but all these writers, including Karen Jensen and her co-authors (whose approach is from our viewpoint relatively congenial), agree in treating ill-formed input as clearly separate from well-formed input, to be processed by subsidiary mechanisms. Weischedel and Sondheimer (1983) suggest that grammatical deviance is governed by rigid rules of its own, parallel to the rules which define grammatical well-formedness.

Within our approach, by contrast, the concept of a grammar which defines "all and only" the forms of the language plays no part at all. Our algorithms deal only with relative frequencies; they recognize no absolute distinctions between "well-formed" and "ill-formed".

The point can be illustrated in connexion with CLAWS, the word-tagging component of the UCREL suite of language-processing systems. CLAWS is discussed in detail in Chapters 3 and 4, and for the sake of conceptual clarity I shall give here only a very simplified account of its operation, omitting a number of complications which are vital to the success of the system in practice. The task of the system is to assign a "tag" or grammatical code, drawn from a set of 133 possibilities, to each word of an input English sentence in which typically many words will be grammatically ambiguous. The system begins by assigning to each orthographic word, considered in isolation, a set of candidate tags paired with probabilities; and it then chooses one of the candidate tags for each word in context, essentially by reference to a table of empirically-observed relative frequencies of transitions between adjacent tags. The likelihood of any path through the candidate tags for successive words of a sentence is equated with the product of the probabilities of each step in the path from one tag to the next (modified by the probabilities of individual pairings of word with tag); the tag predicted by the system for any given word is that candidate tag for which the summed values of all paths passing through the tag is highest.

This system is spectacularly successful. Currently, CLAWS is running at a rate of between 96% and 97% of words of authentic text correctly tagged (and we believe this figure can be further improved). We are unaware of any non-probabilistic system that comes close to matching this performance. What is particularly significant in the present context is that this excellent result is achieved without using any grammatical knowledge (in the generative grammarian's sense) whatever. In the 133×133 matrix of tag-transition frequencies, naturally there are many cells representing transitions which have never occurred in the data on which our statistics were based. Because tag-paths are evaluated by multiplying together the probabilities of individual transitions, a zero figure for any single transition would inevitably mean that any path containing that transition was predicted to be impossible, no matter how likely the other transitions in the path. That outcome was deliberately avoided in constructing the matrix by adding a small positive figure to each cell, so that no value is zero. Thus, not only does CLAWS "know" nothing about the overall grammatical architecture of English sentences: even with respect to the local issue of transitions between tags it knows only that some are more frequent than others – for CLAWS nothing at all is ruled out as impossible.

4. Probabilistic parsing

Word-tagging is of course only a very limited language-processing task (though that does not mean that it is easy to achieve by non-probabilistic techniques). But our approach to the larger task of parsing is very similar in style. The fundamental assumption of "constituent-likelihood grammar" (see Chs. 5 and 6) is that the correct parse-tree for a given sentence will normally be that one among all the logically-possible ways of drawing labelled trees over the words of the sentence which maximizes some simple function of the values of the various productions in the tree, where the value of an individual production (i.e. pairing of a mother node labelled m with a sequence of daughter nodes labelled $d_1, d_2, \ldots, d_n$) is derived from empirical statistics concerning the frequency of the sequence d_1, d_2, ..., d_n relative to other category-sequences as exponent of the category m. Again our technique makes no assumption that certain pairings of mother with daughter-sequence are impossible (even though in practical computational terms there may be no point in modifying the zero statistic for unobserved productions, since it is implausible that multiplication will be a good function for deriving tree-likelihood estimates from constituent-likelihoods). From our standpoint any tree, no matter how inappropriate its structure or how absurd its node-labels, ranks in principle as a possible analysis of any sentence (provided only that the tree has as many terminal nodes as the sentence has words). If a "ridiculous" parse-tree is never in practice selected as the preferred analysis for any input, that is only because for each individual input some higher-valued parse-tree is available. If authentic language were normally "well-formed' in the generative grammarian's sense, this willingness to entertain quantities of perverse candidate-parses would probably be a highly inefficient analytic strategy. But in real life the task confronting a (human or mechanical) language-processer is very often that of locating what one might call a "least ill-formed" analysis; in this situation it is impractical to try to derive an analysis algorithm from a system whose basic function is to divide word-sequences into "grammatical" sheep and "ungrammatical" goats.

No matter how bizarre the input, in principle our algorithms will always yield some (perhaps very low-valued) analysis for it. Our approach does not set a high priority on psychological plausibility, yet ironically this feature of our system is surely much more realistic for a model of human language-processing than the behaviour commonly found in generative-grammar-based systems designed by "cognitively"-oriented CL researchers, which return no output at all in response to ill-formed input.

Admittedly, it is necessary to add an important qualification to the preceding paragraphs. With respect to the current Lancaster implementation of the parsing algorithm (cf. Ch. 6), it is not strictly true that any logically-possible but perverse analysis is treated as a candidate parsing for any sentence. There is a practical reason why this is not so: the number of logically-possible ways of drawing trees with labels conforming to our scheme of grammatical categories is so astronomical, if a sentence is more than two or three words long, that it is not feasible to evaluate each alternative. Instead, absolute (i.e. non-probabilistic) rules are used in order to predict certain limited features of the parse-tree for a given input sentence (see pp. 68–9), and only trees having those features are evaluated. In other words, the many logically-possible labelled trees lacking one or more of the predicted features are not admitted as candidates.

But, in the first place, this aspect of the current implementation is not essential to our approach. At Leeds, Eric Atwell and I are experimenting with the new AI technique of "simulated annealing" in order to develop an algorithm which discovers highest-valued parse-trees without eliminating any logical possibilities *a priori* (Sampson 1986a; forthcoming). (Simulated annealing is a psychologically-realistic computational technique which exploits stochastic concepts drawn from thermodynamics in order to locate optimal solutions among astronomically-numerous ranges of combinatorial possibilities – see e.g. Kirkpatrick *et al.* (1983). A prototype version of the annealing parser, using very crude grammatical statistics, was first successfully run in January 1986; at the time of writing we are developing a more efficient version incorporating refined probabilistic data.)

Secondly, even if it eventually transpires that the most effective parsing algorithm resembles the current Lancaster technique rather than the Leeds annealing technique, it would remain true that the device of eliminating certain perverse parsings without evaluation ranks merely as a heuristic modification of the probabilistic approach adopted for reasons of practical computational efficiency, rather than as a fundamental intellectual component of our approach. (The "T-tag" assignment rules discussed on pp. 68–9 do not amount to a covert acknowledgement of the well-formed/ill-formed distinction: the analyses eliminated by those rules are also given low but positive values by our tree-evaluation function, only in practice it saves time not to calculate their values.) There is a great difference between a concept of parsing which sees the task as one of maximizing a continuous variable, but adopts a convenient strategy for concentrating computational effort on areas of the scale where high values are known to cluster, and a concept which sees parsing as essentially a matter of finding the unique key to fit a rigid lock, but which resorts to *ad hoc* devices to cope with a situation in which keys are mass-produced but locks are hand-built, imperfectly, by amateur craftsmen.

5. Contrasting workstyles

The texture of day-to-day research activity is markedly different as between the two schools of CL I have portrayed. Contrasts extend even to matters such as choice of programming language. Computational linguists of the cognitive persuasion commonly work with "very high level" languages which facilitate subtle logical analysis – there is a certain professional mystique about using the latest dialect of Lisp, or even a declarative language such as Prolog. Our work, on the other hand, uses Pascal, an unglamorous workhorse of a language which copes relatively efficiently with the repeated numerical calculations on very large data-files that are involved in the empirical/probabilistic approach to language-analysis. More significantly, there is a contrast in manpower requirements. By choosing to focus on a sufficiently narrow range of artificial language-samples, a two-man research partnership or even a single researcher may be able to carry a programme of research in the cognitive style to fruition. Development of systems able to process authentic language, on the other hand, requires large teams willing to collaborate in a reasonably disciplined way: much of the work inevitably consists of laborious routine activities with limited intellectual content (checking through thousands of lines of printout to log the varying usage of punctuation marks in abbreviated words, to quote an example at random) which "cognitive" researchers can exclude from their investigations by fiat.

This last contrast implies that CL research of our empirically-based kind is more easily organized within large commercial undertakings than in universities, with their scanty resources and weak managerial relationships. The group of us working with the LOB Corpus have been very lucky in assembling a reasonably large university-based team, and within the UK university system there is one other comparable group, around John Sinclair at the University of Birmingham. But it has been noticeable in recent years that, increasingly, the research publications we need to read are tending to emanate from industrial rather than academic sources. In one major area of CL, namely machine translation, until quite recently the divorce between academic researchers working in a logic-dominated intellectual framework on non-operational "toy" systems, and industry-based work in an empirical style on large-scale commercially-traded systems, was almost total. There were exceptions – notably the TAUM-METEO system for translating weather forecasts from English into French, which was produced at the University of Montreal but carries out a real, non-toy (even if narrowly delimited) task. But general commercial MT systems such as Petr Toma's SYSTRAN were ignored in the published literature of academic CL, and allusions to them in informal chat at academic conferences were condescending and factually inaccurate – despite the fact that almost all the useful machine translation carried out to date is being executed by systems of this category.

6.   The roots of resistance to probabilistic techniques

The relative success of the empirical approach to CL is by now so unmistakable that academic researchers of the cognitive/logic-based school are perforce beginning to come to terms with it. At the 1984 Lugano Tutorial Week on Machine Translation (King 1986) the virtues of statistical techniques, until recently almost a heretical notion in the academic CL community, were advocated by well-respected university-based researchers such as Pierre Isabelle of the Montreal group and Jonathan Slocum of the University of Texas/Siemens METAL project. But it was still seen as something of a daring break with precedent that at the same conference Peter Wheeler was invited to come from his commercial background to address academic MT researchers on the topic of SYSTRAN.

In its resistance to probabilistic, data-driven rather than hypothesis-driven techniques, CL is beginning to look seriously out of step with wider trends in artificial intelligence in general: some of the most exciting current research in AI, such as that on Boltzmann machines (see e.g. Ackley, Hinton and Sejnowski 1985), is heavily flavoured by probabilistic, empiricist concepts and techniques. But it is easy to discern the reasons why linguists in particular are reluctant to follow this trend. Almost all currently-active academic computational linguists have received a training strongly influenced by the linguistic theories of Noam Chomsky, and Chomsky's theories contain several mutually-reinforcing components which imply that this approach is misguided.

In the first place, Chomsky has been consistently hostile to any use of statistical methods in linguistics, writing for instance in his first book that "one's ability to produce and recognize grammatical utterances is not based on notions of statistical approximation and the like" (Chomsky 1957: 16). It was pointed out by Patrick Suppes many years ago that Chomsky's argument to this effect is straightforwardly fallacious (it may well be true that adding probabilities to the alternatives in a large phrase-structure grammar, say, will yield predicted frequencies for *individual sentences* that are too low to test, but the same grammar will make easily-tested predictions about sentence-*types*: cf. Suppes 1970); yet the argument has continued to convince many linguists. Chomsky's conflation of the separate processes of language-production and language-recognition in this context is too glib. It is very reasonable to argue that a *writer* chooses between, say, a nominal clause and a relative clause as final IC of a noun-phrase in terms of how best to achieve his communicative purpose on a given occasion rather than in terms of maintaining statistical norms of English grammar; but, if such decisions fairly regularly led to relative clauses being chosen, say, three times as often as nominal clauses in a particular genre, then it is perfectly plausible that a *reader* would exploit this information in seeking an interpretation for a sequence such as *the idea that they developed* (and, if human recognition strategies exploit statistical information, then it is further plausible that this will in turn influence production strategies, since writers' – and speakers' – need to express themselves must be balanced with their need to be understood).[†]

A second point is that much of the force of Chomsky's *Syntactic Structures* lay in its argument that simple models in terms of transitions between adjacent words are grossly inadequate to capture the grammatical structure of NL, which must rather be stated in terms of far more complex formalisms, many of which are only distantly related to the surface properties of language as it actually appears on the page. Large-scale statistical research on authentic language inevitably tends to deal in properties which are more superficial and simpler than those posited by scholars developing speculative theories about the analysis of small, artificially-delimited subsets of language, and this causes linguists of the latter category to perceive probabilistic CL as theoretically naive.

But again there seems to be a confusion between language production and language recognition. Generative systems such as Chomskyan transformational grammars do not claim to include any algorithm for recognition; the subtler and more complex the appropriate formalisms for describing language production are, the likelier it seems to be that those formalisms will be specific to that one mode, so that the recognition mode would have to exploit different (perhaps simpler) formalisms. A concrete example here might be the asymmetry that exists in practice between left-branching and right-branching structures in English. In principle one might expect no difference in the incidence of the two kinds of branching, since, formally speaking, the burdens which left-branching imposes on a speaker appear to be precisely mirrored by the burdens which right-branching imposes on a hearer. However, authentic English contains many deeply right-branching structures, while left-branching is very limited.

[†] The relative-clause/nominal-clause example is hypothetical; as it happens, LOB statistics suggest that frequency of use of these two categories in the stated environment is roughly equal.

A plausible explanation is that, whereas speakers are required to ensure that their utterances are grammatically correct in all respects, hearers do not systematically check each grammatical detail of a complex utterance but instead interpret it heuristically by sampling a limited number of its properties. (Cf. Fodor, Bever and Garrett 1974: 409.)

In any case, even if it were certain that human language-recognition used analytic categories possessing a degree of abstract subtlety comparable to that of transformational grammar, this would not affect the argument that the most effective techniques for automatic language-recognition in the 1980s are techniques based on cruder categories, because we know quite a lot about how to apply these and we are not close to knowing how to make subtler techniques work. "Cognitive" computational linguists sometimes react to results in probabilistic CL such as the 96–97% success-rate of CLAWS by saying, in effect, "So what? – a system is uninteresting unless it has the potential to deliver 100%, human-like performance; and, for this, subtle AI techniques are essential". One response to this is that the notion of intelligent human language-understanding as an activity which normally proceeds with 100% accuracy is a misconception (cf. Sampson 1986b). But in any case this brand of criticism represents a failure to compare like with like: it is senseless to observe that the performance of a system which is actually running today is inferior to that of a hypothetical system which may or may not be invented at some future time.

Nobody claims that the algorithms currently incorporated in empirical, probabilistic CL systems represent an ultimate ideal. Like other researchers, we are learning as we progress. Perhaps it is arguable whether the best route towards an eventual optimum system for automatically processing authentic language lies through an approach which emphasizes methodological purity irrespective of the cost in terms of failure to deliver results, or through an approach which maximizes concrete results initially by using whatever methods can be made to work – but surely most outsiders to the field would emphatically favour the latter on general common-sense grounds? This point does not lose its force even if one's aim is to produce a system which models human cognitive processes rather than merely a system that works. Some "cognitive" researchers appear to feel that the question whether a language-processing system runs or fails to run counts for little or nothing, and the nature of the techniques involved for virtually everything, in an assessment of the system as a model of human cognition (cf. Ades 1981); yet, in twenty years' time, present-day ideas about which techniques are psychologically realistic may look very foolish, while results are results.

In case the point is not already clear, let me say explicitly that we are well aware that a system which uses exclusively information about transition-frequencies between adjacent parts of speech cannot be completely adequate as a model of how humans disambiguate words in context, and likewise a model based purely on constituent likelihood cannot be the whole story about human parsing behaviour. Sometimes a human can resolve a grammatical ambiguity only by reference to semantic or extra-linguistic considerations which at present are not incorporated into our algorithms in any way. But what we find significant about CLAWS is not the fact that its performance is less than 100% accurate, but that with authentic material it comes as close to 100% as it does. We have noticed that the performance of CLAWS commonly degrades sharply when a visiting linguist is invited to submit an example of his choice to it – the reason being that examples which occur readily to professional linguists tend to be "trick" cases making unusual demands on the reader's/hearer's intelligence. One lesson of CLAWS is that "trick" sentences seem to be much rarer in authentic usage than exposure to the intellectual climate of academic linguistics might lead one to assume. As Gerry Knowles and Lita Lawrence put it in Chapter 11 below, real-life language is usually not "linguistically interesting".

Of course logically-subtle sentences do sometimes occur in authentic usage, and when they occur people understand them (if they do understand them) by virtue of intellectual processes which go beyond the algorithms that we have exploited to date. But the situation with respect to human language-understanding seems rather, as Sapir put it (1921: 14), "as though a dynamo capable of generating enough power to run an elevator were operated almost exclusively to feed an electric doorbell": higher-level processes are available in reserve but rarely need to be invoked. Even when semantic rather than purely grammatical considerations are needed to resolve an ambiguity in authentic material, it does not follow that the resolution process will necessarily involve subtle chains of deductive inference. Recent work by John Sinclair of Birmingham and Andrew Beale at Lancaster suggests that there may be a surprising amount of mileage to be got out of very crude semantic considerations such as frequency of collocation.

It is interesting to notice that one leading proponent of the "cognitive" style of CL, Mark Steedman, recently announced a change of heart about why (as he believes) linguists ought to hold aloof from practical language-processing research. It is not that successful practical systems are impossible in principle, as Steedman once thought: he now believes they may be quite feasible to construct, but the work involved is too "boring" (Steedman 1983: 139). Tastes differ; for some of us, the fascination of working with real rather than artificial data more than offsets the somewhat banausic flavour of the research.

7. The competence concept

One reason why logic-based approaches tend to perform poorly at best with authentic input is that authentic language, as we have seen, is so much more complex than theoretical linguists' descriptions commonly imply. The third point to make about Chomsky's influence on CL is that his doctrine of "linguistic competence" actively encourages researchers to ignore many of these complexities as in some sense not genuinely part of the language. The competence/performance distinction implies that the messy complexity of NL as it is actually encountered on the page or in speech masks a far more orderly, elegant Platonic ideal language lurking below the surface – and it implies furthermore that the proper object of a linguist's attention is the elegant ideal competence rather than the real but relatively intractable performance. A linguistic theorist faced with the example quoted on p. 19 of a reflexive pronoun acting as subject might react by saying, not that an accepted rule of English grammar needs revision, but that the example is a "performance deviation" (compare the use of the deviance concept quoted on p. 17 from the Pisa conference). If competence is more elegant than performance, then it is possible that the subtle but restricted systems being developed by "cognitive" computational linguists might come close to being adequate to handle "competent" NL. From this viewpoint, the fact that these systems are quite inadequate to handle authentic language (i.e. performance) would not be a criticism of the systems: it would be a criticism of authentic language.

One response to this is that, while the distinction between performance and competence may be persuasive so long as it concerns the distinction between utterances interrupted by throat-clearing, broken off prematurely, etc., and the ideally complete, uninterrupted behaviour-patterns from which the former are derived, it becomes very unpersuasive if it is extended to discriminate against usage which is merely quirky or solecistic. The construction quoted on p. 19 occurs, twice, in a reputable publication, with every sign of having been carefully written; there is no reason to doubt that it is "competent" English other than the fact that it complicates the grammar of English (and if this is admitted as evidence, then the claim that linguistic competence is relatively elegant and accessible to the aprioristic type of CL analysis becomes circular).

More important, though, even if solid theoretical grounds could be found for positing simple competence structures underlying the far messier structures found in authentic language, this fact would be entirely irrelevant for the computational linguist. Theoretical linguists, in many cases, are engaged in a largely philosophical enterprise which aims to bring insights derived from the structure of language to bear on an investigation of the nature of human knowledge and the human mind. If some version of the competence/performance distinction can be made to stand up then it is possible that competence is more relevant than performance to this enterprise. I do not wish to undervalue this philosophical brand of linguistics, to which much of my own career has been devoted; but computational linguistics is a different enterprise. An automatic language-processing system which works adequately for "competent" language but fails on "performance" is a futile system, because all there is to be processed is performance. The fact that our discipline is nowadays smiled on by those who control the distribution of research resources, where ten years ago it was seen as an eccentric intellectual byway, is a consequence of the hope (which I believe is well-founded) that computational linguistics may be capable of delivering systems that will offer genuine economic benefits to society. We shall ill repay this new generosity if we squander it self-indulgently on abstract academic games.

8.   The precedent of speech research

The final point worth making is that, although the contrast we have examined between rival research styles is still a live issue in the areas of CL with which this book deals, in another important branch of the subject our battle was fought and won long ago. I have been discussing exclusively systems which process written inputs, which is what all members of our own group are so far concerned with (even though some of us are interested in generating *outputs* that relate to speech – see Chapter 11). With respect to the issue under discussion, though, computational research on written language is quite backward by comparison with research on automatic speech analysis. The current state of the art in our field is in fact very reminiscent of the situation in speech-analysis research fifteen years ago, before the ARPA Speech Understanding Project (on which see e.g. Lea 1980; Cole 1980).

At that time it was widely assumed by phoneticians, on grounds of *a priori* linguistic and psychological theorizing, that the problem of automatically interpreting acoustic signals as sequences of words would require subtle logical inferencing techniques simulating general intelligence and native-speaker-like linguistic competence. There was hostility towards researchers who attacked the problem in a less "cognitive" style; in a famously extravagant 1969 communication in the *Journal of the Acoustical Society of America*, John Pierce of the Bell Laboratories castigated the latter group as "mad scientists and untrustworthy engineers" (Pierce 1969: 1050). Over the years 1971–76 the issue was put to empirical test, as the Advanced Research Projects Agency ("ARPA") of the US Department of Defence funded rival research groups to develop speech-understanding systems that should meet specified desirable performance criteria.

Among the systems produced, the clear winner (the only one which fulfilled, indeed over-fulfilled, all the criteria) was Carnegie-Mellon University's HARPY, which contrasted with its rival systems in eschewing logic-based techniques and instead making heavy use of simple transition probabilities between linguistic units and heuristic methods to eliminate low-probability analyses. Subsequently, it has become accepted wisdom among researchers on spoken-language analysis that the earlier enthusiasm for "intelligent", "top-down" approaches was misplaced, and that systems which succeed in delivering usable results are likely to be statistics-based rather than logic-based and to use simple (e.g. Markovian) models of language structure which lend themselves to empirical statistics-gathering and arithmetical calculation even though they are known to be too crude to be fully adequate as a representation of native-speaker linguistic ability. (See e.g. Bahl *et al.* 1983; de Mori 1983; Cravero *et al.* 1984; Derouault and Mérialdo 1984; Smith *et al.* 1985.) A few researchers who are interested only in psychological theory rather than practical applications continue to oppose this trend in somewhat emotive terms (cf. for instance the title and contents of Ades (1981)); on the other hand, some researchers find the success of HARPY-like systems so impressive as to suggest that our models of human language-processing should become more statistical, less logic-based (Newell 1980).

No doubt it is harder to avoid recognizing the need for statistical methods when dealing with continuous acoustic data than it is when dealing with written language, where units are discrete and clearly individuated. But the programmatic quality that continues to pervade much of the cognitive approach to CL suggests strongly that, in truth, the need for probabilistic techniques is as strong in the written-language field as it is in speech research. To my mind the case is overwhelming.

CHAPTER 3

The CLAWS word-tagging system

Roger Garside

1. Introduction

This chapter describes CLAWS (Constituent-Likelihood Automatic Word-Tagging System), a system for tagging English-language texts: that is, for assigning to each word in a text an unambiguous indication of the grammatical class to which this word belongs in this context. The first version of this system was developed over the period 1981 to 1983 at the Universities of Lancaster, Oslo, and Bergen. This version (CLAWS1) was designed to assign a grammatical tag to each of the million words in the LOB corpus, and achieved 96–97% accuracy (the precise degree of accuracy varying according to the type of text); the remaining errors were removed by a manual post-editing phase. Work is at present proceeding at Lancaster to develop a second generation of the tagging system (CLAWS2), to increase its accuracy, and reduce its reliance on manual pre-editing and the particular coding conventions of the LOB Corpus; this enhancement is described in Chapter 8. The present chapter gives a general overview of the complete CLAWS1 tagging system, and describes in detail the mechanism for assigning a set of candidate tags to each word in the text; a later program in the system selects a preferred tag from this set, and this is described in more detail in Chapter 4.

The tagset used in CLAWS1 was derived from the one used in tagging the Brown Corpus (Greene and Rubin 1971). We wished to retain overall comparability of the tagged LOB Corpus with the tagged Brown Corpus, although we did modify the Brown tagset in the area of proper nouns and pronouns, ending up with a total of 133 possible tags for the syntactic units (words and punctuation marks) of the corpus. For CLAWS2 we decided to develop the tagset in the light of our experience with automatic tagging and parsing systems, resulting in a new set of 166 tags. In both sets the tags each consist of from one to five characters, and are intended to have mnemonic significance; the tagsets are discussed in detail in Appendix B. In most chapters (including this one) we use the first set of tags, called in Appendix B the "LOB tagset"; whenever the second, "Lancaster" tagset is referred to, attention will be drawn to the fact.

There is a general assumption in tagging that there is a one-to-one correspondence between tags and orthographic units. However, this correspondence breaks down with contracted forms (as, for example, in *can't, they'd, I'll*) and certain idiomatic phrases. It was decided that the CLAWS system would use a different mechanism for dealing with contracted forms from that used in the Brown tagging system. In the Brown system an orthographic unit such as *can't* is assigned two tags representing "modal + *not*": in CLAWS *can't* is split into two syntactic units, *can* and *n't* (with an indication that the two syntactic units are a single othographic unit), and the two units are separately tagged. A late addition to CLAWS allowed for "multi-word units", where two or more orthographic units are assigned a single tag (which the UCREL team generally refer to as a "ditto-tag"): thus *because of* and *such as* are each tagged as a preposition, *as if* as a subordinating conjunction, and *at once* as an adverb. This is discussed further in Chapter 9.

2.   Overview of the tagging system

The input to the CLAWS1 tagging system is a text in the format of the LOB Corpus. An example is:

```
D01    2  |^*0With so many problems to solve, it would be a great help to
D01    3  select some one problem which might be the key to all the others, and
D01    4  begin there. ^If there is any such key-problem, then it is undoubtedly
```

This extract is from text category D text extract 1 lines 2 to 4, as indicated by the reference numbers on the left. Notice the symbol ^ marking the beginning of each sentence, and the symbols | and *0 meaning (respectively) "new paragraph" and "normal (roman) typeface". The Corpus is unrestricted in vocabulary and syntax, and contains foreign words and phrases, dialogue, incomplete and non-standard English, etc.

The output from the tagging system is a tagged text. For example, the first sentence in the above excerpt would appear as overleaf in the table on p. 32. The text has been reformated or "verticalized", with each word or punctuation mark occupying its own line, and being at a fixed position within the line. Each such line has a reference number linking it back to the line, and position within the line, of the word in the original "horizontal" text; punctuation marks are given a reference number subordinating them to the preceding word, and sentences are "framed" by a special new-sentence-marker line. The remainder of the line is taken up with the word itself, the associated tag, and special markers (there are none in this extract) for such things as headings, foreign words, contracted words, etc. The tags are from the LOB tagset, listed and discussed in Appendix B.

There are two problems with an automatic tagging approach: first, the large number of homographs in English, and second, the open-ended nature of English vocabulary. There are about 50 000 word types in the LOB Corpus; we did not wish to rely on a

D01	2	001		– – – –
D01	2	010	with	IN
D01	2	020	so	QL
D01	2	030	many	AP
D01	2	040	problems	NNS
D01	2	050	to	TO
D01	2	060	solve	VB
D01	2	061	,	,
D01	2	070	it	PP3
D01	2	080	would	MD
D01	2	090	be	BE
D01	2	100	a	AT
D01	2	110	great	JJ
D01	2	120	help	NN
D01	2	130	to	TO
D01	3	010	select	VB
D01	3	020	some	DTI
D01	3	030	one	CD1
D01	3	040	problem	NN
D01	3	050	which	WDT
D01	3	060	might	MD
D01	3	070	be	BE
D01	3	080	the	ATI
D01	3	090	key	NN
D01	3	100	to	IN
D01	3	110	all	ABN
D01	3	120	the	ATI
D01	3	130	others	APS
D01	3	131	,	,
D01	3	140	and	CC
D01	4	010	begin	VB
D01	4	020	there	RN
D01	4	021		.
D01	4	022		– – – –

dictionary of this size designed for the LOB Corpus, but preferred a mechanism involving a smaller dictionary which had the potential of being used on other texts. The Brown Corpus had already been automatically tagged with an accuracy of something like 77% (Greene and Rubin 1971), and we aimed to design algorithms which would ensure a significantly higher success rate than this. In achieving this goal we had the benefit of three tools, made available by the Brown team: (a) a set of tags which had been used for the Brown tagging: (b) the tagged Brown Corpus, a database of information about the associations between words, tags and contexts; and (c) a tagging program, TAGGIT, which carried out the automatic tagging of the Brown corpus, and which we used to investigate the areas where the automatic tagging system worked least well.

The CLAWS tagging system consists of five separate stages applied successively to a text to be tagged:

(a)   **A pre-editing phase**   This stage, partly automatic and partly manual, prepares the text for the tagging system proper; it is described in section 3.

(b)   **Tag assignment**   Each word in the input text is assigned a set of one or more tags. This assignment phase does not look at the context in which the word appears, so the assigned set of tags should include any tag that could be appropriate to the word in some possible context. This stage (the program WORDTAG) is described in sections 4 and 5.

(c)   **Idiom-tagging**   This stage looks for a number of special word or tag patterns where a limited amount of context could narrow down the set of possible tags assigned to a word. This stage (the program IDIOMTAG) is described briefly in section 7, and in more detail in Chapter 9.

(d)   **Tag disambiguation**   This stage inspects all cases where a word has been assigned more than one tag, and attempts to choose a preferred tag by considering the context in which the word appears, and assessing the probability of any particular sequence of tags. This stage (the program CHAINPROBS) is described briefly in section 6, and in more detail in Chapter 4.

(e)   **A post-editing phase**   This stage involves a manual process in which erroneous tagging decisions by the computer are corrected, followed by a reformating stage (the program LOBFORMAT) to eliminate unnecessary subsidiary information provided by the tagging system and produce a final tagged corpus. This is described in section 8.

In the Brown system, stages (b) to (d) are all executed by a single program TAGGIT. In our system we kept the separate operations as three separate programs (WORDTAG, IDIOMTAG and CHAINPROBS). However, when the programs had been developed, a command-language procedure was written which automatically applied each program in turn to a portion of the corpus.

3.   Verticalizing and pre-editing

The CLAWS1 system was developed for use primarily on the LOB Corpus, and is now being revised to deal with other formats of input text. The LOB Corpus consists of a series of lines of running text, with extra information relating to the typographic layout, such as new paragraph, change of typeface, etc., and with markers for special items such as abbreviations, foreign words, or substandard English. The first phase of the tagging system involves a program (PREEDIT) which "verticalizes" the text, followed by a manual pre-editing stage.

The main task of the PREEDIT Program is to create a separate line for each word or punctuation mark in the corpus, with the word or punctuation mark in a standard place in the line, and with a reference number so that it can be traced back to its original category, text extract, line, and position in the line. However, there are a number of subsidiary tasks for the program:

(a)   Certain typographic information which is of no help to the automatic tagging system is discarded at this stage. This includes new-paragraph symbols, changes of typeface, indications of the position of diagrams, etc.

(b)   Certain information which may be of use to the tagging system, or which should be retained as possibly of interest in the final tagged corpus, is moved to a subsidiary position in the line. This includes an indication of whether the current word is part of a heading, and the markers for special items mentioned above.

(c)   As mentioned above, a contracted form such as *he'll* is treated as two separate syntactic units each with its own tag. The PREEDIT program therefore recognizes these cases and splits them into the appropriate units, leaving markers in a subsidiary position in the lines to show that the two units are orthographically joined.

(d)   It is the task of the remaining programs in the suite to assign a tag to each word. However, as can be seen from Appendix B, the tag symbol associated with a punctuation mark is the punctuation mark itself, so this trivial tagging operation is performed by the PREEDIT program.

(e)   The running text of the Corpus is in lower case, but upper case occurs in a number of places: in words where the upper case should be retained (*McDonald, NATO, I'm*), but also in the first word of a sentence (where the initial capital should be retained only if it would have occurred if the word were found in the middle of a sentence), and in a number of rarer situations with continuously capitalized texts. The PREEDIT program attempts to recognize words where the upper case should be retained, and converts the rest to lower case, relying on manual intervention to correct this where necessary. This is a place where significant manual intervention is currently required, so the new version of CLAWS is being written to attempt to deal with capitalization without manual intervention.

After the PREEDIT program has been run, the verticalized corpus is manually pre-edited to correct the text where necessary, and to tag certain words manually where it is known that the automatic tagging system is likely to fail. In order to help with this manual pre-editing, a suite of programs was written to extract from the original Corpus lists of cases needing consideration. Since the CLAWS1 system was being designed and constructed at the same time as the earlier parts of the pre-editing, several of these lists (such as lists of arithmetic formulae and of abbreviations) were used mainly in suggesting types of linguistic feature which the tagging system had to cope with, and would not be used in pre-editing a new corpus.

Other lists were more central to the pre-editing process, such as lists of words where the verticalizing program retains a word-initial capital letter or where it changes the letter to lower case; the editor would check each example, and correct the verticalized text where the program was in error. As mentioned above, it is planned that the enhanced tagging system currently being developed will make more use of automatic methods of selecting the appropriate case-shift in these situations. Lists were also prepared of more rarely occurring features (such as non-English words) so that they could be manually tagged. Our policy with CLAWS2 is similarly to eliminate manual insertion of tags at this stage, in the expectation that consequential errors will be rare and can be dealt with during manual post-editing.

4.   The tag assignment program (WORDTAG)

It is the task of the WORDTAG program to assign one or more tags to each word in the corpus. If it assigns a single tag, it is assumed that this is the correct tag and it will not be changed by CHAINPROBS; however, it may be altered by the IDIOMTAG program or during manual post-editing. If WORDTAG assigns more than one candidate tag, then CHAINPROBS will attempt to choose one of these candidates as the preferred one. An attempt is made by WORDTAG to order such a set of candidate tags in approximately decreasing likelihood, and a "rarity marker" may be attached to a tag (see below).

   WORDTAG assigns tags to a word considering it in isolation; it is the task of the CHAINPROBS program to select a tag on the basis of the context in which the word appears. The basic plan of WORDTAG is provided by the first half of the Brown TAGGIT program, but enhanced by the experience of using TAGGIT and by the availability of larger dictionaries derived from the data extracted from the Brown and LOB Corpora. It is designed to be open-ended in the sense of coping as far as possible with unrestricted English, including neologisms, deviant spellings, etc. The program consists of a sequence of rules, ordered so that later rules are applied to a word only if all earlier rules have failed. These rules were constructed by an iterative process, involving the testing of WORDTAG over a portion of the Corpus, an analysis of the results, and subsequent modifications to the WORDTAG rules. The program proceeds as follows:

(a)   Some syntactic units will already have been tagged before WORDTAG is reached, either automatically or manually by the first stage of the tagging system, as described above. WORDTAG simply accepts these tagging decisions.

(b)   The next step is to look up the syntactic unit in a lexicon. A lexicon of some 7200 words is used, containing the word and up to six possible tags for the word; thus the word *round*, for instance, has possible tags JJ, RI, NN, VB, and IN (i.e. adjective, a certain type of adverb, noun, verb, and preposition). The tags are listed in approximately decreasing likelihood, and may be marked "@" meaning "rare" (likelihood nominally less than 10%) or "%" meaning "very rare" (likelihood nominally less than 1%). Thus the lexicon entry for *round* is in fact:

   round   JJ RI NN VB@ IN@

If the word is found in the lexicon it is assigned all the tags listed in its entry; otherwise the program applies a sequence of further tagging rules which are to be described.

   The lexicon contains all function words (*in, my, was, that*, etc.), the most frequent words in the open classes noun, verb, and adjective, and any words which are exceptions to the general tagging rules which will be applied to unlisted words. Conversely, certain types of derived forms (plurals of nouns, comparatives of adjectives) do not need to appear in the lexicon, since the general tagging rules will correctly assign the appropriate tags. Thus the construction of the lexicon has been an iterative process, taking into account the tagging rules added to WORDTAG and their exceptions. The original version of the lexicon together with the word-ending list or "suffixlist" was constructed in Oslo and Bergen (Johansson and Jahr 1982), and it was extended in Lancaster by adding some 200–300 common abbreviations, some 400–500 common words with a word-initial capital, and a number of other words or syntactic units. This lexicon accounts for a large proportion (65–70%) of the tagging decisions made by WORDTAG.

(c)   The next step is to eliminate a wide class of syntactic units which are not strictly speaking words. The types of tagging decision made here cover such cases as:

- *$37.00* and *£2* are tagged NNU (unit of measure)
- *i, b27, x″* are tagged ZZ (letter of the alphabet; *I* and *a*, being exceptions, are in the lexicon)
- *27th, 1st* are tagged OD (ordinal)
- *1940s* is tagged CDS ("plural" cardinal)
- *1950–7* is tagged CD–CD (hyphenated cardinal)
- *1940's, 3's* are ambiguously tagged CDS or CD$ ("plural" cardinal, or cardinal with genitive, as in *Louis 14's reign*: in this example the LOB Corpus includes a marker for "type shift into Roman numerals", which has been ignored by the PREEDIT program)
- Other numbers (*2, 19.6, 4,000,000, $\frac{1}{2}$,* etc.) are tagged CD (cardinal)
- Various expressions like H_2SO_4, *a−4*, $E=mc^2$ are tagged &FO (formula).

All other orthographic units, containing only letters and accents, apostrophes and hyphens, together with such partially-numeric expressions as *12-year-old*, are left for later rules to process. Notice here that a certain amount of care has been taken to assign a correct tag to these non-word structures despite their low frequency, and the examples illustrate the types of thing to be met in unrestricted English text.

(d)   The next step deals with words containing hyphens, and is discussed in detail in the following section.

(e)   The next step deals with words which retain an initial capital letter after the manual pre-editing phase. (The same set of rules is used within the procedure for dealing with hyphenated words, if there is a capital letter after the (last) hyphen.) The rules are as follows:

- Look the word up in a special list of suffixes or word-endings for words with initial capitals. This includes such endings as *-ish* and *-ian*, which commonly occur in capitalized words, with the appropriate tags.
- Strip any final *-s*, and look the word up in the lexicon or, failing that, the special word-ending list mentioned above.
- Assign a default tag of NP (proper noun). This is the most commonly applied rule for words retaining an initial capital.

(f)   If the above steps fail, the next step is to look up the word in a list of word-endings, the "suffixlist"; this consists of about 720 word-endings (for words *without* initial capitals) with their associated tag or tags. The suffixlist contains sequences of up to five letters, including "suffixes" in the ordinary sense, such as *-ness* (noun), but also any word endings which are associated invariably (or at least with high frequency) with certain word classes, for example *-mp* (noun or verb) – the letters *-mp* do not constitute a morphological suffix, but it is a fact that almost all words ending with these letters are either nouns or verbs (the few exceptions, such as *damp* and *limp*, are listed in the lexicon).

The suffixlist is searched for the longest matching word-ending. Thus there are entries in the list for *-able* (adjective), *-ble* (noun or verb), and *-le* (noun), and these will be tested for in that order; exceptions (such as *cable* and *enable*) are in the lexicon. This step succeeds for most of the words not found in the lexicon, typically 7–12% of the words in the text.

While this step is quite successful, it is being extended in the revised tagging system. It is possible to envisage a generalized morphological analysis, which would successively strip a sequence of suffixes. Instead we are concentrating on particular troublesome suffixes; for instance, if the suffix *-er* is stripped and a test made of the word-class of the stem, it enables this step in many cases to disambiguate between agentive noun and comparative adjective.

(g)   The suffix *-s* is not dealt with by the above test. Instead the suffix *-s* (but not *-ss*) is stripped; and action taken to construct a putative singular noun or first person singular verb by stripping a trailing *-e* or changing *-ie* to *-y* in the appropriate cases. The resulting character-sequence is looked up first in the lexicon and, if that fails, in the suffixlist. If any tags are assigned by this procedure, then only those compatible with the final *-s* are retained as possible tags for the original word. The possible cases are that the base form of a verb becomes a third person singular form, and various noun classes become plural. Thus the word *kinds* found in a text would have its final *-s* stripped to become *kind*, which is found in the lexicon with tags NN JJ@ (i.e. noun or more rarely adjective); the JJ tag is rejected as incompatible with the *-s* suffix, and the NN tag is converted to NNS (i.e. plural noun), which is therefore the (unique) tag assigned to the word *kinds* by WORDTAG. If none of the tags selected for the s-stripped word are compatible with the *-s* suffix, then the tags NNS VBZ (i.e. plural noun or third person singular verb) are assigned, but the word is marked for possible manual attention.

(h)   If all the above rules fail, certain tags are assigned by default. We have just seen that the default tagging for words ending in *-s* is NNS VBZ; all other words are by default tagged NN VB JJ (i.e. noun, verb, or adjective). Very few words receive this default tagging (a total of about 200 out of the million words of the Corpus, mostly foreign words and deviant spellings).

(i)   Before step (a), a test is made for the genitive markers *'s* and *s'*; if found they are stripped off the word, and their occurrence noted. Constructions like *1940's* are dealt with in step (c). Any other syntactic unit which is associated with a genitive marker is considered when all the above rules have been tried and some tag assignment made.

Only those tags compatible with a genitive marker are retained; thus, for example, NP (proper noun) becomes NP$. If no tags are compatible, a default tag (either NN$ or NNS$) is assigned and the word marked for possible manual attention.

5. Hyphenated words

If a syntactic unit is a word (by the criteria mentioned in (c) above) and contains one or more hyphens, then the following steps are performed:

(a)   The first step is to search before the (first) hyphen for a special set of prefixes which do not generally affect the classification of the word of which they are part. If any of the prefixes *a-, co-, counter-, de-, hyper-, mis-, out-, over-, re-, retro-, super-* and *trans-* are found, then the prefix is stripped off and the remaining word tagged by trying all the rules in the preceding section (starting with the lexicon look-up); that is, the word is tagged as if the prefix was not present, so that (for example) the word *a-dying* receives the tags of *dying*.

(b)   Similary, if the first letter after the hyphen is a capital letter, that part before the hyphen is ignored and the remaining word is tagged by the rules given in step (e) of the preceding section (for words with an initial capital), so that (for example) the word *un-American* is tagged as if it were *American*.

(c)   Next, the part of the word after the (last) hyphen is looked up in the lexicon and, failing that, the suffixlist. If this search is successful, the program attempts to deduce tags for the complete word from the tags found for the "part-word" applying the following rules in sequence:
- If the tags of the part-word include IN (preposition), assign tags NN (noun) and JJ@ (rarely adjective), for example *washing-up, well-off*.
- If the tags of the part-word include VBN (past participle), assign tag JJ (adjective), for example *self-employed, so-called*.
- If the tags of the part-word include VBG (present participle), assign tags JJ (adjective) NN (noun) and VBG@ (rarely present participle), for example *fact-finding, fierce-looking*.
- If the tags of the part-word include NN (noun) unmarked for rarity, assign tag NN (noun) and JJB (attributive adjective), for example *income-tax, long-term*.

A similar sequence of steps is followed for hyphenated words ending in -*s*.

(d)   Various special-purpose procedures are inserted in this sequence of steps. For example, before step (c) a check is made to see whether the part of the word after the (last) hyphen is one of the set -*class*, -*free*, -*hand*, -*like*, -*price*, -*proof*, -*quality*, -*range*, -*rate* and -*scale*; any one of these causes the full word to be tagged JJ (adjective). An example would be *middle-class*; exceptions like *price-range* must be in the lexicon.

Failing all else a default (NN VB JJB) is assigned; there were about 100 words tagged in this way in the Corpus.

6. The tag-disambiguation program

After WORDTAG has run, every syntactic unit has one or more tags associated with it, and about 35% are ambiguously tagged with two or more tags. The program CHAINPROBS attempts to disambiguate such words by considering their context, and then reordering the list of tags associated with each word in decreasing order of preference, so that the preferred tag appears first. With each tag is associated a figure representing the likelihood of this tag being the correct one, and if this figure is high enough CHAINPROBS simply eliminates the remaining tags. Thus some ambiguities will be removed, while others are left for the manual post-editor to check; in most cases the first tag, as preferred by CHAINPROBS, is the correct one.

This disambiguation mechanism requires a source of information as to the strengths of links between pairs of tags; much of this information was derived from a sample taken from the tagged Brown Corpus, and effectively gives us a matrix of probabilities of tag y occurring given tag x on the immediately preceding word. Given a sequence of ambiguously tagged words, the CHAINPROBS program uses these one-step probabilities to generate a probability for each sequence of ambiguous tags. Thus given words w_1 and w_4 unambiguously tagged t_1 and t_4 respectively, and words w_2 and w_3 each with two tags:

$$w_1\ w_2\ w_3\ w_4$$
$$t_1\ \ t_{21}\ t_{31}\ t_4$$
$$t_{22}\ t_{32}$$

CHAINPROBS calculates the probabilities of the sequences:

$$t_1\ t_{21}\ t_{31}\ t_4$$
$$t_1\ t_{21}\ t_{32}\ t_4$$
$$t_1\ t_{22}\ t_{31}\ t_4$$

and

$$t_1\ t_{22}\ t_{32}\ t_4$$

and from these derives a probability for each ambiguous tag. More details of this process are given in Chapter 4.

7. Multiple syntactic units and IDIOMTAG

The tagging system as originally conceived consisted of WORDTAG, to assign plausible tags to individual words, followed by CHAINPROBS to disambiguate the tags in context. After we had tested this system over some portions of the Corpus, it became clear that a useful addition would be a mechanism for assigning plausible tags to *groups* of words, since with this we could eliminate certain obvious classes of error. For simplicity this is a separate program, IDIOMTAG, which modifies some of the decisions made by WORDTAG, and the output of which is fed for disambiguation into CHAINPROBS.

IDIOMTAG looks for any of a specified list of about 150 phrases, and modifies the tags accordingly. For example, suppose it finds the word *as*, followed by a word to which WORDTAG has assigned a set of candidate tags which include JJ (adjective), followed by the word *as*, for example *as old as*. IDIOMTAG assigns the tag QL (qualifier) to the first *as* and the tags IN CS@ (preposition or rarely subordinating conjunction) to the second *as*. WORDTAG would have assigned all three of these tags to each of the occurrences of *as*, so the amount of ambiguity to be dealt with by CHAINPROBS is reduced.

One minor modification to the tagset was introduced with IDIOMTAG. There are a number of cases where two or more separate orthographic units function syntactically as a single unit. A number of examples were given in section 1 (p. 31), and another is *as well as*, which is an exception to the pattern described in the previous paragraph. To deal with this we introduced a "ditto-tag" marking which represents a single grammatical tag covering a sequence of two or more orthographic units in the tagged Corpus, and these markings are assigned by IDIOMTAG; *as well as* would for example be tagged CC (conjunction). Chapter 9 of this book discusses the IDIOMTAG program in more detail, and some of the problems it raises.

8.   The post-edit phase

After the LOB Corpus had been processed by CLAWS1, it was manually post-edited. This was done in two passes: the first was to look at all the remaining ambiguous taggings, and decide whether CHAINPROBS's preferred tag was in fact correct, and the second was a manual check of the whole Corpus, since we required the tags assigned to the words of the LOB Corpus to be as accurate as possible. For other uses of the tagging system this manual post-editing phase might be reduced in scope or even omitted. Subsequently a third phase of checking has been performed on the tagged LOB Corpus in Oslo and Bergen; this has involved extracting various lists of particular tags in context, in order to check the consistency of the final published tagged Corpus.

Corrections were made to the Corpus in such a way as to preserve an indication of the type of correction needed; since this version of the Corpus also retains information as to how WORDTAG selected the appropriate tags, whether IDIOMTAG was involved, and what probabilities were calculated by CHAINPROBS, it is possible to make a detailed analysis of the source and type of all tagging errors. The results of such an error analysis have guided the construction of CLAWS2.

For distribution a further program (LOBFORMAT) removes all the extra information, leaving only the correct tag, and it can if desired reformat the corpus into a "horizontal" running text form, with the correct tag immediately next to the word to which it refers.

9. Conclusions

This chapter has described a system for assigning grammatical parts of speech to words in running text, a task which it performs with a high degree of accuracy over texts which are unrestricted in vocabulary and contain passages of learned English, dialogue, non-standard English, etc. The system is robust in the sense that, given a text, it will always assign some tag to each word, however complex or erroneous the text.

Our current work at Lancaster includes further development of this tagging system. Our analysis of the errors arising from application of the current system will lead to enhancements to the three main tagging programs, and the tagged LOB Corpus is being used to derive a new matrix of probabilities for use by CHAINPROBS. Thus the development of these tagging programs is an incremental process, in that each tagged corpus can be used as a database of information for tagging the next.

CHAPTER 4

Tag selection using probabilistic methods

Ian Marshall

1. Introduction

Chapter 3 describes the CLAWS tagging system in general, and describes in detail the WORDTAG program for assigning to each word in a text a set of one or more possible tags. If a single tag is assigned, the CLAWS system assumes that this is the correct one, but if more than one tag is assigned a disambiguation procedure is required. This is the task of the program CHAINPROBS, which is described in detail in this chapter. The program receives a sequence of words, each with one or more tags, and attempts to choose a preferred tag. Depending on its level of certainty that the preferred tag is the correct one, it will either eliminate all but the preferred tag, or simply retain a sequence of tags and associated information displayed in order of decreasing likelihood. The associated information is an indication of how confident CHAINPROBS is in its choice of preferred tag. All this information is made available to the next stage of the tagging system, the manual post-editing procedure, which is also briefly discussed in the previous chapter. If no manual post-editing is performed then the first or only tag in the sequence is the CLAWS suite's choice as the appropriate tag for the word, a choice which is correct in 96–97% of cases.

In designing CHAINPROBS we were aware of the techniques used in the TAGGIT program to carry out the tag disambiguation task on the Brown Corpus. In this chapter we therefore first discuss the disambiguation algorithm used in the TAGGIT program, and indicate the type of problems we expected in applying a similar algorithm to the LOB Corpus. We then describe the first, simple mechanism we designed to disambiguate tags in the LOB Corpus, giving a detailed example of how it works. Finally we discuss the areas in which this simple mechanism did not work well, and describe enhancements to the disambiguation procedure to get around these problems.

2.   The TAGGIT approach to disambiguation

Lexical disambiguation in the TAGGIT program is based upon rules which use a word's local context to determine its syntactic category. TAGGIT contains a collection of 3300 "context frame rules", each of the form:

$$W \ X \ ? \ Y \ Z \rightarrow A$$

Such a rule specifies that, in a syntactic context where an ambiguous word (represented by "?") is surrounded by words tagged W and X on the left and Y and Z on the right, the tag of the word is A, provided that A was among the possible tags specified for that word. A variant type of context frame rule has the right-hand side negated:

$$W \ X \ ? \ Y \ Z \rightarrow \text{not } A$$

This indicates that the tag A is to be eliminated from the list of possible tags in the context specified by the left-hand side of the rule.

One or more of the context tags (represented by W, X, Y, Z) may be left unspecified in a rule, subject to the requirement that if W is specified then X must be specified and if Z is specified then Y must be specified. The set of context frame rules is ordered in such a way that rules with more specific (wider) context frames are applied first, and, if the ambiguity is resolved, block the application of rules with less specific context frames. Thus, in the design of the rule set, the more specific rules represent exceptions to the more general rules. For further details of how this mechanism works see Greene and Rubin (1971: 32–40).

The application of such rules is restricted to cases where words in the context of the word under consideration are unambiguously tagged with the tags specified in a rule. To see why this is problematic, consider the two context frame rules:

$$? \ VBZ \rightarrow \text{not } NNS$$
$$NNS \ ? \rightarrow \text{not } VBZ$$

These rules state that before the third person singular form of a verb (VBZ) a word is unlikely to be a plural noun (NNS), and conversely that a plural noun is unlikely to be followed by the third person singular form of a verb.

Suppose we are confronted by the (hypothetical) sentence:

Henry likes stews.

Since both *likes* and *stews* are ambiguous between being plural nouns and third person singular verb forms, neither of the rules quoted could be applied: the failure to apply either rule prevents application of the other. In such sequences of ambiguously-tagged words the TAGGIT program attempts to disambiguate words by working inwards from the unambiguous words at either end of the sequence and using other context frame rules. In this particular case, no other rules are applicable, and disambiguation is not achieved. As a result of experimental runs of the TAGGIT program over parts of the LOB Corpus, it became clear that this type of problem would leave many words ambiguously tagged, if this disambiguation mechanism was applied to the complete LOB Corpus.

In such cases we felt that it should still be possible to use the information about the tags of the adjacent words to assist in the choice of the appropriate tag for the current word, even when the choice of the appropriate tags for the adjacent words is not unambiguous. Thus in the above example it *is* relevant that a tag of NNS for *likes* precludes a tag of VBZ for *stews*, even though the allocation of a tag to *likes* is ambiguous. In this case one could attempt to make the quoted rules select the desired tags by removing the restriction that context words must be unambiguously tagged, but this would lead to unpredictable consequences for the application of the entire body of rules to other examples. In particular, it would tend to increase the proportion of cases in which rules with wide context frames were applied in preference to rules with narrower frames.

However, the experimental run of TAGGIT over parts of the LOB Corpus suggested a different approach. Some of the TAGGIT context frame rules specified only one context tag: that is, they had one of the forms:

$$? \ X \rightarrow A$$
$$? \ X \rightarrow \text{not } A$$
$$X \ ? \rightarrow A$$
$$X \ ? \rightarrow \text{not } A$$

and we noticed that, although rules of these forms comprised fewer that 25% of TAGGIT's context frame rules, approximately 80% of the actual rule applications were of rules of this form. This disproportionate usage of minimally specified contexts suggested that a more effective method of tag disambiguation might be produced by a system which exploited only the relationship between adjacent tags (rather than a wider context), but coupled it with a mechanism that would apply through a sequence of ambiguous words.

3.   Disambiguation in CLAWS

In computational linguistic research, statistical analyses of distribution have been used fairly widely to investigate semantic associations between words, but less commonly to investigate syntactic relationships. Efforts to formulate explanatorily-adequate linguistic theories have emphasized introspective judgements of grammaticality, and work on the development of automatic parsers has followed this trend. While significant progress has been achieved through such approaches, the state of the art is such that a comprehensive parser for English remains to be developed. The LOB Corpus contains a range of texts reflecting how English is used across a number of genres. For the purpose of tagging the Corpus we wished each word to be given the best possible analysis, despite the fact that Corpus texts represent diverse styles and indeed contain many incomplete or "ungrammatical" sentences.

The observation noted above, that most applications of context frame rules in TAGGIT involved rules with minimal frame specifications, suggested that the task of disambiguating words in the LOB Corpus might be approached through a statistical analysis of co-occurring tags in the already-tagged Brown Corpus, which would yield a transition matrix showing the probability of any one tag following any other. A large proportion of the tagged Brown Corpus was used to generate statistics on the overall frequency of each tag, and on the frequency with which any two tags were found adjacent to each other. It was pointed out in the previous chapter that there were some small differences between the Brown tagset and the LOB tagset, so some adjustment of the Brown frequency figures was required to take account of these differences. Disambiguation of words in the LOB Corpus was then based on these statistics.

We initially assumed that, if w_1, w_2 were two adjacent words in the LOB Corpus and w_1 was known to be correctly tagged A, then the probability of B being the correct tag for w_2 could be estimated from the ratio of the number of cases in the Brown Corpus where tag B immediately follows A to the number of cases in the Brown Corpus where *any* tag follows tag A (i.e. effectively the frequency of the tag A). That is, we supposed that a prediction of the probability of the occurrence of tag B conditional on the fact that we have observed tag A on the word immediately preceding is:

$$\frac{\text{frequency of the tag-sequence "A followed by B" in the Brown Corpus}}{\text{frequency of the tag A in the Brown Corpus}}$$

Our transition matrix stored a figure representing conditional probabilities of "tag B given tag A" derived in this way, for each pair of tags A, B in the tagset. For practical computational reasons the figures derived from the above formula were multiplied by one thousand and rounded to the nearest integer before being stored in the matrix, and then converted back to a probability figure when used; in the following discussion we will use the probability values in this "per-thousand" form.

Although the transition matrix only takes into account statistical relationships between consecutive tags, the disambiguation algorithm incorporated in the CHAINPROBS program has to deal with sequences of more than one adjacent ambiguously-tagged word. Where an ambiguously-tagged word in the text happens to be surrounded on either side by words which are unambiguously tagged by the tag-assignment program WORDTAG. this is treated merely as a special case of an ambiguous sequence where the length is one (rather than the central case, as in TAGGIT). A sequence of ambiguously tagged words, bounded at either end by a word which has been assigned a single unambiguous tag by WORDTAG, defines a number of possible tag-sequences (i.e. different pathways through the possible alternative tags for the successive words). Since punctuation marks are treated as unambiguously tagged "words", a sequence of ambiguities will usually be reasonably short (up to about ten words long). The algorithm calculates the probability of each of the tag-sequences: in most cases, the correct tag for a word is the one among those assigned by WORDTAG which lies on the sequence with the highest probability.

For example, consider again the sentence:

Henry likes stews.

This would receive the following tags from WORDTAG:

Henry   NP
likes   NNS VBZ
stews   NNS VBZ

For each of the four possible tag sequences spanning the ambiguity, a value is generated by calculating the product of the values for successive tag transitions taken from the transition matrix. Thus:

$$val(NP\text{-}NNS\text{-}NNS\text{-}.) = 17 \times 5 \times 135 = 11\ 475$$
$$val(NP\text{-}NNS\text{-}VBZ\text{-}.) = 17 \times 1 \times 37 = 629$$
$$val(NP\text{-}VBZ\text{-}NNS\text{-}.) = 7 \times 28 \times 135 = 26\ 460$$
$$val(NP\text{-}VBZ\text{-}VBZ\text{-}.) = 7 \times 0 \times 37 = 0$$

The probability of a sequence of tags X_j is then determined by dividing the value obtained for the sequence by the sum of the values for all possible sequences:

$$prob\ (X_j) = \frac{val(X_j)}{\sum_{i=1}^{n} val(X_i)}$$

where n is the number of possible sequence of tags, X_i is the ith sequence, and $val(X_i)$ is the value calculated for the ith sequence by the method above.

Thus the probability of the sequence NP-VBZ-NNS-. as compared to the other possible sequences is:

$$\frac{val(NP\text{-}VBZ\text{-}NNS\text{-}.)}{val(NP\text{-}NNS\text{-}NNS\text{-}.) + val(NP\text{-}NNS\text{-}VBZ\text{-}.) + \ldots}$$

or

$$\frac{26\ 460}{11\ 475 + 629 + 26\ 460 + 0} = 69\%$$

This algorithm allows lexical disambiguation to be undertaken without regard for the extent of ambiguity in the local context, and makes maximum use of the information available in the matrix of transition probabilities throughout a sequence of ambiguities.

In the previous chapter it was indicated that, where a word is assigned ambiguous tags by WORDTAG, some of the tags may have associated "rarity markers", the symbol @ indicating that the tag is appropriate nominally less than once in ten occurrences of the word and the symbol % indicating that the tag is appropriate nominally less than once in one hundred occurrences of the word. If such a rarity marker occurs on one of the tags in a sequence, then the value of that sequence is "scaled down" by a factor to take account of the rare or very rare association between tag and word. If a rarity marker occurs more than once on a particular sequence then the scaling factor is applied the appropriate number of times. The scaling factors used were chosen by a process of trial and error; the values currently used are $\frac{1}{2}$ for the @ symbol and $\frac{1}{8}$ for the % symbol. Thus if, in the above example, the NNS tag for *likes* had the @ rarity marker, the two associated sequences would have the values 5738 and 315, instead of 11 475 and 629.

Although the final version of CHAINPROBS incorporated further mechanisms to be described later, even the simple algorithm described here, which uses only information about frequencies of transitions between immediately adjacent tags, provides a remarkably good approximation to the correct tagging of words. In a sample of sentences comprising more than 15 000 words, 94% of all words were correctly tagged by the CLAWS suite of programs before incorporation of later refinements. Approximately 65% of words were tagged unambiguously by the tag-assignment program WORDTAG, which implies that the disambiguating program CHAINPROBS itself achieved better than 80% success on the words which were ambiguously tagged.

4.   Additive probabilities and thresholds

In addition to marking the most probable sequence of tags, the CHAINPROBS program also performs a cross-check intended to estimate the likelihood that a given tag selection for a word is correct independently of the correctness of tags selected for surrounding words. For each tag assigned to a word by WORDTAG, CHAINPROBS calculates a figure representing the probability that this tag is correct, by summing the values of all the tag-sequences which select this tag for the word in question, and dividing by the sum of the values for all possible tag-sequences.

More formally, suppose that:

> n is the number of different tag-sequences;
> X_i is the ith sequence of tags;
> val (X_i) is the value of the ith sequence;
> tag_j is the jth tag in a tag-sequence;
> Z is a tag associated with a word.

Then the probability calculated for tag Z being associated with the jth word is:

$$\frac{\sum_{i=1}^{n} (\text{if } tag_j \text{ in } X_i \text{ is } Z \text{ then val}(X_i) \text{ else } 0)}{\sum_{i=1}^{n} \text{val}(X_i)}$$

Here the numerator is the sum of the values of all tag-sequences which select Z as the tag associated with the *j*th word, and the denominator is the sum of the values of all tag-sequences.

In the example discussed above the probability of *likes* being correctly tagged as a plural noun is given by

$$\frac{\text{val(NP-NNS-NNS-.)} + \text{val(NP-NNS-VBZ-.)}}{\text{val(NP-NNS-NNS-.)} + \text{val(NP-NNS-VBZ-.)} + \text{val(NP-VBZ-NNS-.)} + \text{val(NP-VBZ-VBZ-.)}}$$

or

$$\frac{11\ 475 + 629}{11\ 475 + 629 + 26\ 460 + 0} = 31\%$$

In most cases, the fact that a tag lies on the most likely tag-sequence is enough to ensure that this "additive" probability for the tag is greater than those of competing tags for the same word. However, in cases where other tag-sequences have probabilities only slightly lower than that of the most likely tag-sequence, the tag with the highest additive probability might not be the one on the most likely tag-sequence. Since the CHAINPROBS program is designed so that its output can be used directly or passed to a manual post-editing stage, this output is arranged to indicate both methods of calculating the preferred tag. In all cases where the output from CHAINPROBS indicates an ambiguity in tag-assignment, the tags are ordered by decreasing additive probability and this probability is given as a numerical value. The tag on the most likely tag-sequence is marked by enclosing it in square brackets; this will usually be the first tag in the list (that is, the tag with the highest additive probability) but occasionally it will be the second. The subsequent programs in the CLAWS suite, in particular the reformating program LOBFORMAT, are set up to assume that the first tag in the list is the preferred one (unless action has been taken by the manual post-editor). In other words it is assumed that, where the methods of calculating the preferred tag yield different results, it is the additive probability method that is decisive.

Some feeling for the implementation of the CHAINPROBS tag-disambiguation program may be gained from examining the processing of the sentence:

> *This task involved a very great deal of detailed work for the Committee.*
> (G04 116–7)

The type of output generated by the CHAINPROBS program for this sentence would be:

this	DT
task	NN
involved	[VBD]/90 VBN/10 JJ@/0
a	AT
very	[QL]/99 AP@/1
great	[JJ]/96 RB/4
deal	[NN]/98 VB/2
of	IN

detailed	[JJ]/98 VBN/2 VBD/0
work	[NN]/100 VB/0
for	[IN]/94 CS/6
the	ATI
committee	NN

(Actual output from the current version of CLAWS1 is in fact slightly different from this, because of the effect of some of the refinements to the program which are described later.) Words shown with only one tag were assigned that single tag by the WORDTAG program (or in principle by the IDIOMTAG program mentioned in the previous chapter and described in more detail in Chapter 9, but in fact no alterations were made by IDIOMTAG to the WORDTAG output for this particular sentence). Where there are several tags associated with each word each is followed by its "additive" probability (as a percentage), and the most likely tag-sequence is marked by square brackets. Probabilities of 100% or 0% arise from the fact that all figures are rounded to the nearest integer. Note in the above sentence that the initial capital letters on the words *this* and *committee* have been replaced by lower-case letters in an earlier stage of CLAWS.

The CHAINPROBS program generates three trees (as shown in Figure 4) representing the possible tag-sequences for the three blocks of ambiguously-tagged words in the sentence. If the program runs out of space when constructing such a tree (in the case of a long sequence of words, each with several possible tags), then it defaults to a simpler method for calculating the likelihood of each tag, which is an approximation to the method described here but requires less storage. Once it has generated a tree the program associates with the links in the tree the transition probabilities from the transition matrix (here shown as "per-thousand" values). Each path through a tree from a root to a leaf node represents a possible tag-sequence, and the end of a path holds the computed product of the transition probabilities corresponding to the links forming that path. If a rarity marker is present there will be a "scaling-down" of the value of the path as described earlier; here the notation "/2" associated with the NN-JJ link in the first tree and the AT-AP link in the second tree are meant to represent the scaling factors for the JJ tag assigned to the word *involved* and the AP tag assigned to the word *very*, and these scaling factors have been taken into account in the values shown for the tag-sequences. Subsequently the program computes the additive probabilities, re-orders the tags and outputs the tags and the associated information.

The additive probability information not only indicates a preferred tag, but also gives us some idea of the strength of the preference shown by CHAINPROBS for that tag. In the example given CHAINPROBS was reasonably sure about all the preferred tags. However it is possible for CHAINPROBS to show no very conclusive preference for one particular tag, for example if two possible tags for a word lie on tag-sequences whose values are similar. Examples of such inconclusive assignments can be seen in the tagging of the sentence discussed in the next section (pp. 51–2).

The CHAINPROBS program is designed not only to calculate a preference for each

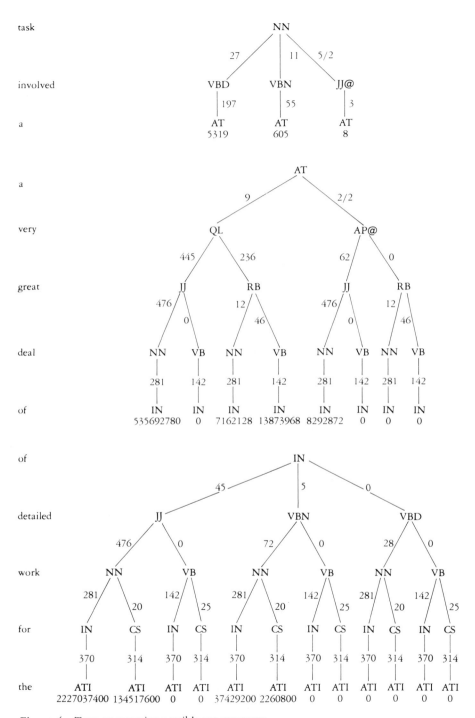

Figure 4   Trees representing possible tag-sequences

tag in an ambiguous situation, but also to act on that calculation if the evidence is firm enough. Thus a threshold is set such that, if the additive probability of a tag is higher than the threshold, that tag is assumed to be the correct one, and all other tags can be eliminated from the word. The choice of setting for the threshold is dependent on our wish to eliminate ambiguities from further consideration, and our wish not to eliminate ambiguities where CHAINPROBS is likely to be in error. With a threshold set at 90%, 86% of the output from this early version of CHAINPROBS had a single tag, and less than 1% of these unambiguously tagged words were in error. In fact CHAINPROBS has a slightly more sophisticated thresholding function, since the error rate for a given threshold will vary from tag to tag. We therefore use an array of thresholds, one for each tag in the tagset; if the preferred tag has an additive probability greater than the threshold associated with that tag, then all the other tags associated with that word are eliminated. In the example given earlier in this section, the final version of CHAINPROBS in fact eliminated all the ambiguities except for the ones associated with the words *involved* and *very*.

5. Analysis of errors from CHAINPROBS

As indicated above, early runs of the disambiguation program over preliminary samples of the LOB Corpus resulted in an error rate of approximately 6%. The types of error produced by these early runs of the CHAINPROBS program are illustrated by the tagging of a sentence taken from GO5 133–5 in the LOB Corpus, where asterisks indicate the erroneous selection of a tag:

*so	[RB]/83 CS/17
that	[CS]/100 DT/0 WP/0 QL%/0
we	PP1AS
were	BED
in	[IN]/98 RP%/0
the	ATI
worst	[JJT]/100 RBT/0 VB%/0
possible	JJ
shape	[NN]/100 VB/0
*to	[IN]/80 TO/0
*deal	[NN]/80 VB/20
with	IN
the	ATI
immediate	JJ
task	NN
of	IN
trying	[VBG]/55 JJ/45
*to	[IN]/53 TO/47

*co-operate	[NN]/50 VB/47 JJ/3
with	IN
the	ATI
Russians	NNPS
who	WP
suffered	[VBD]/100 VBN/0 JJ@/0
from	IN
no	[ATI]/100 UH/0
*such	[RB]/100 ABL/0
*disadvantages	[VBZ]/87 NNS/13
as	[CS]/71 QL@/29
did	DOD
we	PP1AS

The word *so* is incorrectly tagged as an adverb; the opening words of two infinitival clauses are incorrectly tagged, as if they constituted prepositional phrases; and *such* and *disadvantages* are incorrectly tagged as adverb and verb respectively.

This last pair of errors is a consequence of an erroneous lexicon entry which included an adverb tag RB as a possible tag for *such*; the fact that RB-VBZ (i.e. adverb followed by verb) is a very high-frequency tag transition meant that inclusion of this possibility for *such* led to an incorrect choice of the VBZ tag rather than the NNS tag for *disadvantages*. The lexicon entry for *such* has since been amended to remove the RB tag. This example illustrates the need for accuracy in specifying the possible tags for each word.

Since the WORDTAG lexicon is necessarily limited in size, a percentage of errors is of course inevitably introduced through the fact that the WORDTAG program makes many of its assignments in terms of classes of word satisfying the conditions of some rule (such as sharing a common suffix), rather than in terms of specific information about an individual word. However, analysis of the errors found in the preliminary runs of CHAINPROBS has led to the recognition of certain types of error which can be corrected by various methods before or within CHAINPROBS.

One means of reducing the CHAINPROBS error rate is by reducing the numbers of problems in the input text by the introduction of the IDIOMTAG program, which is mentioned in the previous chapter and discussed in more detail in Chapter 9. It was clear from the examination of preliminary output from CHAINPROBS that there were a number of rather specific word sequences which, because of their idiosyncratic nature, CHAINPROBS tended to tag incorrectly. Thus the IDIOMTAG program was designed to scan the output from the tag-assignment program WORDTAG for particular patterns of words and tags, and either select a single tag for some of the words or delete some of the tags where these were not possible in context, in both cases reducing the total amount of ambiguity in the input to CHAINPROBS. Furthermore, the fact that the IDIOMTAG program will assign tags to certain words when these words occur in idiomatic structures means that the tag-assignment program WORDTAG needs to assign to these words only the tags which occur in normal non-idiomatic grammatical contexts, again reducing the amount of ambiguity to be dealt with by CHAINPROBS. In the final version of CLAWS1 the words *so that* in the above example are tagged by IDIOMTAG as a multi-word sequence with a single (CS) "ditto-tag".

6. Errors stemming from the transition matrix

In several cases the disambiguation program proves to be excessively inclined to choose tags which have a relatively high frequency in the language over alternative, lower-frequency tags: even when the lower-frequency tag was in fact correct it would often not be selected. In particular, words were often wrongly tagged as nouns, since nouns are the commonest part of speech in the Brown Corpus from which the statistics were derived (and presumably in English in general). Other examples are that the word *there* was often tagged as an adverb (a high-frequency tag), even when it occurred preceding a form of *have* or *be*, when it is more likely that the correct choice is the low-frequency tag EX (existential *there*); and *to* followed by a word ambiguous between noun and verb was tagged as a preposition followed by a noun (both high-frequency tags), whereas in most cases of this ambiguous configuration (at least in the LOB Corpus) the correct analysis is infinitival *to* (a less-frequent tag) followed by a verb.

This pattern of errors suggested that the formula used for determining the values to be inserted in the cells of the transition matrix might be inappropriate. Recall that the formula is that, for each tagpair (A, B), the value in the corresponding matrix cell is:

$$\frac{\text{frequency of the tag-sequence "A followed by B" in the Brown Corpus}}{\text{frequency of the tag A in the Brown Corpus}}$$

The problem with this formula is that it does not take into account the frequency of the tag B in the sample.

Accordingly, we experimented with different formulae for calculating the transition-matrix values. Rather than using conditional probabilities, the formula used in the final version of the CHAINPROBS program for the value stored for the tagpair (A, B) is:

$$\frac{\text{frequency of the tag-sequence "A followed by B"}}{\text{frequency of tag A} \times \text{frequency of tag B}}$$

This value reflects the strength of the bond between the two tags; the effect of including the frequency of the second tag in the denominator is to weaken the tendency to prefer individual high-frequency tags, so that low frequency tags are more often chosen.

Another modification relates to zero entries in the transition matrix. Since tag-sequences are evaluated by multiplying together the values of their individual transitions, a zero figure for any one transition automatically leads to a zero value for the tag-sequence as a whole, even if it is a sequence in which several other transitions have high values. Yet this result is often misleading: no matter how large the sample from which the matrix is derived, there is always the possibility that some relatively rare co-occurrence of tags will fail to be represented. To circumvent this problem, we arranged that no value in the matrix should be zero; instead a small positive value is associated with any transition that fails to occur in the sample. Thus no co-occurrence of tags is outlawed, although the co-occurrence of certain tagpairs is specified as far less likely than the co-occurrence of others. Consequently the program is now very robust; the possibility of the value of any tag-sequence evaluating to zero is eliminated, and it is guaranteed that the program will always produce some analysis, even on texts employing obscure syntax or containing ungrammatical material (particularly common in fictional texts including representations of spoken English).

7.   Errors involving relationships between non-adjacent words

In several cases, the statistical relationship between the tags of adjacent words is less useful for disambiguation than the relationship between the tags of the first and third words in a three-word sequence. It was therefore necessary to modify the algorithm so that in a number of situations figures for tagpairs separated by an intermediate word supersede figures for tags of adjacent words. For example, many words emerge from the tag-assignment program as ambiguous between past tense verb and past participle (and, often, adjective); if such a word is preceded by an adverb, this is less useful for disambiguation than the word before the adverb. In particular, if a form of *have* or *be* precedes the adverb, this is strong evidence for the following word being a past participle.

To meet this problem, the algorithm incorporates a number of "tag-triples", each associated with a scaling factor which is used either to upgrade or to downgrade the values in the tree which have been computed on the basis of tagpair values. For example, the tag-triple:

BE RB VBD

(i.e. the word *be* followed by adverb and then past tense of verb) has been assigned a scaling factor which downgrades the value of any tag-sequence containing this triple, as compared with a competing tag-sequence containing a tag for past participle instead of past tense.

Again, with the co-ordinating conjunctions *and* and *or*, it is a generally useful heuristic to bias the algorithm in favour of selecting the same grammatical category (where possible) for the words on either side of the conjunction. This goal is achieved by providing tag-triples which upgrade the value of such sequences in comparison with other possible sequences, while yielding equal values for different three-tag sequences each meeting this condition if they are in competition with one another. For example, if the words on either side of a conjunction are both ambiguously tagged as nouns or adjectives (NN or JJ), then the partial sequences NN-CC-NN and JJ-CC-JJ receive the same value, which is greater than the values for either of the partial sequences NN-CC-JJ or JJ-CC-NN derived from the transition matrix. The choice between the two higher-valued partial sequences is then based upon the strength of the links with tags preceding and following the three-word sequence.

Another example is that the word *not* is less useful in determining the category of the following word than is the word preceding *not*. Since *not* is itself unambiguously tagged XNOT and does not need disambiguating; a mechanism has been built into CHAINPROBS which causes *not* to be ignored, so that the words on either side are treated as if they were adjacent. Opening and closing inverted commas are dealt with in the same manner, for the same reason. The mechanism which deals with *not* and inverted commas is implemented in a different fashion from the tag-triples discussed earlier, but in effect this mechanism abbreviates a long list of tag-triples having the tag for *not* or for inverted commas in the middle position, and in which the associated scaling factors depend only on the first and third tags.

The extension of the disambiguation algorithm to incorporate a limited number of tag-triples, as described, leads to a clear improvement in performance, either resulting in the correct choice of tag in cases where an incorrect choice would have been made without the use of triples, or else causing the correct tag to be strongly preferred where previously the figures for the alternatives would have been inconclusive. In principle, one might envisage systematically using a three-dimensional array of frequency figures for all possible three-tag sequences, in place of the two-dimensional transition matrix on which CHAINPROBS relies. In practice current computer facilities render this expensive; however, even if it were practically possible, it is questionable whether this approach would in fact significantly increase the accuracy of the disambiguation procedure over that of the augmented immediate-transition method outlined here.

8.   The current state of CHAINPROBS

The modifications described above are incorporated in the current version of CHAINPROBS in the CLAWS1 suite, and figures calculated for a number of representative samples of the LOB Corpus indicate that this version achieves a success rate of 96–97% of all words correctly tagged, equivalent to a rate of approximately 90% success on words assigned more than one possible tag on entry to CHAINPROBS.

The above success rate is the appropriate figure for the overall reliability of the

CLAWS1 suite, in selecting the correct tag in the absence of intervention in the form of manual post-editing. But in the task of tagging the LOB Corpus we were also concerned with the amount of post-editing we would need to do to produce an effectively error-free tagged corpus. As explained in the previous chapter, our manual post-editing stage consisted of two phases; a first phase in which all remaining ambiguities were disambiguated, and a second phase which was in effect a proof-reading for outstanding errors. We were therefore interested in the extent to which we could adjust the thresholds described in section 4, so that CHAINPROBS would eliminate ambiguities where the additive probabilities were conclusive (thus reducing the effort in phase one of the manual post-editing) without introducing an excessive number of errors to be found in the second phase of manual post-editing. The new version of the transition matrix, representing as it does the strength of bonds between consecutive tags rather than conditional probabilities, allows a more reliable use of such thresholds to distinguish between cases of conclusive and inconclusive tag selection. A sampling of the output from the CLAWS1 system found, for instance, that 86% of words are either given an unambiguous tag before CHAINPROBS is reached or have a tag with an additive probability sufficiently high for CHAINPROBS to eliminate all other tags (i.e. 86% of words in the output from CHAINPROBS are unambiguously tagged). Among this 86% of words for which CLAWS1 yields a "high-confidence" prediction, less than 0.02% of the predictions are in fact erroneous (as compared with 1% for earlier versions of the suite). In other words, most of the errors which arise in the output from CLAWS1 are associated with values indicating lower confidence in the result.

Finally some comments are in order concerning modifications to the CHAINPROBS program in developing the new CLAWS2 suite. Some of the changes are simply the result of using the new tagset as described on p. 167, and being able to incorporate the results of having tagged the complete LOB Corpus in deriving a new transition matrix. However there are a number of areas where improvements are possible: for example (a) in generalizing and making more use of the "tag-triple" idea to supplement the immediate-transition matrix where appropriate; and (b) in providing for the IDIOMTAG phase to indicate to CHAINPROBS an ambiguity between tagging a sequence of words either individually or as a multi-word unit (something that is not possible with the present version of CHAINPROBS). But in our view the general mechanism described above for probabilistic tag disambiguation has proved extremely successful and is likely to remain unchanged in its general features.

CHAPTER 5

Constituent-likelihood grammar

Eric Atwell

1. Introduction

The previous chapter gives an overview of the CHAINPROBS program, which assigns relative likelihoods to each potential tag of a syntactically ambiguous word. In this chapter, I will concentrate on the underlying theoretical model; and I will show how the principles can be generalized beyond word-tagging to apply to phrase and clause constituent structure analysis.

2. General principles of constituent-likelihood grammar

A "constituent-likelihood" grammar does not define the set of sentences (symbol-strings) which constitute a language, to the exclusion of all other possible sequences of symbols. No linguist (or team of linguists) has yet come up with an adequate generative grammar which truly generates all possible English sentences (and does not generate any non-English sentence); since the syntax of a natural language such as English is extremely complex, large corpora of texts will continue to throw up sentences which are not dealt with adequately. Furthermore, in many applications of syntactic analysis we must assume that the input may be noisy, that is, the text may contain errors; again, noisy text will not be dealt with adequately by a generative grammar. The constituent-likelihood grammar used in the UCREL tagging project is specifically geared to word-tagging; but the general principles can be applied to any level of linguistic analysis. In general, any analysis which involves assigning "labels" to "constituents" can be modelled by a constituent-likelihood grammar. In word-tagging, the "labels" are the tags (part-of-speech markers), and the "constituents" are the words.

The constituent-likelihood method of grammatical analysis involves two steps:
(a)   Each constituent or item is first assigned a set of one or more potential labels by some simple mechanism such as lexicon look-up. If a constituent has more than one potential label, each label may be accompanied by an indication of its context-independent likelihood of co-occurrence with that constituent, relative to the other potential labels for that constituent.

(b)   In the second step, if a constituent has more than one potential label, then each of these potential labels is assigned a relative likelihood figure, using a function which takes into account contextual and other relevant factors (including the context-independent likelihood, if available, from step one). If our application requires a single unambiguous choice of label (as is the case with word-tagging), then we can choose the single "best" label and disregard all the others. The factors which count as "relevant" depend on the nature of the application: in general, we must aim for an acceptable trade-off between the simplicity of the probabilistic model (and hence efficiency of computation) and the proportion of items assigned the wrong tags. An oversimplistic probabilistic model will lead to an unacceptably high error-rate in analysis, but we should use the simplest probabilistic model consistent with an acceptable error-rate, remembering that even an extremely complex model will not analyse all text perfectly.

A constituent-likelihood grammar is not stated in terms of a list of rewrite rules to generate all and only sentences of the language under consideration; rather, it is characterized by:
(a)   an algorithm for assigning a set of possible labels or tags to any given constituent;

·and

(b)   a general *relative likelihood function* which can be used to calculate the relative likelihood of any given label or tag in any given context.

Ideally, the relative likelihood function should take into account *all* relevant contextual information; however, in the case of word-tagging it is not apparent what such an "ideal" formula would look like, except that it would certainly be very complex. In practice, we must use a much simpler formula to compute an approximation to the true relative likelihood function. It turns out that, in word-tagging, extremely simple approximations give remarkably successful results. The simplest possible likelihood formula is one that does not take context into account at all: where the likelihood of a given assignment of tag to word-token depends simply on how common it is for the tag to co-occur with the corresponding word-type – in other words, when a word has more than one possible tag, we simply pick the tag that most commonly co-occurs with that word, regardless of context. There is evidence from both the Brown (Kučera 1985) and LOB tagging projects that even this simple model would be surprisingly successful.

Although this model is very crude, it is not a trivial task to gather the necessary frequency information. This is largely due to the type–token distribution found in large text samples. A *type* corresponds to a word-form or dictionary entry, while a *token* is an occurrence of a type in the text sample. Typically in a large text sample, a small number of types occur very frequently (i.e. there are very many tokens for each of these types); so it is possible to collect reasonably representative statistics for these words. However, the great majority of types or word-forms occur only a few times, so these tokens cannot be assumed to be representative; for example, if the word *waters* appears three times in a sample, each time a plural noun, can we assume that no other tags are valid? Sinclair *et al.* (1970) suggest that at least 100 tokens are needed for a reasonable sample of a word's usage. The LOB Corpus contains approximately 50 000 types or word-forms, of which about 42 000 occur less than ten times each. (See Renouf (1984), Carroll *et al.* (1971), Hofland and Johansson (1982), and Sinclair (1986) for further discussion of word frequency distributions in large corpora.)

In attempting to assign relative probabilities to tags of rare ambiguous words, grammatical idioms, and suffixes in the CLAWS lexicon, idiomlist, and suffixlist respectively (see Ch. 3, pp. 35–40), we were forced to rely heavily on intuition, since printed dictionaries contain no information on relative likelihoods of alternative parts of speech for a word (other than giving commoner parts of speech first), although to a limited extent initial estimates could be corrected if they clearly caused errors in tagging. Assigning relative probabilities to ambiguously-tagged suffixes in the suffixlist was even more complicated than the corresponding exercises for the lexicon and idiomlist: we could not base figures for a particular suffix on figures for all words ending with that suffix, since generally most of these words would be tagged using the lexicon or a longer suffix. The words taken into account in deciding relative probabilities for the alternative tags in a given suffixlist entry ought therefore to be only those words whose tags would actually be assigned by that entry.

Because accurate frequency statistics are so difficult to assemble, we decided to attempt only a very crude weighting system: a logarithmic scale with only four points (common, rare, very rare, omitted: see p. 35). The high success rate of CLAWS suggests that replacing these values with more accurate data (which would be very difficult to do) would probably yield at best a marginal improvement in the performance of the system.

In order to improve on this crude model we need to take context into account, but still avoid having to consider the full syntactic structure of the sentence. A fundamental principle in constituent-likelihood analysis is that we should use the simplest mathematical model which does the job "reasonably well". To begin with we can assume that, when considering the likelihood of a potential tag for a word, we need consider only the immediately preceding tag (rather than all the earlier tags and syntactic structure in the sentence), and the immediately following tag (rather than all the tags and structure in the sentence still to come). This model is called a *first order Markov model* in information theory, because the likelihood function "looks at" only one tag in each direction. A *second order Markov model* would use a formula involving the previous *two* and the next *two* tags to calculate probabilities, and higher-order models would involve larger contexts (but these involve great increases in computation). Chapter 4 describes in detail the application of such a first order Markov model to the problem of word-tagging, and shows how its success rate can be improved by a *restricted* second order Markov model. That is, probabilities based on a second order Markov model are used only in a few special cases (centred on the tag RB or CC), and all other cases are handled by a first order Markov model. This allows the increased accuracy of a second order model where it is necessary, without incurring the increased computational cost of a full second order model. (The formal definition of the restricted second order relative likelihood function is too technical to cover here, but is explained in Atwell (1983).) CLAWS therefore incorporates information about contextual likelihood, but the use of figures on relative co-occurrence frequencies of immediately adjacent wordtags means that the system abstracts a very small proportion of information from the enormously complex wealth of considerations by which contexts in fact influence wordtag likelihoods in any particular case. Yet what is in essence a first order Markov model gives a success rate of 96–97%. The residual errors are analysed in Atwell (1982) and Lawrence (1984); most could be cured only via a full syntactic-analysis extension to the model. A small minority of errors (perhaps 1%) could not be corrected without somehow incorporating semantics into the model. Computational linguists generally accept as a truism the tenet that a parser attempting syntactic disambiguation often requires recourse to a semantic analysis component. One interesting, and perhaps significant, finding of UCREL research is that, in word-class disambiguation, a "semantic component" is actually required for only about 1% of all words.

3. Extending constituent-likelihood analysis to higher-level constituents

In word-tagging, the labels added during analysis are part-of-speech markers. The constituent-likelihood model can be extended to deal with higher-level groups of word-sequences such as phrases and clauses by incorporating labelled bracket symbols (corresponding to clause and phrase boundaries) into the model, to be inserted *between* pairs of words. Elsewhere in this book, the symbols labelling phrase- and clause-nodes in syntax trees are called *hypertags*; a hypertag begins with a capital letter denoting a primary clause or phrase category (e.g. N for noun phrase, F for subordinate finite clause), followed by some (zero or more) lower-case letters denoting subcategory features. (The set of hypertags, and what the individual letters designate, are discussed in Chapter 7.) A two-dimensional syntax tree can be represented by a one-dimensional sequence including labelled brackets, so that for instance the parse-tree for:

A dog is as much God's handiwork as a man. (D14 106–7)

would be represented as:

[S [Ncs AT NN Ncs] [Vzb BEZ Vzb] [N QL RB [Ns NP$
NN Ns] [P IN [Ncs AT NN Ncs] P] N] . S]

One way of extending the constituent-likelihood approach from word-tagging to parsing involves assuming that the parser is trying to find the "likeliest" assignment of labelled brackets for an input sentence, with the opening-bracket symbol and closing-bracket symbol for each hypertag treated as two separate symbols, which I shall call *hyperbrackets*.

If a parse-tree is represented as a linear sequence of symbols, then we could try applying the simple first order Markov model described above to find the "likeliest" symbol-sequence (i.e. parse-tree) for a given input sentence. The function used in CLAWS which represents degree of bonding between wordtag-pairs would be replaced by a function representing bonding between pairs of symbols drawn from an alphabet including both wordtags and hyperbrackets. (Thus we would need to extract frequency statistics for each symbol-pair from a sample of manually parsed text.) The WORDTAG program in the CLAWS system (see Ch. 3, p 35) would have to be replaced by a more general symbol-assignment program adding both wordtags and hyperbrackets. In fact, since we already have a successful word-tagging system, we can simplify the parsing problem by assuming that hyperbrackets must be added to tag-sequences rather than to word-sequences, i.e. that the leaf-node labels in the corresponding syntax tree are already known; this means that we simply need a hyperbracket-assignment program. This would not need all the "special case" routines from WORDTAG, since the items being assigned labels all come from a small closed set of 133 wordtags (rather than the open set of possible words). Thus it might seem possible to parse sentences using a system very little different from CLAWS. In practice, however, matters are not so simple.

4. Problems with a CLAWS-like approach

Adding hyperbrackets is a much more complex problem than adding wordtags. First, there is a practical problem in gathering symbol-pair frequency statistics. There are 133 different wordtags, but (as explained in Ch. 7) there are many thousands of possible hypertags and hence hyperbrackets. This makes it very difficult to gather adequate frequency statistics for all symbols and symbol-pairs: not only do sample texts have to be fully parsed rather than just word-tagged, but also a much larger sample is required for representative statistics. We have attempted to collate a first approximation to a full symbol-pair table by ignoring most lower-case subcategorization symbols for hyperbrackets (that is, instead of trying to collect separate statistics for Np, Ns, etc., we just collect statistics for a general N class), but this degrades the predictive power of the statistics.

Even if adequate statistics could be assembled, we still could not use the CLAWS approach without modifications. In that approach, the tag-likelihood function is used to choose one wordtag (out of one or more alternatives) for each word; however, there could be zero, one, two, or more hyperbrackets between each tag-pair. In the example sentence on the opposite page, there are no hyperbrackets between QL and RB, one hyperbracket between IN and AT, two between BEZ and QL, and three between NN and "." (sentence-final punctuation). A hyperbracket assignment program would have to associate with each successive pair of wordtags, not a set of alternative hyperbrackets, but a *set of alternative hyperbracket-sequences* of length zero or more; and this would imply that the alternative symbol-sequences passed on to the equivalent program to CHAINPROBS would be of differing lengths. This means that the system for evaluating various paths through the alternatives would have to be modified in some way to normalize the probabilities. (The CHAINPROBS system, which simply multiplies together the fractional probabilities for the various tag-transitions, would artificially favour short paths, corresponding to unduly broad, flat syntax trees.)

Furthermore, the most important feature distinguishing hyperbracketing from word-tagging is that hyperbrackets always occur in pairs. The occurrence of [Na, for example, means that Na] must occur later in the sentence. This information cannot be captured in a straightforward CLAWS-type first order Markov model, since the two symbols may well be quite far apart in linear sequence. Other kinds of "long-distance dependency" may also cause problems for a first order Markov model; for example, if the likelihood of a subtree such as [Ncs AT JJ NN NN Ncs] is computed purely in terms of symbol-pair transition probabilities, the model cannot take account of any "bonding" between mother nodes and their medial daughters (although the bond between mothers and their first and last daughters is built into the transition likelihoods for the opening and closing hyperbrackets).

One solution to these problems might be to use a higher-level model in place of the Markov model. The Markov model can be seen as a finite-state grammar augmented with probabilities on transitions. Chomsky (1957) suggested context-free phrase structure grammar as a more powerful alternative to finite-state grammars, and so by analogy we could use a probabilistic context-free grammar if we wanted to keep the benefits of probabilistic analysis. (A probabilistic context-free grammar has probabilities summing to unity associated with each of the productions expanding a given nonterminal symbol.) This model has been proposed by others for restricted or small grammars with only relatively few symbols and possible productions as compared with the UCREL system discussed in Chapter 7. For example, Baker (1979) outlines how a probabilistic context-free grammar could be used in speech recognition. However, the method described is restricted to grammars in Chomsky normal form (that is, grammars where only binary or unary branching is allowed). Although any context-free grammar may in principle be reduced to Chomsky normal form, this transformation is non-trivial with a probabilistic grammar because production probabilities must not be affected by the transformation.

This problem might be solved by transforming a grammar to Chomsky normal form before deriving probabilities for productions from parsed text. A more serious problem, however, is the amount of computation required even by the dynamic-programming technique proposed by Baker. Where CLAWS effectively generates a set of plausible (one-dimensional) symbol-sequences and computes the likeliest, Baker's algorithm involves generating possible (two-dimensional) *trees* which have nodes labelled with legal symbols, and choosing the "best" tree. The search space is much larger, and also the frequency tables used by the probabilistic parser are much bigger. Whereas a Markov model needs a square matrix with a row and a column for each symbol to hold symbol-pair transition likelihoods, Baker's algorithm uses a cubic matrix a in which each cell $a_{i,j,k}$ represents the probability that the symbol i will immediately dominate the pair of symbols j and k. Even if subcategory features on hypertags are ignored in collating statistics, the UCREL parsing scheme is too complex (there are too many symbols and possible productions) for a probabilistic context-free grammar to be used straightforwardly in parsing.

5. Bracket insertion and tree-closing

The UCREL parser to be described in Chapter 6 is based on a "compromise" model first proposed in Atwell (1983) and modified in Atwell *et al.* (1984). The model is a hybrid of the simple first-order Markov approach, and the full probabilistic context-free approach just discussed. Parsing proceeds in two main stages:

(a) **Bracket insertion** Opening and closing hyperbrackets are inserted between wordtags which usually indicate phrase boundaries; for example, the tag-sequence . . . VB ATI . . . marks the end of a verb phrase and the beginning of a noun phrase, so V] and [N hyperbrackets are inserted between the two tags. The underlying model is basically first order Markovian rather than context-free, since only tagpairs are used as context; there is no requirement at this stage that every opening hyperbracket has a corresponding closing hyperbracket later in the sentence.

(b) **Tree-closing** After hyperbracket insertion, there will be some unmatched brackets. Certain wordtags specifically mark the beginning of a higher-level constituent (e.g. preposition IN, article ATI, subordinating conjunction CS), but often there is no corresponding explicit marker at the end of the phrase or clause. In the tree-closing phase, a tree-testing procedure discovers which brackets have no partners, and then missing brackets are added to turn the symbol sequence into a well-formed tree-structure. Generally there will be more than one possible insertion position which leads to a well-formed tree; when several missing hyperbrackets have to be inserted (as is normally the case), the different combinations of possible insertion positions will lead to many possible parse trees. A constituent-likelihood measure of the likelihood of each parse tree is used to choose the best putative parse; as explained in Chapter 6, this constituent-likelihood function is based on frequency statistics extracted from a sample of manually parsed sentences. Tree evaluation is based on an underlying context-free model of language (the evaluation function refers to relationships between mother-node labels and their successive daughter-node labels, rather than merely to adjacent symbols in the linear representation of a parse-tree); but, because a simpler, Markovian model was used to generate the initial set of symbol-sequences from which trees were derived, the search space is considerably reduced.

However, there are problems associated with the fact that this hybrid approach requires at least one member of each pair of hyperbrackets to be inserted in the first phase. Not all left-hand phrase boundaries are marked explicitly by function words: for instance, in:

I gave the baby milk to drink.

there is no explicit phrase boundary marker between *baby* and *milk*. If examples such as this are handled by assigning N] [N as a possibility at each noun-noun transition, a large number of alternative trees will be available for an input containing sequences of nouns. Furthermore, right-hand boundaries are only rarely marked explicitly in English, so that there will often be many possible locations for insertion of a closing hyperbracket. A sentence which combines several uncertainties of these kinds can lead to combinatorial explosion in the computing process. The implementation discussed in Chapter 6 makes use of various *ad hoc* heuristics to make sure that at least one member of a pair of hyperbrackets is inserted before tree-closing, and to reduce the space of alternative parses to be searched.

6.   Simulated annealing

As a more general response to these problems, we have begun to investigate an alternative search strategy to find the "best-fit" parse-tree, called "simulated annealing". Basically, this involves parsing a sentence by the following steps:

(a)   First, generate a parse-tree at random, with any structure (so long as it is a well-formed tree), and any legal symbols at the nodes.

(b)   Then, make a series of random localized changes to the tree, by randomly deleting nodes or inserting new (randomly-labelled) nodes. At each stage, the likelihood of the resulting tree is measured using a constituent-likelihood function. If the change would cause the tree likelihood to fall by a quantity which exceeds a threshold, then it is disallowed, but alterations which increase the likelihood, or decrease it only by an amount smaller than the threshold, are accepted.

Initially, the threshold of unacceptable likelihood-decrease is set very high, so almost all changes are accepted. However, as the annealing run proceeds, the threshold is gradually lowered, so that fewer and fewer "negative" changes are accepted. This process should converge on a globally optimal parse tree, without getting stuck in "local optima" where all individual changes decrease likelihood even though better solutions are available in distant parts of the search space. Rather than reducing the size of the search space as in the model described in section 5, the annealing approach uses randomization in order to search the full space efficiently.

This is a very simplified statement of the annealing approach to probabilistic parsing; for a fuller description, see Sampson (1986a, forthcoming).[†]

[†] As this book was being prepared for the press, we discovered that simulated annealing has independently been applied to the parsing problem by Bart Selman and Graeme Hirst of the University of Toronto (e.g. Selman 1985). Selman and Hirst's approach uses annealing to search the fixed range of structures generated by a (non-probabilistic) context-free grammar.

7.   Conclusions

Constituent-likelihood grammar is very different from other formalisms for the description of syntactic structure, as it is based on statistical pattern matching rather than generative rewrite rules. It is particularly useful for the syntactic description of unrestricted natural language, including syntactically "noisy" or ill-formed text. It has the great advantage that, once an appropriate general model has been defined, the parameters of the model (the frequency statistics from which likelihoods are calculated) can be automatically extracted from a corpus of analysed text. The constituent-likelihood approach to grammatical description even opens up the intriguing possibility of automatically extracting a grammar from *raw, unanalysed* text corpora, as will be discussed in Chapter 10 (pp. 132–3).

CHAPTER 6

The UCREL probabilistic parsing system

Roger Garside and Fanny Leech

1. Introduction

This chapter describes a parsing system currently being designed and implemented at Lancaster, making use of the constituent-likelihood grammar ideas described in the previous chapter. The parser is designed to analyse a text in which words have already been allocated a grammatical word-class by the CLAWS1 tagging system described in Chapters 3 and 4, and produces a text annotated with the boundaries and type of each grammatical constituent.

It will be recalled that in the CLAWS tagging system there are three main stages. The first stage (WORDTAG) takes a text which has been appropriately formated, and assigns a set of possible tags to each word, considering the word in isolation. This stage uses an ordered set of rules to make this assignment, but the most commonly applied rule is to look up the word in a lexicon of words and their associated tags. The second stage (IDIOMTAG) is designed to look for a number of special patterns of words and tags, and make suitable adjustments to the tags from the first stage. The third stage (CHAINPROBS) takes the results of the first two stages, assigns a numerical value to each combination of tags to indicate its likelihood, and hence chooses a preferred tag for each word in the text.

The parsing system described here can be similarly characterized by three stages. In the initial stage we assign a set of possible parse continuations to each word in the text, based on a lexicon which associates such parse continuations with each possible pair of tags. In the second stage (which in practice is incorporated in the initial stage rather than being separate) a search is made for a number of special patterns of tags and parse fragments, and the parse structure is suitably modified. In the final stage each possible parse is completed, a numerical value is assigned to it, and a preferred parse is hence chosen for each sentence.

2. Input and output in the parsing system

The input to the parsing system is the output from the CLAWS1 system described earlier. We use as our first example a sentence from the tagged Corpus:

I hope it's the right thing to do. (P13 131)

The tagged version of this sentence is as follows:

P13	131	001			– – – – –
P13	131	010	I		PP1A
P13	131	020	hope		VB
P13	131	030	it	>	PP3
P13	131	031	's	<	BEZ
P13	131	040	the		ATI
P13	131	050	right		JJ
P13	131	060	thing		NN
P13	131	070	to		TO
P13	131	080	do		DO
P13	131	081	.		.
P13	131	082			– – – – –

Notice how the contracted form *it's* has been split by the tagging system into *it* (tagged PP3 for third person singular neuter pronoun) and *'s* (tagged BEZ for third person singular present of the verb *to be*), since the two parts function as two distinct syntactic units. The original sentence in the LOB Corpus began with an opening inverted comma (which is not matched by a closing inverted comma, since the sentence is the beginning of an extended passage of direct speech); the tagging system assigns the appropriate tag, but the current version of the parsing system simply ignores opening and closing inverted commas, so we omit them in what follows.

In Chapter 8, work is described on the design of a new version of the CLAWS tagging system, and this has included a thorough revision of the tagset to be used, in the light of our experience with the LOB tagset. It is not of course possible to make use of this new tagset (described in Appendix B as the "Lancaster tagset"), since the work is being done in parallel with the development of the parsing system. However, in a small number of cases we have decided to make changes to the tagging of text input to the parsing system, where these changes are likely to improve the accuracy of the resulting parse. The only changes being made to the tagging are ones which can be made automatically, so that the modifications can be applied by a pre-processor running over a text tagged by CLAWS1 before the parsing system is run. The main changes (yielding the "Leeds tagset" of Appendix B) are as follows:

(a)   It is useful to be able to distinguish between the prepositions *of, for, with* and *without* (all of which are tagged IN in CLAWS1 when they are used as prepositions), so these are given distinctive tags for the parsing system. The subordinating conjunction *as* is similarly distinguished from other subordinating conjunctions.

(b)   A number of multi-word prepositions and subordinating conjunctions receive "ditto-tags", in addition to those receiving such tags in the IDIOMTAG phase of the CLAWS1 tagging system (see Chapter 9), to indicate that they should be treated as single syntactic units. Examples are *instead of* and *provided that*.

The output from the current version of the parsing system for the above tagged text is:

P13	131	001				
					– – – – –	
P13	131	010	I		PP1A	{S[Na}
P13	131	020	hope		VB	[V}
P13	131	030	it	>	PP3	[Fn[N}
P13	131	031	's	<	BEZ	[V}
P13	131	040	the		ATI	[N
P13	131	050	right		JJ	
P13	131	060	thing		NN	
P13	131	070	to		TO	[Ti[Vi
P13	131	080	do		DO	Vi]Ti]N]Fn}
P13	131	081	.		.	S}
P13	131	082			– – – – –	

The parsing system adds the new field on the right, which represents the preferred parse-tree for this sentence. The beginning and end of a grammatical constituent are marked by opening and closing square brackets, with the convention that any opening square brackets on a line precede the word on the line, and any closing square brackets on a line follow the word on the line; thus one of the constituents marked N begins with the word *the* and ends with the word *do*. The opening bracket (and, if separated, the closing bracket) is marked with an indication of the grammatical constituent. This marking is an upper case letter, possibly followed by one or more lower case letters giving more details about the type of constituent. Thus S marks the sentence or top-level constituent, V and N are verb and noun phrases respectively, and F indicates a finite clause whose type is given by the following lower case letter: possible types of finite clause are Fn for a nominal clause, Fr for a relative clause, etc. We call these constituent labels "hypertags". More details of the possible labels for constituents, and of the parsing scheme in general, are given in Chapter 7.

The above text could be rewritten in a more conventional form as the tree at the top of p. 69.

3.   Initial stage: T-tag assignment

As indicated earlier, the rationale for the first stage of parsing is to build a tentative set of parse structures by looking at individual units of the sentence in isolation. The individual unit considered is a pair of consecutive tags, rather than an individual tag, and any such pair of tags is looked up in a lexicon of tagpairs to indicate the possible

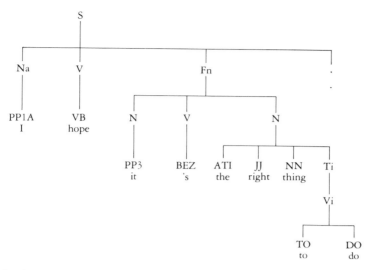

Figure 5   A parse-tree

ways the parse may be continued over one further word. Thus with the example sentence the first stage of the parsing process is to look up the pairs (- - - - -, PP1A), (PP1A, VB), (VB, PP3), etc., and fit together the partial parse structures so found.

It is clear that such a pair of consecutive tags is partially diagnostic of the beginning, continuation or termination of a constituent. Thus, for example, the pair "noun-verb" tends to indicate the end of a noun phrase and the beginning of a verb phrase, and the pair "noun-noun" tends to indicate the continuation of a noun phrase (although it might also indicate the division between two noun phrases). Since the beginnings of constituents are more often marked than the ends, this sequence of markings will often omit some of the right-hand or closing brackets, and these are inserted at a later stage.

The result of looking up the tagpair in the lexicon is one or more possible sequences of opening and closing brackets and constituent labels – each of these sequences is, for obscure historical reasons, called a "T-tag". A T-tag consists of a left-hand and a right-hand part. The left-hand part consists of an indication of what constituent should be current (i.e. at the top of the stack of open constituents) at this stage, or an indication that any constituent is acceptable, perhaps followed by one or more closing brackets. The right-hand part normally consists of an indication that one or more new constituents should be opened, that some particular constituent should be continued, or more rarely that a new constituent should be opened but that it is not yet clear what the constituent should be (and this will be deduced later on in the analysis process). Thus the tagpair (VB, PP3) (i.e. base form of verb followed by the word *it*) indicates two possible T-tags, either "Y] [N" or "Y] [Fn[N". The first means "close the current constituent whatever it is (Y matches any constituent) and open a new noun phrase", while the second means that additionally a nominal clause (Fn) should be opened, and the noun phrase will be the first constituent of the nominal clause.

The left-hand part of the T-tag is assigned to the first tag of the pair, and the right-hand part is assigned to the second tag of the pair. Thus, using the sequence of tags from the above example, we obtain:

```
– – – – –
PP1A          Y  [S[Na        [S[Na]
VB            Y] [V           [V]
PP3           Y] [N           [N]
BEZ           Y] [V           [V]
ATI           Y] [N           [N
JJ            N N
NN            N N
TO            Y [Ti[Vi        [Ti[Vi
DO            V V             Vi]
.             Y] S            S]
– – – – –     S ]
```

The first column gives the wordtags of the example sentence. The second column gives the T-tags as looked up in the lexicon; here the T-tag on a line is the one associated with the tagpair on that and the preceding line; thus the T-tag "V V" is the one associated with the tagpair (TO, DO). Where there are several possible T-tags associated with a tagpair, as with (VB, PP3), only the first T-tag is shown here; how we deal with alternative T-tags is described later. The third column shows the two parts of the T-tag rearranged, so that the left-hand part is correctly associated with the first tag of the pair and the right-hand part is associated with the second tag of the pair. Thus the left-hand part of the T-tag associated with the tagpair (PP3, BEZ), which is the closing bracket for the N constituent formed by the word tagged PP3, is moved to the line containing that word.

The look-up procedure as described requires a lexicon entry for each possible pair of tags, which is inefficient and difficult to relate to meaningful linguistic categories. Instead the 138 tags of the Leeds tagset (including sentence-boundary marker) are subsumed in a set of 36 "cover symbols" (the terms is taken from the Brown tagging system). Thus all the different forms of noun wordtag are subsumed in the cover symbols N* (singular noun), *S (plural noun) and *$ (noun with genitive marker). The required tagpair lexicon therefore requires only an entry for each cover-symbol pair.

A further simplification is that in many cases (because of the admissibility of the "wild" marker Y on the left of a T-tag) the first tag of the pair is irrelevant and the second tag in the pair determines the set of T-tag options. Thus, if the second tag of the pair is infinitival *to*, the appropriate T-tag is "Y] [Ti[Vi": i.e. closure of the current constituent (whatever it is) and opening of an infinitival clause containing an infinitive verb phrase. There will be exceptions to these overall rules – for instance, if the pair is a noun followed by infinitival *to*, then an alternative option is to continue rather than close the current constituent, so that the infinitival clause is subordinate to the current constituent rather than the two being sister constituents (or even "aunt and niece" constituents) in a higher-level constituent.

Thus the T-tag lexicon is in fact divided into three separate sections. The first section is for those cases where the second cover symbol alone is diagnostic of the appropriate set of T-tags, the second section is for the exceptions to the first section (where both cover symbols need to be considered), and the third section is for exceptions to the second (where the individual tags need to be considered). Hence given a pair of tags (tag_1, tag_2), we first convert them to cover symbols, say ($cover_1$, $cover_2$). We then check the three parts of the lexicon for the T-tag entries associated respectively with ($cover_2$), ($cover_1$, $cover_2$), and (tag_1, tag_2), and use the most specific entry found.

It was suggested above that the lexicon look-up would often result in more than one possible T-tag, rather than just one. Thus, using again the sequence of tags from the earlier example, the T-tags actually obtained from the lexicon are:

$- - - - -$	
PP1A	Y [S[Na
VB	Y] [V
PP3	Y] [N : Y] [Fn[N
BEZ	Y] [V
ATI	Y] [N
JJ	N N
NN	N N : J] N
TO	Y [Ti[Vi : Y] [Ti[Vi
DO	V V
.	Y] S
$- - - - -$	S }

Here, alternative T-tags are separated by a colon. Some options can be eliminated immediately by matching the current constituent with the putative extension. Thus the "J] N" option for the tagpair (JJ, NN) specifies that the current constituent for extension must be an adjectival phrase J; since this is not the case (the current constituent is a noun phrase N), this T-tag can be eliminated, leaving only the "N N" T-tag. In other cases the alternatives cannot be eliminated, and must be retained for later disambiguation. Thus the result of the assignment stage is in fact:

$- - - - -$	
PP1A	[S[Na]
VB	[V]
PP3	{:[Fn}[N]
BEZ	[V]
ATI	[N
JJ	
NN	{:]}
TO	[Ti[Vi
DO	Vi]
.	S]
$- - - - -$	

Here the common parts of the alternatives have been "factored out", and the alternatives are enclosed in braces and separated by colons. As an example, at the point in the parse between the VB and PP3 tags, a verb phrase V is closed and a noun phrase N is opened, but a nominal clause Fn may or may not be opened between them. Thus the notation "{:[Fn}" indicates two choices separated by ":" – to insert nothing at this point, or to insert "[Fn". More generally the braces may include more than two alternatives, and the alternatives may extend over a sequence of consecutive words. As an example of the former, consider a second LOB Corpus sentence:

Where are the profligate little terrors I hear about? (R05 122)

This leads to the following output from the first stage:

where	WRB	[S{:[F}[Rq]
are	BER	[V]
the	ATI	[N
profligate	JJ	
little	JJ	
terrors	NNS	
I	PP1A	{[Fr:]:}[F}[Na]
hear	VB	[V]
about	IN	[P]
?	?	S]

Here the notation "{[Fr:]:}[F}[Na" between the words *terrors* and *I* indicates three possibilities: to open a relative clause Fr, to close the noun phrase N, or to close the noun phrase N and open a finite clause F (whose subcategorization is unknown).

4. Constructing the T-tag lexicon

The original version of the first two sections of the T-tag lexicon (i.e. the sections dealing with cover symbols) was generated using linguistic intuition, and the third section (dealing with specific tagpairs) was initially empty. If there are several possible T-tags to an entry, they are given in approximately decreasing likelihood and rare T-tags are marked as such. Now, as described later in this chapter, a number of parsed sentences have been collected in machine-readable form in order to provide information about the structure of constituents. This bank of data can also be used to extract information about what constituent types and boundaries are associated with any pair of tags. We have therefore written a program which takes a current version of the T-tag lexicon and a set of parsed sentences, and generates:

(a)   information about possible exceptions to the current T-tag lexicon, in the form of cases where the effective T-tag in the parsed sentence is not among those proposed by the T-tag lexicon, and

(b)   where the effective T-tag *is* among those proposed by the T-tag lexicon, statistics as to the relative probabilities of the various T-tags associated with a particular tagpair.

The first set of information is used to guide the intuition of a linguist in deciding how to modify the original T-tag lexicon. This cannot (at least at present) be done automatically, since there are various unsystematic differences between the T-tag as looked up in the lexicon and the sequence of constituent types and boundaries as they appear in the parsed sentences. We are thus using information from the parsed Corpus texts to generate improved versions of the T-tag lexicon.

The frequency information about the alternative T-tags associated with a particular tagpair is not at present used by the parsing system, but it may be included later as a further factor to be taken into account when deciding on a preferred parse in the third stage of analysis. The information is of course being used to refine linguistic intuition about the ordering of possible T-tags in the lexicon and their marking for rarity.

5. Final stage: Tree-closing

The output from the first stage consists of indications of the types of a number of constituents and where they begin, but in many cases the ending position of a constituent is unknown, or at least is located ambiguously at one of several positions. Thus, in the first example shown, the positions of the closing brackets for the Fn (if present) and Ti constituents (and the final noun phrase N in one alternative) are not known at the end of the T-tag assignment phase. The main task of the third stage is to insert these constituent closures. There is a second stage, between T-tag assignment and tree closing, but we shall postpone discussion of this until Section 7.

The basic task of the third stage then is to establish the positions of the right-hand brackets marking the ends of those constituents unclosed by earlier stages. This is done by considering the possible positions for closure of constituents, and from this deducing the consequential structure of each constituent in terms of constituents and cover symbols at a lower level. It can then deduce a figure for the probability of any particular parse from the probabilities that the constituents have the respective structures.

Let us consider again the first example sentence above and, for the moment, choose to consider only one of the options at the two places where an alternative is possible (marked with braces "{...}" in the example tabulated on pp. 71). If we choose the second option in both these cases we obtain:

I	P*A	[S[Na]
hope	VB*	[V]
it	P*	{Fn[N]
's	BE*	[V]
the	DT*	[N
right	J*	
thing	N*	N]
to	TO	[Ti[Vi
do	DO*	Vi]
.	.*	S]

In the second column wordtags have been replaced by the associated cover symbols, since the third stage works at this level of aggregated detail. Notice that ".*" is the cover symbol for sentence-terminating punctuation (full stop, exclamation and question mark, etc.), and the wordtag TO constitutes a cover symbol on its own, with the same name as the wordtag it covers. The third column gives the parse as it enters the third stage; it is incomplete, in that the closure positions for Fn and Ti have not yet been decided. It is clear that the only possible logical position at which the Ti constituent can be closed is after the closure of the Vi constituent. However the Fn constituent could in theory be closed after either of the N constituents (on the word *it* or *thing*), after the V constituent (on the word *'s*), or after the now-closed Ti constituent.

The third stage of the parser therefore generates all these possible completion patterns, and examines each one in turn. It is clear from the above example that one needs to start at the bottom and work up, since there we needed to have considered the possible closure positions for Ti before we considered the closure positions for Fn. In a more complicated case the alternative choices for the positioning of lower level closures will affect the positions available for closing constituents higher up the tree. For example, consider the second example sentence above, and choose to consider only the first option at each alternative. This gives us:

where	WRB	[S[Rq]
are	BE*	[V]
the	DT*	[N
profligate	J*	
little	J*	
terrors	*S	
I	P*A	[Fr[Na]
hear	VB*	[V]
about	IN	[P]
?	.*	S]

If the Fr constituent were closed on the word *I*, then the N constituent could be closed on any one of the words *I*, *hear* or *about*; but if the Fr were closed on the word *hear*, then only the second and third closing positions for the N are possible. Any constituents not included in the N will, of course, become daughters of the S constituent.

Having generated all possible completion patterns we need to be able to assign a "figure of merit" to each possible parse. Each parse is made up of a number of constituents, each with a particular structure, and the figure of merit for a complete parse is calculated from a likelihood figure for each of these constituents, which is the probability that a constituent of this type has this structure. Thus, returning to the first example sentence, the figure of merit for the parse:

I	P*A	[S[Na]
hope	VB*	[V]
it	P*	[Fn[N]
's	BE*	[V]
the	DT*	[N
right	J*	
thing	N*	N]Fn]
to	TO	[Ti[Vi
do	DO*	Vi]Ti]
.	.*	S]

(where the Fn constituent is closed after the word *thing*, and Ti is consequently the final constituent of S) is derived from the probabilities that:

    an S constituent has the form [Na V Fn Ti .*]
    an Na constituent has the form [P*A]
    a V constituent has the form [VB*]
    an Fn constituent has the form [N V N]
    an N constituent has the form [P*]
    a V constituent has the form [BE*]
    an N constituent has the form [DT* J* N*]
    a Ti constituent has the form [Vi]
    a Vi constituent has the form [TO DO*]

If the assignment stage has resulted in alternative structures, then the tree-closing stage calculates a figure of merit for each pattern of tree closures for each alternative structure. Thus, when we apply the assignment stage to the first example sentence, four possible incomplete parses are generated:

P*A	[S[Na]	[S[Na]	[S[Na]	[S[Na]
VB*	[V]	[V]	[V]	[V]
P*	[N]	[N]	[Fn[N]	[Fn[N]
BE*	[V]	[V]	[V]	[V]
DT*	[N	[N	[N	[N
J*				
N*		N]		N]
TO	[Ti[Vi	[Ti[Vi	[Ti[Vi	[Ti[Vi
DO*	Vi]	Vi]	Vi]	Vi]
.*	S]	S]	S]	S]

and the third stage considers all possible patterns of closure for each of the possible incomplete parses, and assigns a figure of merit to each one. Notice that there is an explicit representation in the output from the first stage of a possible closure point for the N constituent at the N* cover symbol. This is because of a convention to which the third stage adheres, by which positions within or at the end of a sequence of wordtags are not considered as candidates for closing a constituent unless explicitly marked as such.

We are trying a number of different ways of deriving a figure of merit for a parse tree from the probabilities of the individual constituents: for example multiplying together the individual probabilities, or taking some sort of average of them. However these simple schemes are likely to require modification in the light of experience; for example, it is expected that the probability calculations will have to be normalized with respect to the shape of the tree (i.e. the depth of the tree, and the length of the constituents) if differently-shaped trees are being compared. Another problem is the large number of trees generated by the mechanism of considering all possible logical closure points; here we are experimenting with "figures of merit" for forests of trees (representing incomplete parses of a sentence) derived from the figures for the individual trees, so that these will enable the parser to retain only the more promising candidate partial parses.

6. Constructing the probabilistic grammar

The tree-closing procedure requires a database of statistics on the possible structures of constituents. To this end a "treebank" of manually parsed sentences has been created, comprising some fifty thousand words from the LOB Corpus (cf. Chapter 7). The first example sentence used above to show how the automatic parsing system works has also been manually parsed, and appears in the treebank as follows:

P13	131	001			– – – – –	
P13	131	010	I		PP1A	[S[Nas]
P13	131	020	hope		VB	[V]
P13	131	030	it	>	PP3	[Fn[Ni]
P13	131	031	's	<	BEZ	[Vzb]
P13	131	040	the		ATI	[Ns
P13	131	050	right		JJ	
P13	131	060	thing		NN	
P13	131	070	to		TO	[Ti[Vi
P13	131	080	do		DO	Vi]Ti]Ns]Fn}
P13	131	081	.		.	S}
P13	131	082			– – – – –	

Notice here further manual subcategorization of constituent markers, which we do not at present expect the automatic parser to produce (although most of it can be generated automatically from the wordtags and the current output of the automatic parser, and the parser may later be refined to do this).

We have already explained how the treebank is used as a source of data on constituent boundaries for improving the T-tag table. A further program in the suite goes through the treebank, using it to construct a probabilistic grammar – essentially a lexicon containing information on the probabilities of different structures for each constituent. Thus from the example we obtain (among other things) an example of an S having the structure "Nas V Fn .*", an example of an Fn having the structure "Ni Vzb Ns", and an example of an Ns having the structure "DT* J* N* Ti". The structure is specified in terms of labels (i.e. hypertags), or cover symbols, of immediate constituents of nonterminal nodes. (The program which extracts the statistics is also used to provide a useful check on the consistency of the treebank.)

An example of a portion of the statistics generated from the treebank is:

Po	1595		
[INO]	7	B10 216 070
[INO *S]	98	A05 123 090
[INO CD*]	14	A13 219 060
[INO DT*]	15	A13 226 020
[INO F]	4	G43 81 010
[INO N]	1056	A01 64 090
[INO N*]	315	A02 81 030
[INO P*]	26	A20 111 100
[INO Tg]	45	A14 20 060

These are the statistics relating to the Po constituent, representing prepositional phrases introduced by the word *of*, which is assigned the wordtag INO in the Leeds tagset (and also has its own cover symbol INO). There are 1595 examples of this constituent in the treebank, and it can be seen that the majority (1056 examples) have the internal structure "[INO N]": i.e. the word *of* followed by a noun phrase (N). The next most common structure (315 examples) is "[INO N*]": i.e. the word *of* followed by a singular noun (with cover symbol N*) – note that our scheme for manual parsing does not assign a separate noun-phrase node to a one-word complement of a preposition (cf. p. 88). Omitted from the above example, but of course present in the statistics, are a number of other possible structures, for example "[INO AB*]" (*of all*), which occur only once or twice in the treebank. The final column is a reference number to the point in the treebank where the first example of the given structure occurred, which is useful for cross-checking the statistics back to the treebank.

These structures, usually termed *productions* in grammatical theory, consist of a "mother" symbol (here Po) associated with a sequence of "daughter" symbols, which may be cover symbols or non-terminal labels (i.e. hypertags), for example "INO N". We could of course rewrite the rules in the form (for example):

Po → INO N with probability 1056/1595

to show that this set of statistics is simply a set of productions for a probabilistic context-free phrase-structure grammar. In this grammar the non-terminals are the set of hypertags (N, V, Fn, Ti, Po, etc.) with the designated "sentence" symbol S, and the terminals are the set of cover symbols (N*, *S, P*A, INO, etc.).

The program can be adjusted to collect the statistics at different levels of detail for different constituents. For example, we could collect statistics on the structures of all examples of N, all examples of N with subcategory s (for singular), all examples of Ns also having subcategory a (subject-marked, e.g. *I, he*), etc. At present we are collecting statistics with as much aggregation of detail (i.e. as little subcategorization) as possible, since the treebank is quite small to attempt to capture the syntactic richness of the English language. However, we are retaining the subcategorization where it is reflected in substantial differences in the statistics. Thus we retain the separate statistics for Po, as they are sufficiently different from the statistics for P as a whole; and there are, for example, statistics for Fn and Fr as well as F as a whole, and for Tb, Tg, Ti, and Tn as well as T as a whole. The level of subcategorization of the statistics may be adjusted in the light of experience (and the size of the treebank). The third stage of the parser attempts to fit the most specific statistics available to the partial parses encountered, and if necessary falls back on more aggregated statistics.

Initially the statistics were collected only as a set of productions in the form illustrated above: i.e., for a "mother", say S, the possible "daughter" sequences would be "N V F .*" with some frequency, "N V .*" with some frequency, "N V N .*" with some frequency, etc. However, the small size of the treebank, and the wide variety of possible constituent structures in the English language, led us to consider ways of "generalizing" the statistics we have gathered. Thus the possible structures for the category noun phrase (N) represented in the treebank might happen to include statistics for

DT* J* N*
DT* J* J* N*
DT* J* N* T

but not for

DT* J* J* N* T

because noun phrases such as *the final decision, a slick combined move, the undiscriminating hatred known .. as Vansittartism* happened to occur among the sentences in the treebank, but there were no noun phrases of the form *a single young man waiting for a dead man's shoes* in the treebank. More generally, for rarely occurring structures, there are unlikely to be sufficient examples to give us reliable statistics of occurrences.

Two approaches have been considered to deal with this problem. The first attempted to use linguistic intuition to amalgamate the statistics for different structures. For example, a typical sentence S would contain a "kernel" (N V, N V N, N V N N, etc.) optionally preceded and followed by peripheral structures (typically adverbial phrases and punctuation). If we had the program which processes the treebank recognize these and produce separate statistics for the kernel and the peripheral structures, then the parser could reconstruct the statistics for a full S structure by multiplying together the probabilities for the separate portions. The problem with this is that it requires *ad hoc* linguistic decisions for each constituent (or at least each constituent where there is a wide variety of possible structures).

The second approach is more radical. This is to hold the information about constituency of each grammatical category as a set of probabilities for each pair of successive IC categories or cover symbols for that category. Thus, the information for N would include frequency statistics on

```
[   DT*
DT*  J*
J*  J*
J*   N*
N* ]
N* T
T   ]
```

and from these we could reconstruct the frequency statistics for

```
DT*  J* N*
DT*  J* J*  N*
DT*  J* N* T
```

and

```
DT* J* J* N* T
```

generalizing from what actually occurs in the treebank. (Here "[DT*" represents DT* occurring as the first IC of an N, and "N*]" and "T]" represent occurrence of the respective categories as final IC.)

7.   Intermediate stage: heuristics

The first stage of T-tag assignment introduces constituent types and boundary markings only if they can be expressed in terms of look-up in a lexicon of tagpairs. However there are a number of cases where a more complex form of processing seems desirable, in order to reduce the number of potential parses which would otherwise have to be dealt with in the third stage. The parser therefore incorporates a second stage, analogous to the second stage of the tagging system, which is able to look for various patterns of tags and constituent markings already assigned by the first stage, and then add to or modify the constituent markings passed to the third stage.

There are a number of linguistic constructs that we process at this stage, and we expect to add to the cases considered in the light of our experience with using the system. Four examples of the type of processing we are currently using are as follows:

(a)   The processing of "preposition + *which*" constructs, such as *in which*. The normal lexicon look-up for the tagpair Y IN (anything followed by preposition) would open a prepositional phrase, and the look-up for the pair (preposition, *wh*-word) would open some form of noun phrase. At stage two the more specific pattern (preposition, *which*) is recognized and a subordinate clause (Fr) is opened before the prepositional phrase.

(b)   If, for a given parse, the opening of a prepositional phrase is immediately followed by the opening of a noun phrase, and the first stage decides to close the noun phrase, then a reasonable heuristic is to close the prepositional phrase as well. Thus in the sequence of cover symbols "CD* INO DT* *S DO*" (for the words ..*one of the propositions must..* (B09 166–7)), the first stage of the parser opens a Po constituent on INO and an N on DT*, and closes the N at *S (plural noun) preparatory to opening a V on DO*. This heuristic therefore closes the Po on *S. If the N constituent had not been closed, then the position for the closure of the P would have to be decided by the third stage of the parser. Thus in the sequence of cover symbols "DT* N* INO J* N* IN P* .*" (for the words .. *some kind of general recognition for it?* (B02 39–40)), this heuristic is invoked to close the second prepositional phase on P*. However, since the first stage of the parser generates two alternative partial parses at the N* IN position (to close or to continue the noun phrase), only the first of these causes the heuristic to close the first prepositional phrase; the alternative parse (in fact the correct one), which closes all the noun and prepositional phrases on the final *it*, must be completed by the third stage of the parser.

(c)   Genitive phrases concluding with *'s* are also dealt with at this stage. Whenever the T-tag assignment decides to open a noun phrase, an alternative option would be to open a noun phrase containing a genitive phrase (G), the latter option to be rejected at a later stage if no *'s* occurs in the phrase. Instead all noun phrases are opened as such at the T-tag assignment stage; then, at the heuristic stage, the occurrence of an *'s* (signalled by the cover symbol *$) causes the current constituent to be changed from noun phrase to genitive phrase, and a new noun phrase to be opened just before it. Of course the heuristic is not quite as straightforward as this; for example, there has to be provision for the heuristic in some cases to indicate more than one possible pattern of constituents to the third stage of the system.

(d)   As a final example of the type of pattern processed at this intermediate stage, consider co-ordination. The occurrence of the co-ordinating conjunction tag CC will have caused the T-tag look-up to open a new constituent and mark it as part of a co-ordinated structure, but it will not have indicated the type of the constituent. A heuristic at this stage attempts to assign the appropriate hypertag type to this constituent, and then searches back for the appropriate constituent with which to co-ordinate it. This is again a simplified explanation of the heuristic, because there is a distinction made in the parsing scheme between co-ordination at the word level (*bread and butter*) and at the phrase level (*the bread and the butter*), and because co-ordination can have dissimilar conjunct types, or more than two conjuncts. Essentially the co-ordination heuristic has three phases; it first tries to co-ordinate at the word level, then at the phrase level, and finally at the clause or sentence level.

We have suggested here that the parsing system is constructed as three separate stages, but in fact the second stage, which applies these and other heuristics, is implemented as a set of finite state machines which scan the partial parse as it is being constructed in the first stage.

8.   Problems and conclusions

This chapter has described the basic structure of the parsing system that we are currently developing at Lancaster. There are of course a number of areas where the techniques described will need to be extended to take account of linguistic structures not presently provided for. But our technique with the tagging project was to develop basic mechanisms to cope with a large proportion of the texts being processed, and then to modify them to perform more accurately in particular areas where they were deficient, and we are following this procedure with the current project.

It is not clear at present what is the appropriate division of responsibility between the various stages of the parsing system: for example, whether it is advantageous for the T-tag assignment program to specify a number of possible positions for closure of constituents, in order to reduce the number of cases to be considered by the third stage, or whether it is better to disregard ambiguous constituent closure at the T-tag assignment stage, and to let the third stage do most of the work.

We have run the current version of the parser over two samples of the tagged LOB Corpus (totalling over 250 sentences, not selected in any way for "tractability" or length), and achieved an approximately 50% success rate in generating an "acceptable" parse for a sentence (bearing in mind that the parser does not currently attempt to match the full subcategorization specified by the manual parsing scheme). These are promising results, and we believe that the technique described can be developed to provide a robust and economic parsing system, able to operate with a high degree of accuracy over unconstrained English text.

CHAPTER 7

The grammatical database and parsing scheme

Geoffrey Sampson

1. The aim of the parsing scheme

If an automatic parsing system is to rely for its performance on statistical information about authentic language, it must be provided with a representative database of manually parsed material from which statistics can be extracted. Irrespective of how a parser works, furthermore, it must be based on an explicit parsing *scheme*: a statement of just what range of structures and categories will be used in parsing, and which among various analyses in terms of those structures and categories will be regarded as correct for any particular debatable construction. A research group claiming a high degree of accuracy for their automatic parser will fail to impress, if they provide no specification, independent of the output of their automatic system, of what counts as correct parsing. And, if the parser is to run over "real-life" texts drawn from unrestricted domains, it is vain to hope that the parsing scheme can be merely a formalization of standard patterns of analysis that linguists already use routinely in their work. True, many aspects of grammatical structure are well-known and uncontroversial: if that were not so then the enterprise of automatic parsing would perhaps make little sense. But real-life English includes masses of phenomena which are ignored by linguists' tacit consensus view of grammatical structure. To take a few examples at random: the Harvard-style reference in:

> *Knighting and Hinds (1960) showed* .. (J10 94)

the hierarchical sequencing of elements in an address such as:

> *26, Boyle Avenue, Stanmore* (B10 192–3)

or the interrogative afterthought in:

> *The secret life of Matthew Helm ... Helm?" she said.* (N15 152–3)

are all normal enough features of one or another genre of written English, but none of them are the sort of thing that one sees included in the tree-diagrams of orthodox linguistics textbooks. Indeed, because linguistics has traditionally concentrated on spoken language, linguists' tree-diagrams totally ignore all punctuation; yet, for automatic parsing of written language, punctuation marks are "words" almost as crucial as *of* or *the*. We want automatic parsing to be based on a scheme that comes as close as possible to the ideal of "total accountability" (cf. Quirk and Svartvik 1979: 204): the scheme should yield an unambiguous analysis for any phenomenon whatever occurring in written English.

For our group, creation of the grammatical database and formulation of the parsing scheme went hand in hand. In what follows I shall begin by describing the database fairly briefly, and then discuss at greater length the parsing scheme and the process by which it was evolved – a process which has lessons to offer for general linguistic theory, quite apart from the special issue of computational analysis.

2. The grammatical database

Our grammatical database, or "treebank", comprises manual parsings of sentences totalling about fifty thousand words (actually, 50 363 words) of the LOB Corpus, counting punctuation marks, and enclitics such as $>n't$, as separate "words". This represents 4.5% of the total Corpus. (The size of the LOB Corpus is nominally one million words, but when punctuation and enclitics are counted separately a more realistic figure is about 1 125 000 words.) The treebank includes parsings of 2284 sentences (mean sentence-length being 22.1 words), whose parse-trees contain about 33 000 non-terminal nodes. Thus our parsing scheme yields trees in which the ratio of non-terminal to terminal nodes averages 0.66. This average falls to 0.64 in Category J, Learned and Scientific Writings, and rises to 0.71 in fiction; that is, there is a slight tendency for technical prose to contain more "daughters" per "mother" in its parse-trees than fiction.

Within each of the fifteen LOB genre categories, the standard deviation of the non-terminal/terminal ratios in different sentences is about 0.12. The lowness of this figure is reassuring, since it suggests that consistency has been achieved in applying the parsing scheme to different sentences. Mean sentence-length, on the other hand, shows large differences between genres – in Category J the mean is 30.3 words, while most fiction categories have means of about fifteen words; and standard deviations are also large, e.g. 16.6 for Category J.[†]

This database was produced by me over the period mid-1983 to mid-1985. Sentences were selected for parsing so as to represent each of the genre categories in proportion to its size, with one major deviation: at an intuitive level it appeared that Category J contained a much higher incidence of unusual grammatical complications than any other single category, and since J is also a rather important category for

---

† The fact that non-terminal/terminal ratios remain highly consistent in sentences of very variable length is psycholinguistically interesting, in view of Lyn Frazier's identification of this statistic as a crucial measure of human language-processing difficulty (Frazier 1985).

many of the practical applications of automatic natural-language analysis it seemed worthwhile to include more than the standard percentage of J in the treebank (even though J is a large category in the Corpus as a whole). In fact the treebank includes 6.1% of Category J, which constitutes more than a fifth of the whole treebank; consequently, the average representation of the other fourteen categories is 4.2%. For several practical reasons it was difficult to adhere to this figure precisely, so a tolerance was allowed about this mean and sample-sizes of different non-J categories vary between 3.6% and 4.8%.

For most categories, the texts were sampled by mechanically extracting from the word-tagged version of the Corpus runs of about four or five contiguous sentences from different locations within different texts included in the category. (In the early days of creating the treebank, much longer runs of sentences were used for two of the fifteen categories.) Each sentence selected was printed out at the bottom of a sheet of line-printer paper as a sequence of words paired with their wordtags; I drew the corresponding labelled tree on the blank area above the sentence, and a representation of the tree was then keyed into the machine. Choice of sentences was neither purely random nor perfectly systematic, but there seems little reason to doubt that the finished treebank is about as representative a sampling as any other method would have yielded; and it produced a database which is arranged in sections corresponding to the Corpus categories, which has important potential advantages with respect to genre-specific language-analysis applications. (It would be easy, for instance, to equip the parser with statistics drawn exclusively from official and technical documents rather than from fiction, or vice versa.)

3. Creation of the parsing scheme

The actual drawing of trees was a very small part of the work involved in creating the database. Far more effort was required by the associated task of developing the parsing scheme to which the trees conform.

The scheme began life in early 1983 as a few pages of notes by Geoffrey Leech laying down a set of categories and symbols to be used in node-labels, with examples; after drawing a few experimental trees I supplemented these notes with some further material defining certain of the categories a little more tightly and adding explicit rules governing the structure to be recognized in trees. In my naivety, I remember hoping that the resulting 25 pages of typescript could stand as an essentially complete statement of our parsing scheme, though I did suspect that we would occasionally encounter quirky linguistic forms not provided for in the scheme.

I soon learned. As I began to parse fresh sentences, again and again they would throw up novel problems for which the existing draft scheme offered no guidance – frequently there would be several separate issues to be resolved in a single shortish sentence. A routine developed whereby I would make provisional decisions whose details were logged in documents circulated periodically among the group: often my decisions were ratified, but sometimes another member would point out arguments I had overlooked in favour of a different solution, and a final decision would be made in discussion between us. Occasionally an issue of this kind would be thrashed out in quite lengthy discussions at one of the weekly meetings of the whole group. The documentation circulated in the process of evolving the parsing scheme amounts to well over 100 000 words of dense prose, full of quoted examples, cross-references to earlier decisions, and the like. (The whole has been cumulated into a systematic exposition of the parsing scheme, which is likely to be published separately.) The categories of the original draft remain largely intact (though there have been a few changes even to this fundamental component of the scheme); but around each category has grown up a complex structure of rules and precedents for applying it to debatable cases.

Thus the scheme as it now stands does represent a consensus rather than one linguist's private view of English grammar, but it is much more detailed than any scheme which is tacitly taken for granted by the profession in general. Indeed, so far as I know our parsing scheme represents the *only* extant attempt to lay down explicit rules defining a specific grammatical analysis for whatever occurs in modern written English. (Alvar Ellegård (1978) has done valuable work along similar lines, but, while his database of parsed text is larger than ours, he uses a less comprehensively specified parsing scheme.)

4. The nature of the scheme

The scheme is founded on a few very general principles. In the first place, as indicated above, it should provide an analysis for anything found in written English, no matter how substandard or solecistic it may appear, with the sole exception of actual misprints. If we were convinced that a form as it stands on the page could not have been what its writer intended to write, then we would not require the scheme to be able to cope with it; an example is:

> *The evidence suggest that* .. (E06 87)

where it does not seem credible that the writer could have intended the form *suggest*, and it is corrected in the treebank to *suggests*. But we strove to be conservative in postulating misprints. If an odd sequence might conceivably have been intended, we assume that it was: thus it was tempting to "correct" the *to* of:

> .. *between £25 to £30 million* .. (A27 13)

to *and*, but this could have been sloppy writing rather than a printer's error so *to* stands in the treebank. The fiction categories of the Corpus contain many passages of dialogue in which the author has deliberately used substandard dialect or imitations of foreigners' broken English: such passages are parsed, by analogy with their nearest standard-English equivalents. (These and other special cases are segregated from the bulk of the material within the treebank, since, for many practical applications of automatic language-analysis – e.g. text-critiquing, cf. Chapter 10 below – it is desirable to have access to statistics representing exclusively standard language; but that does not affect the principle that such cases are required to be parsable.)

Where there is consensus in the discipline about the analysis of a grammatical construction, our scheme respects that consensus: it seems reasonable to assume that the consensus analysis has the greatest chance of proving to be the analysis which fits well into yet-to-be-created automatic systems for mapping between all the various levels of language structure, from orthography to semantics. Where alternative analyses can each be defended as "respectable" in terms of linguistic theory, we allowed ourselves to opt for the choice which harmonized best with the existing UCREL word-tagging scheme and with our approach to automatic parsing; but we resisted the temptation to postulate unorthodox structures in order to simplify the task of designing the parser. (It would be a poor achievement to build a parser which succeeded in detecting structures that had been designed to be easily detectable.) Probably the nearest our scheme comes to positive grammatical unorthodoxy is in its treatment of co-ordination, which we assimilate to subordination: co-ordinate noun-phrases or sentences are analysed as in:

> [*my mother* [*and my father*]]
> [*John played,* [*Wendy sang*], [*and Anne danced*].]

– with the second and any subsequent conjunct treated as subordinate to the first. This may seem illogical, since semantically the function of co-ordination is to express equivalence between the conjuncts; but we do not normally require grammar to mirror logic so directly. (To give an analogy: we do not require plural forms to be analysed as containing more morphemes than singulars, and in the case of English verbs the opposite is the case.) Co-ordination is a notorious focus of grammatical controversy, and I would defend our approach as psychologically more plausible than the usual analysis which makes the conjuncts grammatically equivalent, as in:

> [[*my mother*] *and* [*my father*]]

Human beings parse (and, presumably, construct) utterances sequentially. It is hard to believe in an analysis which forces a choice between opening one and more than one bracket at a stage when no indication is available of whether co-ordination will in fact occur.

Our scheme is designed to yield trees that are relatively "flat" rather than "tall". So, for instance, there are tight limits on the use of singulary branching (i.e. nodes with unique daughters); and the scheme treats endocentric constructions as built by concatenation rather than recursion – a noun phrase such as:

> *two sprightly elderly ladies* (C09 190)

is analysed as a sequence of four sister-nodes rather than as:

> *two* [*sprightly* [*elderly ladies*]]

(This conforms to the kind of structuring described by Terry Winograd (1983: 198) as characteristic of transition-network rather than rewrite-rule grammars. Lyn Frazier (1985: 153) cites research suggesting that relatively flat structures are psychologically realistic.)

In transformational terms, our scheme provides analyses which are "surfacy" rather than "deep". Where constituents are broken up by movement rules, commonly nothing in our parsing indicates their underlying unity, and constituents are labelled in terms of surface rather than deep grammatical roles. (Likewise, where the form of a constituent conflicts with the function it performs in its environment, parsing follows form rather than function.) Surface and deep are relative terms, and there are many exceptions to the tendency I am describing. Conjuncts which have undergone co-ordination reduction are identified as reduced examples of their original categories, and clauses deformed by "unbounded movement rules" are labelled in terms of their underlying rather than surface form – in:

> .. *the original lead-210 solution .. which we concluded was radiochemically pure.*
> (J04 42–3)

the sequence *was radiochemically pure* is identified as a nominal clause despite the fact that Wh-fronting has removed its subject. Again, where a verb phrase has been split, by question-formation or otherwise, as in

> .. *never before had such tremendous innovations and plans for the future been*
> *contemplated.* (A30 60–1)

the underlying unity of the phrase, in this case *had been contemplated*, is expressed by labelling its two parts Vo, Vr for "operator" and "remainder". But, within the spectrum of current approaches to grammatical analysis, ours is located towards the "surfacy" end.

Undoubtedly it is true that for many potential IT applications a system which delivered deeper parses would be much more useful. That said, I believe that it is quite inevitable in the present state of the art that our scheme has to be fairly surfacy. Deep grammatical analyses are often highly contentious even with respect to the restricted domain of artificially simple, polished sentences which theorists of linguistic competence discuss. Questions about the deep-structure location of commas, or about the underlying analyses of the quirky or colloquial turns of phrase which are very common in authentic data but have no links with issues of general theory, are never raised within mainstream generative linguistics. To quote an extreme case: a sentence such as:

> *"I – I just wanted – people sometimes like to be alone together – please try to*
> *understand."* (P14 145–6)

would be dismissed by a generative linguist as containing several "performance" deviations, and therefore not really English at all. We cannot allow ourselves the luxury of such an attitude. Accordingly, a pioneer approach to the analysis of authentic language must necessarily be a surface approach, although incorporation of deeper levels of analysis is a desirable future development.

5.   Grammatical categories

Our parsing scheme assigns each non-terminal node of a parse-tree to one of a range of major categories coded by capital letters. (We use the term "hypertag" for the label of a non-terminal node. The distinction between wordtags and hypertags is reflected in their coding: wordtags other than punctuation-tags include at least two capitals and no lower-case letters, hypertags include just one capital and other letters are lower case.) Constituent-types are divided into two classes: clause-types coded by letters S, F, T, W, A, L, and phrase-types coded by V, N, J, R, P, M, D, G, X, E, U. (In addition, certain multi-word constituents are tagged as grammatically equivalent to individual words, thus the grammatical idiom *out of* is labelled IN=, that is as the equivalent of a preposition – see "ditto-tags", p. 40.)

The distinction between clauses and phrases is relevant for the rules limiting singulary branching: broadly, every clause must be fully mirrored in the parse-tree, but where some linguists would recognize a phrase-node which was immediately dominated by a higher phrase-node while itself dominating a single phrase-node or word, our scheme ignores the intermediate node as redundant. (For instance, if an adjective occurs as IC of a clause, as in *this specimen is unusual*, it is parsed as an adjectival phrase, J, consisting of a single word tagged JJ; but no J node is postulated when a one-word adjectival "phrase" occurs as IC of a noun phrase as in *an unusual specimen*.)

Our categories are defined briefly as follows:

S   independent sentence (or sentential conjunct), together with:

        Si   interpolation (e.g. author's "aside")

        Sq   direct quotation

F   finite clause, divided into:

        Fa   adverbial clause

        Fn   nominal clause

        Fr   relative clause

        Ff   antecedentless relative, as in '*But [whoever did it] got clean away* .. (L04 150–1)

        Fc   comparative clause, as in .. *found the evidence less clear-cut [than he might have desired]*. (J35 179–80)

T   non-finite clause, divided into:

        Tg   clause with present-participle head

        Tn   clause with past-participle head

        Ti   clause with infinitive head

        Tq   infinitival relative or indirect question as in *a good time of year [at which to lay turf]* (E08 108–9)

        Tf   *for-to* clause, as in *It just remains [for the afterbirth to come away]*. (F32 140)

        Tb   "bare" non-finite clause, as in .. *would have us [run risks]* .. (B02 28)

W   *with* clause, as in [*With events in Brazil leading to fears of anarchy*], *Dr. Fidel Castro today urged* .. (A29 227–8)

A   non-standard *as* clause, as in *Weber saw sociology* .. [*as dialectically related to reality*] (G67 131–2)

L   "verbless" clause, as in *Marcel Dupré,* [*himself in his seventies and a pioneer of organ records*], *has re-recorded it* .. (C10 196–7)

V   verb phrase (sequence of auxiliary and main verbs, excluding object, complement, etc.)

N   noun phrase

J   adjectival phrase

R   adverbial phrase

P   prepositional phrase

M   phrase with numeral head, as in .. [*nine out of ten*] *men* .. (F21 21)

D   phrase with determiner head, as in [*practically no*] *new houses* .. (E28 62)

G   genitive phrase, as in [*his master's*] *voice*

X   *not* as independent phrase

E   existential *there*

U   interjection

For most phrase categories a number of lower-case subcategory symbols are defined: e.g. Nqp stands for a noun phrase containing a *wh*-word and marked as plural, such as *which recipes*. There is a difference in kind between lower-case subcategory symbols added to phrase tags and those added to clause tags: clause subcategories, e.g. Fa v. Fn v. Fr, stand for functional properties of the constituents they label, and they are part of the output which a successful automatic parser should produce, whereas phrase subcategory symbols are merely a mechanical reflection of grammatically-relevant features which are overtly marked within the relevant phrases, and they serve as data for the parsing process rather than as output required from it. (The verb-phrase subcategories Vo and Vr, mentioned above, are an exception to this point.)

Apart from lower-case subcategory symbols there are also a small number of non-alphabetic supplementary symbols which apply to both clause and phrase nodes. The hypertag for a co-ordination ends in an ampersand, and the "subordinate conjuncts" of a co-ordination end in a plus or minus sign according as they do or do not begin with a co-ordinating conjunction:

[S& *John sang*, [S— *Wendy played*], [S+ *and Anne danced*].]

Where the conjuncts of a co-ordination are of different types, the hypertag of the co-ordination includes each relevant symbol linked by solidi:

[R/P& *orally* [P+ *or on paper*]] (E24 156)

Finally, the symbol "t" marks a form used as a book title or the like, which will often be grammatically disharmonious with its context:

When his famous [Nst *The Green Hat*] *appeared,* .. (G30 122–3)

The possibilities of combining these various symbols mean that in theory the parsing scheme offers upwards of 60 000 distinct hypertags. In practice a small number of these are very frequent and many of them vanishingly rare. (The rarity of many combinations is of little practical consequence for our approach, since statistics are gathered on individual subcategories rather than their combinations.)

It may be helpful to display the structure of a sample sentence. An example of average length and complexity is the following sentence (taken from a *Guardian* film review):

> *Here, the guests arrive in ghost-like yachts, the wildly flapping white sails slashed by the glaring beacon of a lighthouse.* (C02 49–51)

The structure assigned by our scheme to this sentence is shown in Figure 6.

Our motive in creating this database was to use it for automatic parsing. But the mass of statistics it yields is a mine of information, potentially relevant to all kinds of linguistic enterprises. Consider, for example, the statistics on sentence-patterns, treated as sequences of ICs analysed in terms of elementary categories (ignoring phrase subcategories, etc.). Many of us have been brought up to believe that the most basic type of English sentence is the subject-verb-object type, as in *John kissed Mary*. Sure enough, the pattern N V N. is the most frequent single sentence pattern, accounting for 6.1% of all cases. Contrary to what linguistics textbooks might suggest, though, the corresponding intransitive pattern, as in *Mary shrieked.*, is very far from enjoying similar popularity. In fact, at 0.64% of all cases, the pattern N V. is merely thirteenth equals, on a par with the patterns N V R P. and N V J, S. The runner-up to N V N. in frequency is N. – a "sentence" consisting of just a noun phrase followed by full stop, particularly common in headings and the like in technical prose – which accounts for 4.6% of all sentences. (The third, fourth, and fifth commonest patterns are N V P. (3.7%), N V Fn. (2.9%), and N V Ti. (2.0%).) Our treebank allows detailed figures of this kind to be retrieved easily, not just for sentences but for individual constructions – and not just for the language as a whole but for particular genres of writing. (Cf. the work of Ellegård (1978) on the Brown Corpus of American English.)

6.   Grammar as case law

Having sketched the parsing scheme as it stands, let me turn now to the processes by which the scheme was worked out – processes which were often quite alien to my past experience as a theoretical linguist.

When a theorist of linguistic competence sets out to provide a descriptive framework for a language, his work tends to resemble in general flavour the work of a physical scientist (sometimes the resemblance is explicit). The linguist seeks a parsimonious, elegant set of laws or "grammatical rules" to generate the language in question; often an initial attempt to state a law/rule for a given area proves too

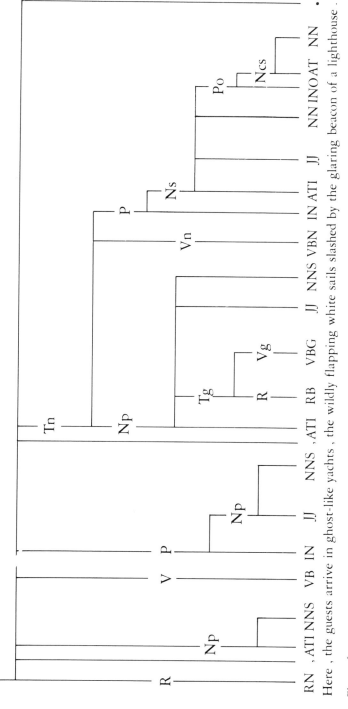

Figure 6

simplistic to work, for both the physicist and the generative linguist, but in both cases the reaction is to seek the minimal sacrifice of elegance that will allow the recalcitrant facts to be accommodated. Both categories of scholar share a fundamental axiom that reality is essentially simple.

The discipline of developing a parsing scheme for authentic language is very different in mood. Not that, in undertaking this task, we did not aim to keep the scheme as simple as possible; of course we did. But the axioms of the philosophy of science lose their relevance in practice, when the aim is not to find psychologically-sophisticated explanatory theories of the "core" aspects of grammar but rather to construct a descriptive framework with a place for everything that occurs, core or peripheral. Instead, two other disciplines suggested analogies for our work: law, and biology.

The resemblances between the process of evolving the parsing scheme and the processes by which the Common Law evolves were very striking indeed. By lawyers' fiction, the Common Law contains within itself an answer to every issue that may arise in litigation: the problem in a particular case is to find it. If the case has a precedent, that settles the issue – unless rival precedents seem to point in different directions, in which case one has to try to discern what is the relevant distinction between the precedents and hence which of them is the true model for the instant case. If no particular case seems to offer a relevant precedent, the judgement is made in terms of the set of consistent and all-embracing principles which the Common Law is deemed to express. The truth is, of course, that no set of principles and precedents can possibly suffice to settle unambiguously all the endlessly novel cases which arise: when a judge applies the law, it is inevitable that he must often make a choice which cannot be called "correct" or "incorrect". Yet a useful purpose is served by the fiction that the law leaves no gaps. It discourages judges from making decisions in a merely capricious fashion, and holds the evolving body of law as close to the unattainable ideals of total consistency and predictability as is compatible with the unpredictability of human life.

Working out the details of the parsing scheme, likewise, was a matter of "broadening down from precedent to precedent". Often, a sequence of precedents would direct the evolution of a rule in a direction far removed from what had been envisaged when the rule was first laid down. Consider, as one example among many, the case of comparative expressions. Two of the points stated by Geoffrey Leech in his original act of law-giving were these: the category J, adjectival phrase, covers sequences such as *so* + adjective + Fc, e.g. [J *so useful* [Fc *that you will want several*]]; and the category Fc, comparative clause, covers not only "clauses" in the ordinary sense which include verbs, but also verbless comparative expressions like *as at Easter*. Some time after beginning to apply the rules, I encountered the case:

> *.. is due as much to Wicki the photographer as to Wicki the director.* (C02 29–30)

It was far from clear, intuitively, what constituent structure should be postulated in this sequence. The best analogy I could find was the rule about J just quoted, which suggested that if *so useful that you will want several* is a single constituent with *useful* as head then *as much to Wicki the photographer as to Wicki the director* must be one constituent with *much* as head; so I parsed it:

[R *as much to Wicki the photographer* [Fc *as to Wicki the director*]]

and I made explicit the implied generalization by enunciating the maxim that all such comparative phrases:

> *more X than ..*
> *so X that ..*
> *as much X as ..*

were to be treated as single constituents (in which the X element is the head). Only later did I encounter the sentence:

A dog is as much God's handiwork as a man. (D14 106–7)

By the piece of "judge-made law" just quoted, [*as much God's handiwork as a man*] must be a constituent, with *handiwork* as head – hence a noun phrase. Yet, if I had encountered this example at the outset, I doubt whether I would have chosen to analyse this sequence as a noun-phrase constituent: there are very few N slots into which it can fit (it cannot be subject, or object, or complement of a preposition).

In this case, I accepted the consequences of following precedent despite misgivings. With some other grammatical issues, a rule which looked reasonable when first enunciated led to such intolerable implications for later, unforeseen examples that eventually it became necessary to change the rule; and of course such developments occur in the course of legal evolution too, despite the theory that the prior state of the law has authority over later decision-making. (Here there is one important disanalogy, though: whenever one of the established parsing rules was changed, it was necessary to search laboriously through the existing treebank to bring all earlier decisions into line with the new rule. When laws are changed, only subsequent cases are affected.) In the physical sciences, there is a tacit assumption that somewhere, in the mind of God as it were, a wholly adequate theory is waiting for Man to formulate; perhaps no one expects that humans will ever succeed in creating the ultimate theory, yet the enterprise of scientific research is difficult to make sense of unless one accepts that there is a final truth to which various theories are closer or more distant approximations. Generative linguists, too, while they may accept with Sapir that in practice "All grammars leak", have in the back of their mind the idea that a linguist who was sufficiently patient and lucky should in principle be able to produce a totally leak-free grammar. Law is not like that. Lawyers write systematizations of the law on a given topic as it exists at a particular time; everyone knows that such a survey will become outdated, but that does not imply that the work was defective when written – what outdates it is genuinely new law which could not have been anticipated before it came into being (even if we consider only case law, ignoring statutes). As I moved on from one batch of sentences to the next in constructing the treebank, it was certainly true that the frequency of issues calling for new decisions fell to a much lower level than it had been at the start, and the problems which did crop up tended to be increasingly narrow ones; but these declines, I am sure, approached zero only asymptotically. True, fifty thousand words of English is not a great deal, but I doubt whether anyone who became seriously involved in this work would envisage that the point could *ever* come when there were no more grammatical issues left to be decided. (Cf. Sampson 1987.)

One way of giving an impression of how far fifty thousand words go towards representing the grammatical possibilities of English might be to identify a "marginal construction" – a construction which occurs just once in the treebank, so that the sampling has all but missed it outright. Perhaps the most significant marginal construction in this sense is the "correlative" construction which occurs in *the more the merrier*. The correlative seems to be a distinct construction not easily assimilable to any commoner grammatical phenomenon (the German translation of such a phrase includes a closed-class word, *desto*, which has no other use); the treebank has only one correlative, and not a straightforward example at that:

> .. *the non-diagonal d_{ij} being the smaller the better the waviness of Ω_1 is retained ..*
> (J80 110–1)

(One feature of work with authentic data is that clearcut, "textbook" cases of any given phenomenon tend to be elusive.) Clearly, statistics derived from a database of this size will not be adequate for automatic analysis of a passage containing a correlative, and if the correlative construction has "just made it" into the treebank then no doubt there are a few constructions of comparable frequency in the language as a whole which "just failed to make it". But the peripheral status of the correlative construction in English suggests to me that our database should serve very well in practice as an initial source of information for automatic parsing. (It is intended as no more than an initial source; one of the beauties of our approach to language processing is that performance can be improved recursively, as manually-corrected output from earlier versions of the system is fed back into the database used by later versions. This was an important mechanism in the development of CLAWS, and should be equally applicable to our parsing system.)

7.   Lumping and splitting

Law is one subject with strong parallels to the work of creating the parsing scheme. Another is biological taxonomy, with its ambiguities about which differences between individuals justify the recognition of distinct varieties or species. Biologists classify one another as "lumpers" or "splitters", recognizing that there is often no objectively correct answer to the question whether two variants are "the same" or "different" species and that subjective tendencies are bound to play a part in taxonomy. For us too the arguments between splitting and lumping of grammatical categories were often finely balanced.

In the case of relative clauses "fused" with their antecedents, for instance, as in:

> .. *share* .. [*whatever light God has given them*] .. (B03 55–6)

we decided to give them a tag of their own, Ff, distinct from the tag Fn which covers nominal clauses, including indirect questions and clauses introduced by the complementizer *that*: Ff and Fn both function nominally, and often they are indistinguishable with respect to internal structure (the phrase *what one has learnt* is an Ff in the context:

> *Is there no such thing as .. forgetting what one has learnt?* (D14 83–4)

while the identical sequence would be tagged Fn if it occurred as object of *wonder* or *ask*); but there are also important differences. An antecedentless relative with plural subject can govern a plural verb in the clause containing it, while an Fn is always grammatically singular; Fn's are rare as surface subjects and are commonly extraposed, Ef's often occur as surface subjects; some *wh*-words, such as *who*, associate with Fn while others, such as *whoever*, associate with Ff: differences such as these were deemed sufficient to justify splitting. In the case of Tf, *for-to* clauses, on the other hand, we lumped. The tag Tf was invented in order to handle the classic generative-linguists' *for-to* complement, as in:

> [*For John to know the answer*] *would surprise me.*

In our database this construction, functioning nominally within a clause, turned out to be quite rare, though examples do occur. A commoner construction is the one exemplified in:

> .. *little* [*for the West to do*] .. (B02 52–3)

where the clause acts as post-modifier within a noun phrase, and where one of the noun phrase slots within the clause (in this case, the object of *do*) is omitted as corresponding to the antecedent. Since this construction differs both formally and functionally from the construction for which the Tf tag was originally coined, it seemed appropriate at one stage to give it a separate label despite the considerable resemblances between the two varieties of *for-to* clause. But then we observed that there exist intermediate possibilities, as in:

> *that's difficult* [*for me to put up with*]

and eventually the decision was to lump all *for-to* clauses under the hypertag Tf. (Commonly, Geoffrey Leech tended to lump while I was a splitter; reassuringly, however, on occasion we found these roles reversed.)

Within the generative paradigm, it might seem objectionable to treat issues of this sort as ones where personal predilections have any legitimate part to play. A given node either belongs or does not belong to the same category as another node, and the task is to discover the objective "God's-truth" of the matter (to use the phrase which F. W. Householder (1952) coined for this conception of linguistics). That truth would not necessarily be simple; a generative linguist might argue that our debates stemmed from a naive failure to appreciate that two constituents can belong to the same category in deep structure and different categories in surface structure, or that categories are not atomic symbols but sets of features which may display partial resemblances with other sets. But this would not affect the claim that subjective analytic styles are irrelevant.

The generativist's view may be correct; clearly, the fact that we made decisions about lumping or splitting "core" constructions such as *for-to* clauses in a partly subjective fashion is no argument at all against the possibility that such questions can be resolved in terms of objective evidence that we were not perceptive enough to notice. What might be an argument, though, is that questions of just the same type arose equally often in connexion with "peripheral" grammatical issues where the generative writ scarcely runs.

For instance, should a Harvard-style reference, e.g. the *(1960)* in:

Knighting and Hinds (1960) showed .. (J10 94)

be lumped under the hypertag Si, along with bracketed interpolations such as *(iv)* or *(it is claimed)*? The fact of enclosure in brackets is an important formal similarity, and the slots where such sequences can occur overlap heavily; but there are also some consistent differences. In the event we "split" in this case, and chose to link Harvard-style references with the preceding names as a special class of appositional elements. But in an area like this it is difficult to believe that one choice would be an accurate reflection of the psychologically-real linguistic competence determined by our innate language-acquisition device, with other choices simply "incorrect". Once one becomes used to the idea that only judicious weighing of the balance of convenience can settle issues of this kind, it seems implausible that comparable questions have a qualitatively different status when one happens to be dealing with an aspect of grammar falling within the generativists' purview. Where is the borderline, and how would one know that one had crossed it?

It may be that theorists of linguistic competence have answers for such questions. My purpose here is not to claim that their style of language description is necessarily mistaken in its own terms. What seems undeniable, though, is that, for the practical purpose of building natural-language processing systems which achieve usable results with authentic input, the approach to linguistic description associated with the phrase "linguistic competence" is irrelevant, and will remain so at least for the foreseeable future.

A sociologist may spin webs of deep theory by focusing on just those aspects of human behaviour which express individuals' class affiliation, or their family relationships. A judge, on the other hand, has to confront human behaviour in all its rich and unpredictable diversity, and the legal structure he helps to build is a developing filigree of detailed rules rather than a geometrical construct of elegant, eternal axioms. In computational linguistics, likewise, the researcher who aims to cope successfully with real-life data cannot pick and choose just theoretically-interesting bits of language. His approach must be catholic and pragmatic, not absolutist. But to be pragmatic is not to be unprincipled. The opposite of God's-truth need not be "hocus-pocus"; it may be jurisprudence.

CHAPTER 8

Text input and pre-processing: Dealing with the orthographic form of texts

Barbara Booth

1. Introduction

The problem of analysing the orthographic features of texts is an important but neglected area in natural-language text processing, and current enhancement work to CLAWS has brought this problem area very much into focus. Previous chapters have emphasized that the aim of our work is the automatic analysis of large quantities of unrestricted text. But if we are to make credible claims about the practical usefulness of our systems it is clearly essential that all the orthographic features of texts, especially such ambiguous features as capitalization, full stops, and abbreviations, should be as far as possible correctly processed without manual intervention. CLAWS1 was developed specifically for the tagging of the LOB Corpus, from which the orthographic ambiguities had been virtually eliminated at the coding stage, with a few remaining problems forestalled during manual pre-editing. With CLAWS2 we are aiming for a more general and ambitious system, which will run over any machine-readable text without recoding or pre-editing. This chapter explores the problems of dealing automatically with the orthographic form of texts, first, by describing how the automatic process in CLAWS1 used information made available by manual coding and pre-editing, and secondly by examining how the process was elaborated so that CLAWS2 could function from the text alone, once this manual intervention was eliminated.

2. The LOB orthographic coding scheme

The anticipated uses of the LOB Corpus influenced the format in which the Corpus was held, as well as the initial selection of material. The "guiding principle" was to produce "a faithful representation of the text with as little loss of information as possible" (Johansson *et al*. 1978: 7).

The compositors of the original printed texts were able to exploit the options of a very large symbol system: the letters of the Roman alphabet in a variety of sizes and styles; alternative alphabets and diacritic markings for non-English language material; a vast assortment of symbols for mathematical data or information from other specialized fields.

But computer character sets are far more restricted in size. The LOB editors limited themselves to the 95 printable symbols of the international standard 128-member ASCII character set. So only a certain number of the symbols in the original text could be represented on a one-for-one basis in the Corpus coding scheme. In addition to "simple" coding symbols, where one character in the Corpus represented a single, usually the same, character in the original text, there were also "compound" coding symbols, where strings of more than one character represented a single character in the original. For example, a percent sign, %, in the Corpus represented the same character in the text, whereas the string *?22 was used to represent the square root sign, √. And because the character * was a prefix distinguishing compound coding symbols, when an asterisk actually occurred in a text it also had to be represented by a compound symbol, in this case */.

The Corpus was to provide a representative sample of written English at a particular moment in history, so the coders needed to distinguish data within the Corpus which might be unrepresentative or non-contemporary. It was particularly important to mark quotations, which might be taken from earlier texts, or might be direct speech, with the rather special linguistic features of dialogue. Although opening and closing inverted commas are usually differentiated in print, in computer character sets they are not normally distinguished. Opening and closing single and double inverted commas (', ', ", ") were all allocated unique compound coding symbols (*', **', *", **"), so that quotations could be unambiguously identified within the Corpus.

Besides such "designator" symbols, both simple and compound, corresponding to the symbols of the original text, the Corpus also contained "marker" symbols (see Johansson *et al.* 1978: 28). A marker symbol gave information about one or more of the preceding or following designators, and had no direct correlate in the original. Again, markers might be simple or compound. For instance, the compound marker symbol *1 indicated a typographical shift and showed that the following characters (up to the next typographical shift marker) appeared in italics in the original text. The simple symbol " indicated that there was an umlaut or diaeresis on the preceding character in the original. Again, because of the need to distinguish possible unrepresentative material, mathematical formulae and headings were delimited by markers, as were foreign-language excerpts, and all forms of non-standard English.

The coding scheme as described so far was an attempt to prevent loss of information when representing a printed text within the far more limited constraints of a machine-readable format. But the devisers of the scheme went beyond this in anticipating problems which might be met when processing printed data automatically. Despite the wide range of symbols available to the printer, some symbols are still conventionally used for more than one purpose. A full stop, for instance, may mark the end of a sentence, or an abbreviation, or both, or might appear as a decimal point within a numerical expression. Similarly, the same printed symbol is used for an apostrophe and for a closing single quotation mark, and an apostrophe may indicate a possessive case form (*John's father*) or a contraction (*don't*, *he's*). These local ambiguities would pose no problem for the competent reader, and would in all probability be unconsciously resolved. But for the linguistically incompetent machine they remain problematic.

Where the coders felt that an ambiguity would cause processing problems they again usually introduced separate coding symbols to resolve the ambiguity. Since the closing single quotation mark had been allocated a compound coding symbol, * ', the simple symbol ' was reserved for apostrophe. Similarly, the compound symbol * − was allocated to the dash punctuation mark and the simple symbol − was reserved for hyphen or minus.

The full-stop symbol remained ambiguous, but all abbreviations were overtly marked as such in the Corpus, so the ambiguity could be automatically resolved from the context. For instance, the abbreviation for *inch* would be coded as \0*in.* and could be distinguished from the preposition *in* even at the end of a sentence.

Various other coding conventions were adopted in relation to spacing and ordering of punctuation, to standardize the Corpus, and to simplify later processing by researchers. For instance, where words in the original text were linked by a solidus (/), the symbol would be followed by a space in the Corpus to facilitate the automatic division of the Corpus into its minimal grammatical units. Similarly, the Corpus coders introduced a special marker symbol, ^, to indicate the start of each sentence, since the sentence is the maximal grammatical structure usually analysed by linguists.

A coding scheme which represents a single original symbol by a variable- length string of characters will necessarily involve more sophisticated processing than a one-for-one scheme at the character-handling level. But the recoding of ambiguous symbols, the inclusion of interpretative codings, and other explicit marking of covert information in the LOB Corpus, all helped to simplify the language processing tasks to be performed automatically.

3. CLAWS1: The automatic pre-editing phase

The first phase of the automatic processing was known as the "pre-edit" phase (see Chapter 3, pp. 33–4). At this stage, the text was segmented into the units which were to be tagged, and at the same time various other amendments were made to simplify the later tagging procedures.

The conventions adopted for spacing and ordering of punctuation made the automatic segmentation of the text relatively straightforward. Each sequence of characters delimited by spaces was treated as a word, and any punctuation marks at the start or end of the word were stripped off. A separate line was generated in the "verticalized" output text for each word or punctuation symbol, a line which would eventually also hold the correct tag. In general, because of the coding scheme, the recognition of punctuation was unproblematic, and it was decided that punctuation tagging could also be done at this early verticalization stage, each line created for a punctuation symbol being generated with an unambiguous tag. A full stop was treated as a punctuation symbol unless it fell within the scope of an abbreviation marker or followed a digit. The special marker for start of sentence was also put on a separate line, but recoded as a line of dashes so that sentence divisions would be clearly visible in the output text (see the example on p. 32).

Because the later tagging procedures would process the "verticalized" text output from this procedure with each word on its own separate line, marker symbols in the Corpus with a scope of more than one word were recoded as flags on every word within their scope. So, for instance, the delimiters for foreign-language excerpts were removed, and the line generated for each word within the excerpt was written with the character F in a certain column to indicate a foreign word. Abbreviations were flagged in another column, but the abbreviation marker symbol was left on the front of each abbreviated form and the final full stop was removed, to simplify lexical look-up at the next stage. Besides generating flags for words within their scope, certain other marker symbols – heading delimiters, for instance – were also recoded as start-of-sentence lines; and where there was no terminating punctuation before such markers, a full-stop record was inserted in the output text, to standardize sentence divisions in the verticalized Corpus. Because the automatic pre-editing involved this recognition and recoding of marker symbols, any tagging which could be carried out by reference to the marker symbols alone was also done at this verticalization stage. Thus, foreign words and formulae explicitly marked in the text were tagged as &FW and &FO respectively.

The segmentation task also involved the recognition of certain contracted forms. The automatic procedure looked for the words *I'm* and *cannot* and forms ending *'ve*, *'re*, *'d*, *'ll*, or *n't*. These forms were split into two separate lines and were flagged to show that they were originally part of the same orthographic unit.

The other major amendment made to the text at this automatic pre-editing phase was the conversion of letters from upper to lower case in certain contexts. The procedure assumed that, where a word occurred with a capital letter immediately after a start-of-sentence marker, the capitalization was irrelevant for tagging purposes, and changed the capital to its lower-case equivalent. But, if a word started with a capital letter in the middle of a sentence, this was assumed to signal some sort of proper name, and the automatic pre-editor left the word unchanged because the word-initial capital expressed information which was needed for tagging. However, where a whole word appeared in upper case, the assumption was that this was for typographical emphasis only, and the whole word was changed to lower case.

4.   CLAWS1: The manual pre-editing phase

Obviously there were exceptions to the kinds of general rules used by the automatic pre-editing procedure. Proper names might occur at the start of sentences as well as in mid-sentence, and in such cases the automatic pre-editor would throw away the word-initial capital, leaving the tagging procedures with insufficient information to make the correct tagging decision. In CLAWS1 it was thought necessary to have some additional manual pre-editing between the automatic pre- editing and the tagging procedures proper, to deal with problems like this.

In fact, the major task of the human pre-editor was dealing with the problem of capitalization. A list was produced of all the words in upper case or with word-initial capitals which had been automatically changed to lower case. The editor then checked these to see if any of the words were actually proper names, and, if so, the word-initial capital was restored. In the sentence *ˆGaunt was compelled to return to England* .. (G01 21–2), for example, the first word was changed to *gaunt* by the automatic pre-editor and then restored as *Gaunt* by the manual editor, to ensure that it would be tagged as a proper noun rather than an adjective. Similarly, a list was also produced of all words with word-initial capitals which had *not* been changed automatically, and this was checked for any words which were *not* proper names. Consider the example *.. the handling of the *1Lady Chatterley's Lover *0case ..* (A11 163). After automatic pre-editing the typographical shift indicators would be removed, but the word-initial capitals of the title would be left unchanged. The manual editor would then flag each word of the title, and reduce *Lover* to lower case, so that it would then be tagged as a singular common noun, while *Lady* and *Chatterley's* would be tagged as titular noun and proper noun, respectively:

A11 163 070 Lady	A11 163 070 Lady	T
A11 163 080 Chatterley's	A11 163 080 Chatterley's	T
A11 163 090 Lover	A11 163 090 lover	T
(after automatic pre-editing)	(after manual pre-editing)	

This last example also shows up another failing of the automatic pre-editing procedure requiring manual intervention, this time in the area of text segmentation. Enclitic forms of *is* and *has*, as in *It's the spring* .. (E15 157) and *.. it's got to be ..* (A33 36), and enclitic forms of *us*, as in *Let's face it* .. (A19 213), all needed to be split off from their preceding words. But, in CLAWS1, genitive forms, like *Chatterley's* above, were tagged as a single grammatical unit. The automatic procedure had no way of distinguishing between these various uses of *'s* without access to grammatical information. So, in the automatic phase, all *'s* forms were left attached, and the manual pre-editor had to put the enclitic *is*, *has*, and *us* forms onto separate lines later.

Because the manual pre-editing phase already involved some very detailed checking of problematic data, some predictable failures of the automatic tagging system could also be detected at this stage, and a very small number of words (approximately 0.2%) were tagged by hand to prevent these failures. More details are given below.

5. CLAWS1: Tagging

Both the initial coding of the texts in LOB coding scheme format, and the amendments made to the texts during the pre-editing phase, allowed certain generalizations to be made which simplified the task of the automatic tagging procedures proper.

WORDTAG, the automatic tag assignment program, contained special procedures for dealing with words starting with a capital. These relied on the fact that, after pre-editing, only proper names or words habitually written with word-initial capital would remain capitalized in the verticalized text. The lexicon contained both lower-case entries and words with initial capital; for example, there were entries both for *may*, tagged as modal verb, and for *May*, tagged as adverbial noun. At tag assignment, a word would be looked up in the form in which it occurred in the text, and, if found, would receive the appropriate set of tags. If the word was not in the lexicon, a special suffixlist was consulted for words with initial capitals; and, if all else failed, capitalized words would be tagged by default as proper nouns. Approximately 35 000 words were tagged as proper nouns by this default procedure, and of these only 700 had to be corrected during post-editing. Virtually all of these errors were because the manual pre-editor had failed to reduce capitalized words to lower case where necessary.

Since the manual pre-editing phase had involved looking through all capitalized words in the Corpus, any which would predictably be tagged incorrectly by WORDTAG were manually tagged at the same time. So about 300 plural proper nouns were manually tagged, as were about 200 proper names which would not correctly drop through to the default procedure. For example, *May* in *Dora May rose to the bait* (L05 127), and *Cyprian* in .. *Chief of the Zulus, Cyprian Dinizulu* (A28 63), were both manually tagged as proper nouns, because otherwise they would have been tagged incorrectly from the lexicon and the special suffixlist, respectively.

Similarly, WORDTAG relied on explicit marking, inserted when the corpus was constructed, for tagging abbreviations. The lexicon contained both full word entries and entries for abbreviated forms with the same marker symbol used in the Corpus; there were entries both for *in*, tagged as a preposition or adverbial particle, and for \0*in*, tagged as a unit of measurement. All abbreviated forms also appeared in the lexicon without a final full stop. So abbreviations could be looked up exactly as they occurred in the verticalized text, with a preceding marker symbol but without any final full stop. This avoided the necessity of having two entries in the lexicon for, say, \0*Mr* and \0*Mr.*, since many common abbreviations are written both with and without final full stops. (Any forms which might occur with or without medial full stops had two entries, e.g. \0*m.p.h* and \0*mph*, both with identical sets of tags). Abbreviations not tagged from the lexicon were tagged as units of measurement by default. Again some manual tagging had been done at the pre-edit phase, for rare abbreviations which would predictably be tagged incorrectly. Compass bearings, for instance, like \0*ESE*, were manually tagged as adverbial nouns. This combination of explicit coding and manual pre-tagging of problematic cases again ensured a very high accuracy rate for abbreviated forms under CLAWS1.

The procedures in WORDTAG dealing with words ending in *'s* could also rely on the fact that all contracted forms of *is*, *has*, and *us* had been split off manually and any remaining *'s* words could be assumed to be genitive forms. Where the *'s* was a contraction of *us* or *has*, the form was tagged manually at the pre-editing stage. The entry *'s* itself appeared in the lexicon tagged as a contraction of *is*. WORDTAG tagged all other words ending in *'s* by ignoring the *'s* ending, assigning tags to the rest of the word through the usual procedures, then changing these tags to equivalent genitive tags, discarding any tags with no corresponding genitive form. For example, *board's* in *the board's share* would first be assigned the tags associated with *board* in the lexicon – singular common noun and verb – then the verb tag would be discarded, and the noun tag changed to the tag for singular common noun plus genitive. In the entire Corpus only 86 words ending in *'s* were mistagged, and again most of these errors were because the manual pre-editor had failed to deal correctly with some capitalized forms.

As explained above, before the texts were submitted to WORDTAG some tagging had already been done at the pre-editing stage. In fact, this amounted to just over 12% of the Corpus – 149 603 syntactic units. The vast majority of these were punctuation symbols, plus the small number of foreign words and formulae tagged by the automatic pre-editor, and the even smaller number of words tagged by the human pre-editor (approximately 2500). This unambiguous pre-tagging together with the generalizations made possible because of the explicit marking of abbreviated forms, and the manual checking of enclitics and capitalized forms, all helped to reduce the amount of tag disambiguation left for CHAINPROBS and must have improved the overall performance of CLAWS1.

6. The motivation for CLAWS2

Although those involved in the development of CLAWS1 were delighted with the accuracy rate they had achieved, they were well aware how time-consuming the initial coding and pre-editing phases had been and were interested to discover how much of this manual work could be avoided if the tagging system were to be made available to other users.

The LOB coding scheme was complex, with multi-character variable-length symbols introduced by a number of different prefixes. Some of the initial coding was valuable for CLAWS1 but other information was not used at all. Markings for typographical distinctions other than capitalization were removed before tagging took place, and heading delimiters were recoded as flags but otherwise ignored. When coding new texts, those unfamiliar with the tagging system would find it difficult to work out exactly what was necessary and what was not, and it would also be far easier for a new user to run the CLAWS system and then correct any errors at the post-editing stage, than to try to anticipate possible errors at the manual pre-editing stage. Moreover, many texts already exist in some sort of machine-readable format, and improvements to optical character readers over recent years have made it possible to input and archive printed texts fairly speedily. Who would want to use an automatic tagging system that required all such texts to be recoded?

It was therefore decided to enhance the tagging system to avoid the need for special coding and manual pre-editing. This entailed modifying the system to deal automatically with ambiguous punctuation marks, all capitalized words, abbreviations without explicit markers, and all the consequential problems of text segmentation.

7.   CLAWS2: A simplified input format

The first stage of this enhancement work was the specification of a new simplified input format. The recognized elements of this new format are either characters from a standard computer character set, or special coding symbols from a limited set used to represent non-standard characters such as foreign orthographic symbols.

The standard characters are those in the ISO/ASCII 95 printable character set, omitting "_" underline, "‾" overline, "|" vertical bar, "\" backslash, "`" grave, and "^" circumflex: 89 characters in all. But it would be a relatively simple matter to alter the composition of this character set if required. The system assumes that all standard characters are used in the text as they would be in normal English orthography and punctuation, except that there is no distinction between opening and closing inverted commas. The character – might represent dash, hyphen, or minus, depending on context, and the character ' might represent apostrophe, or opening or closing single quotation mark.

All special coding symbols have the same format, one or two digits prefixed by *?. This allows 99 special symbols in all. Certain of these special symbols are fixed in meaning: those appearing in the lexicon, or those specifically tested within the tag assignment program. So the symbol *?2 should always be used to represent an acute accent, because it occurs in the lexicon in such entries as *applique*?2 and *cafe*?2; and the symbols *?7 and *?8 should be used for single and double prime marks respectively because WORDTAG uses them to recognize some non-word strings. But other special coding symbols have been left unallocated for the user to assign as required.

With the new input format there are no "marker" symbols, only "designator" symbols. So sentence divisions and abbreviations are no longer explicitly marked in the text. The system has been amended to allow for this. Also there is no coding to pick out typographical shifts, non-English expressions, headings or comments. If this information is required in the output, it would be best to use the existing LOB coding scheme.

8. CLAWS2: The pre-editing phase

In CLAWS2 there is no manual pre-editing phase between the initial verticalization stage and the tagging procedures proper, and the tasks of the manual pre-editor are divided between a new automatic pre-editing program and a revised version of WORDTAG, with any residual errors left for correction at the post-editing stage.

Essentially, the new pre-editing program concerns itself with the verticalization task alone; that is, segmenting the text into syntactic units for tagging. The program puts each word and punctuation symbol on a separate line, and splits contracted forms over two lines, as did the CLAWS1 pre-editor. In addition it recognizes sentence-boundaries, which are no longer explicitly marked in the text. But the pre-editor does not change any capital letters to lower case, nor does it tag punctuation. All tagging decisions are now left to the tagging procedures proper. The problems of capitalization and abbreviations, except with respect to segmenting the text, are handled by WORDTAG; the other amendments made to the text by the CLAWS1 pre-editor are omitted because they operate on information no longer encoded in the simplified input format.

The recognition of sentence-boundaries is not entirely straightforward because it depends on distinguishing abbreviatory from sentence-terminating full stops, another problematic task now that abbreviations are unmarked. The program recognizes potential sentence-boundaries between words that end with sentence-terminating punctuation and words that start with a capital letter, optionally preceded by an inverted comma or bracket. Question marks and exclamation marks, again optionally followed by inverted comma or bracket, are always regarded as sentence-terminating, and so are full stops if followed by inverted comma, bracket, or more than one space. The problem arises when a word ends with a full stop followed by a single space. Certain strings that end with a full stop – abbreviations or initials, for instance – can occur in mid-sentence, and might be followed by other strings starting with a capital, such as proper nouns or initials. The sentence-boundary recognition procedure must try to exclude these cases.

At present a full stop is not considered to be sentence-terminating in the following cases:

(a)   After a single capital letter (assumed to be an initial).

(b)   After an abbreviated title (*e.g. Mr.*, *Mrs.*, *Dr.*) preceding a name. (These abbreviations are tagged NNSB in the lexicon.)

(c)   After an abbreviation for a qualification or award following a name (*e.g. M.A.*, *Ph.D.*, *M.B.E.*) when the next string is also such an abbreviation. (These abbreviations are tagged NNSA in the lexicon.)

In all other circumstances, a full stop is considered to be sentence-terminating punctuation and, if the following word starts with a capital letter, a sentence-boundary is assumed to occur after the full stop. Obviously this procedure is not foolproof. It will fail to recognize a sentence boundary after a single capital letter, and will wrongly insert sentence-boundaries when abbreviations are followed by proper nouns in mid-sentence, if these abbreviations are not in the lexicon tagged NNSA or NNSB. But it is thought that such cases will be so rare that few errors will result.

As before, each string of characters preceded and followed by space is treated as a word, any punctuation stripped off, and a separate line generated for each word or punctuation mark. The following characters are always treated as punctuation at the start or end of character strings:

' " ( ) [ ] , ; : ? ! ...

But the character – is treated as a punctuation mark (i.e. dash) only when at the end of a character string, followed by a space; otherwise it is assumed to be a hyphen or a minus sign and is left as part of the word. Full stops are stripped off only if they occur at a recognized sentence-boundary point; all other full stops are treated as abbreviatory and left attached. A line of dashes is inserted in the verticalized file at the start of the text and at sentence-boundary points.

The new pre-editor handles contracted forms just like the CLAWS1 pre-editor, but it also deals with *'s* in the same way. It is left to the rest of the tagging procedures to decide whether the form is a genitive, reduced auxiliary, or enclitic *us*. Words ending in *s'* get the same treatment, with the character ' put on a separate line and flagged as detached. Because in the simplified input format there is now no coding distinction between apostrophe and single quotation mark, this also implies a tagging ambiguity later. (It may be necessary to try to distinguish quotation marks from apostrophes at verticalization – by pairing quotation marks, for instance – if it proves difficult to resolve this ambiguity later.)

9. CLAWS2: Tagging

CLAWS2 is designed to work with the new "Lancaster" wordtag set (see Appendix B), which makes more distinctions between different classes of words than the LOB tagset used by CLAWS1. (Because of this, tags quoted for various words in this chapter will not in general be identical to the tags quoted for the same words in other chapters.) In the Lancaster tagset, the tags for punctuation marks are generally identical to the punctuation marks themselves, except that both single and double inverted commas share the same tag. There is also now a separate tag for the genitive suffix, namely the symbol $. All punctuation is tagged unambiguously from the lexicon, except that when the new WORDTAG encounters ' on a separate line of text, flagged as detached from a preceding word ending in *s*, then WORDTAG overrides the unambiguous tagging in the lexicon and substitutes an ambiguity between genitive and quotation mark. The lexicon also contains an entry for *'s* with the tags VBZ VHZ $ PPIO2 (i.e. *is, has*, genitive, or *us*).

The problems of capitalization and abbreviation are also now handled at this stage. In CLAWS1, lower-case words, initial-capital words, and abbreviated forms all appeared in the lexicon, and, because of the unambiguous input format and manual pre-editing procedures, a string of characters in the verticalized text could be matched exactly to the entries in the lexicon and receive the relevant set of tags. In CLAWS2, all capital letters are left unchanged in the verticalized text, whether at the start of a sentence or in mid-sentence; initial capital letters might or might not indicate some sort of proper name; abbreviations might or might not be marked with full stops. So the principle in CLAWS2 is to have a single entry in the lexicon or suffixlist for each string of letters, rather than having a separate entry for each possible orthographic variation on that string. But the single entry has a complete list of all possible tags the string could receive, each marked in some way to indicate the conditions under which it is appropriate. All tags compatible with the input orthographic form are selected at the tag-assignment stage and it is left to CHAINPROBS to choose between the options.

Entries in the lexicon are now entirely in lower case, but may have both the normal "lower case" set of tags, and also an "upper case" set, members of which are marked with a colon, and are relevant only if a word starts with a capital. So the lexicon entry:

> may   VM NPM1:

indicates that the form *may* always gets a modal verb tag (VM), but the singular month noun tag (NPM1) is assigned only to the form *May*. For some words, one or the other of these sets might be empty:

> enquiry   NN1
> england   NP1:

Similarly, the suffixes in the suffixlist may also have two sorts of tag. The suffixlist entry:

> aul   NN1 VV0 NP1:

indicates that the form *haul* would get singular noun and verb tags (NN1 VV0), but the proper noun tag (NP1) would apply only to capitalized forms like *Saul*.

WORDTAG reduces all words in the verticalized text entirely to lower case before matching them with the lexicon or suffixlist, but remembers whether or not the words occurred at the start of a sentence or with an initial capital. These factors determine which tags are assigned, and with what probability weightings.

So, for instance, if a word that was originally in lower case is found in the lexicon, then the word is assigned only the lower-case tags in the lexicon entry; if the word has an initial capital at the start of a sentence, it will be given the upper-case tags as well but with reduced probability weightings; and a word with an initial capital in mid-sentence will get the upper-case tags first with the lower-case tags added with reduced probabilities. The word *may* would receive three different tag assignments in these three different contexts:

> *I may go* ..   VM
> *May I go* ..   VM NPM1@
> *In May* ..   NPM1 VM@

The "at" sign, @, is a low-probability marker – see p. 35.

If an initial-capital word has only lower-case tags in the lexicon then that set is used without any reduction in probability. For example, *enquiry* is always tagged NN1 even if capitalized. But if there are no lower-case tags in the lexicon for a lower case word, then WORDTAG behaves as though the word had not been found in the lexicon and tries out its other rules for tag assignment.

The same sort of procedure for selecting appropriate tags applies when words are tagged from the suffixlist; and the final default for initial-capital words is now singular proper noun, NP1, together with the lower case default tagset, NN1 VV0 JJ (singular common noun, verb, adjective). The relative probability of these tags will depend on whether the word occurred at the start or middle of a sentence.

Abbreviations are handled in much the same way. In the simplified input format abbreviations are no longer explicitly marked, and the revised system is not always certain whether a particular form is abbreviatory or not. Some abbreviations, *NATO* for example, will occur without any full stops. Some abbreviations written with final full stops will occur at the end of sentences, in which case it will not be clear to the automatic system whether the full stop is abbreviatory or not; if the new pre-editor has recognized a sentence boundary, the full stop will have been stripped off and treated as punctuation.

All entries now appear in the lexicon without any full stops, final or medial. So a form which might occur with or without medial full stops will now have only one entry; and a word and an abbreviated form which share the same letters (for example *in* and *in.*) will also share the same entry, with any tags relevant to abbreviatory forms marked with a preceding full-stop, thus:

> *in* II RL .NNU

(II = preposition; RL = locative adverb; .NNU = abbreviated unit of measurement.) WORDTAG removes all full stops from forms in the verticalized text before matching them against the lexicon, but remembers if the form occurred with medial or final full stops, in order to determine which tags are appropriate. Forms which occur without stops will be given all the tags which would be assigned by the upper/lower-case selection procedure described above, whether the tags are marked with a stop or not, but forms with stops will be given only those tags marked with a stop which are appropriate for their case. So *in* will receive all three tags, but *in.* will be assigned only the unit of measurement tag, NNU, unless it occurs at the end of a sentence and the full stop has been stripped off by the pre-editor. If a form with stops matches a lexicon entry which has no tags marked with a stop, then WORDTAG behaves as though the form had not been found in the lexicon, and assigns the default tags for abbreviated forms, namely NNU (unit of measurement) for lower-case forms and NP1 (singular proper noun) for forms with an initial capital.

Some entries in the lexicon also have tags which apply only to forms which are entirely in capitals; these tags are marked with a double colon. Again WORDTAG will throw away these tags when processing a lower-case word, but will give them the highest probability if processing a form all in capitals.

Once these changes are implemented it will be possible to run CLAWS without the time-consuming and error-prone tasks of manual coding and pre-editing. There may be a small loss of accuracy when dealing automatically with orthographic ambiguities, but any tagging errors caused by the new procedures can be picked up in the later post-editing phase. Possibly other changes might be made in the future to improve the accuracy of the new system even further: the system might treat as a lower-case word any word with an initial capital that occurs in a cluster of capitalized words; or it could look to see whether a capitalized word at the start of a sentence occurred elsewhere in the text with a capital; or, as suggested above, it could disambiguate a final *s'* by pairing quotation marks. These approaches all involve processing the text in "chunks" rather than single word units. But even without these more sophisticated techniques to improve accuracy, we feel that CLAWS2 will still be a great improvement for an unfamiliar user who wishes to tag new texts.

CHAPTER 9

Syntax versus orthography: Problems in the automatic parsing of idioms

Susan Blackwell

1. Introduction – tagging the LOB Corpus

Because of the general similarities between the LOB and Brown Corpora, initial approaches to the problem of tagging the LOB Corpus drew heavily on the tagging method employed by the Brown team. The CLAWS1 programs WORDTAG and CHAINPROBS reflected the two parts of the Brown program TAGGIT, the first of which assigned one or more possible tags to each word by lexicon look-up or other rules while the second sought to disambiguate those words which had been given multiple tags (Greene and Rubin 1971).

In attempting to improve on the Brown team's 77% success rate, those working on the LOB Corpus retained the general Brown principles of tag *assignment*, but sought to develop a more efficient method of tag *disambiguation*, which in TAGGIT had depended upon a battery of some 3300 context-frame rules. After observing that some 80% of TAGGIT rule-applications were applications of one of the minority of context-frame rules which mentioned only a single neighbouring tag (cf. p. 44 above), the UCREL team jettisoned the Brown context-frame rules and instead designed CHAINPROBS to disambiguate tags by a statistical method based on a probability matrix derived solely from the co-occurrence of tag *pairs*.

2. Problems arising from CHAINPROBS

The strategy of using tagpair statistics had the general effect of making CHAINPROBS more streamlined and efficient than TAGGIT had been. It was now possible to calculate the likeliest tags in the case of multiple ambiguities, since the program assigned a probability to every possible pathway through the sentence. The probability matrix required less storage capacity than the cumbersome context-frame rules.

Several kinds of error occurred in the output from this first version of CHAINPROBS. Some of these were due to incorrect entries in the lexicon or to imbalanced weighting of the probability matrix, and were amended accordingly.

However, a more serious problem remained: the program's reliance on more limited contexts rendered it susceptible to certain weaknesses. In particular, it was unable to deal with situations where more information could be derived from a more distant neighbour than from the immediately adjacent word. In disambiguating an *-ed* verb form, for instance, which might be either a past tense or a past participle, it would be useful to be able to ignore a preceding adverb and look at the word before the adverb. In this respect the initial version of CHAINPROBS offered no improvement on TAGGIT; but this problem was partially overcome by the use of "tag-triples", as described in Chapter 4, pp. 54–5.

3. The purpose of IDIOMTAG

The reliance on tagpairs has proved to be too restrictive in certain syntactic configurations, and the modifications to CHAINPROBS which this necessitated have been described in Chapter 4 and summarized above. However, the same narrowing of syntactic context has given rise to a more complex problem in the CLAWS1 tagging suite.

It can be argued that the orthography of the original text does not accurately reflect the syntactic units of the sentence in question. This position has been implicit in the work of the UCREL team from the outset, as can be seen in the early decision to divide words like *can't* and *she'd* into two distinct units and to place them on separate lines in the verticalized text. This obviously entailed either restoring enclitics to their full, unreduced version, or else adding somewhat contrived entries to the lexicon, which would not otherwise contain items such as *wo* and *n't*. The CLAWS1 system employs a combination of both these strategies, splitting enclitics over two lines of verticalized text and restoring *wo* to *will*, *sha* to *shall* and *ca* to *can*, while leaving *n't* and *'d* in their reduced form.

The converse also applies: sometimes a sequence of words can act as a single lexical item. The device adopted to deal with this problem was what the UCREL team have termed the "ditto-tag", as described in the next section. More generally, it can be said that certain combinations of words assume a "gestalt" identity: their grammatical function differs from the syntactic sum of their parts. It was to accommodate this phenomenon that a new program called IDIOMTAG was introduced to run over the output from WORDTAG before feeding it into CHAINPROBS. IDIOMTAG, as its name suggests, searches the text for specific sequences of words, or words and tags (but not tags alone), whose syntactic role in combination differs from the syntactic role played by the same words in other contexts. (A similar strategy was used in tagging the London–Lund Corpus of Spoken English: see Eeg-Olofsson and Svartvik 1984.)

IDIOMTAG makes a note of the original tags of such sequences and then replaces them. This chapter uses the word "idiom" in the specialized sense outlined above, i.e. to denote a grammatical idiom as defined for the purposes of the program IDIOMTAG, and not an idiom in the linguistic and semantic sense.

In some cases the correct (i.e. "idiomatic") tag is among the choices offered by WORDTAG, and the role of IDIOMTAG is merely to facilitate the process of disambiguation and to forestall possible errors by CHAINPROBS. For example, WORDTAG might output the following ambiguously tagged string:

at	IN
first	OD RB
sight	NN VB

IDIOMTAG will digest the information that in this context the word *first* is preceded by the word *at* and succeeded by a possible noun, and will resolve the ambiguity:

at	IN
first	OD
sight	NN

– thereby reducing the burden of work which would otherwise have fallen on CHAINPROBS.

In other cases, IDIOMTAG inserts tags which were never considered by WORDTAG, because they apply exclusively in the context of one or more idioms. Thus, the phrase *to and fro* will now be tagged:

to	RB
and	CC
fro	RB

– where WORDTAG had previously tagged it:

to	TO IN
and	CC
fro	RB

The word *to* has now been tagged as an adverb, a role for *to* which is peculiar to this particular idiom. It would make no sense to include the adverb tag (RB) in the lexicon entry for *to*, since in almost every other instance this option would prove disastrously misleading to the tagging system.

4. Ditto-tags

In the majority of cases, the tags assigned by IDIOMTAG are "ditto-tags", so-called because they are denoted by dittos or double inverted commas on all but the first tag of the phrase. This indicates that the whole phrase is considered to constitute a single syntactic unit, and is to be treated as such in any further processing. For example:

so	QL CS PN RB
as	CS QL IN
to	TO IN

becomes

so	TO
as	TO''
to	TO''

(the three words are classed as equivalent to a single infinitival *to*), and:

| according | VBG NN CS JJ |
| to | TO IN |

becomes:

| according | IN |
| to | IN'' |

(the two words are classed as equivalent to a single preposition).

5.   The flexible format of the idiomlist

The position that IDIOMTAG occupies within the tagging suite – specifically, the fact that it runs after WORDTAG – means that tags as well as words are available to it. The format of the idiomlist used by the program exploits this potential to the full, allowing almost any combination of words and tags (or words alone) to be specified. Each entry in the idiomlist comprises a line made up of two or more "idiom items" (see the Appendix to this chapter on p. 119 for examples). The format of each idiom item is as follows:

> word   NEW TAG(s)   (DISPLACED TAG)

Idiom items within the same idiom are separated by commas.

An example of a typical entry in the idiomlist is:

> *none* RB (PN), *the* RB'' (AT), *less* RB'' (AP)

The tags in brackets are the "displaced tags" which are overwritten by IDIOMTAG; the unbracketed tags are "new tags" which replace these.

Several variations on this format are permitted. The displaced tag may be omitted entirely, and, if it is, the new tag may also be omitted, as in the following examples:

> *a, little* AP RB JJ@

(both displaced tag and new tag omitted from the first idiom item, and displaced tag omitted from the second);

for IN, *long* RB JJ%

(displaced tag omitted from both idiom items).

The function of the displaced tag is to provide information to the user at a later stage. Since the main purpose of IDIOMTAG is to replace incorrect tags with correct ones, the existing tag will be overwritten. However, the displaced tag, as specified in the idiomlist, reappears in the displaced tag column to the left of the tagging decision column. It is these displaced tags, along with the tagging decision number 99, which enable the user to see immediately from the output from CLAWS1 that IDIOMTAG has made some changes to the tags. If no displaced tag is specified in the idiomlist, the displaced tag column is left blank. In fact, the displaced tag is specified only when the replacement tag is part of a ditto-sequence. This is because ditto-tags are likely to be completely different from any of the original tags selected for the words by WORDTAG, whereas with other "idioms" the new correct tag (as chosen by IDIOMTAG) is probably one of the original tags. This is not a hard-and-fast rule, however, and leaves scope for improvement (see the further discussion on p. 52).

Idiomlist format permits two kinds of "wildcards", both distinguished by the use of square brackets. If the brackets are empty, then any word and any tag whatsoever will match. For example, the idiomlist entry:

either DTX, [ ], *or*

means that *either*, which will have been assigned the two tags DTX and RB by WORDTAG, will now be tagged unambiguously as DTX if the next word but one is *or*, regardless of the word between them.

A more restricted use of the wildcard can be seen in the "wildtag". In this case, the square brackets are occupied by a tag, indicating that any word currently having that tag assigned to it (possibly among other tags) will match the idiom. Thus:

no RB, [RBR]

means that *no* followed by any comparative adverb (*no farther, no better*) will always be tagged RB, while in any other position the tags ATI (article) and UH (interjection) would also have to be considered as possibilities, with ATI being preferred. Similarly:

no CS (ATI), *matter* CS'' (NN), [WRB]

means that *no matter* will be tagged as a single subordinating conjunction whenever the following word is tagged WRB. Thus the properties of *no matter why, no matter how, no matter when*, and *no matter where* can all be captured in a single idiomlist entry.

6.   Problems with IDIOMTAG

It is clear that this approach has its advantages. As Marshall points out (p. 52), IDIOMTAG simplifies the task of CHAINPROBS by relieving it of the task of dealing with 'idiosyncratic constructs'. However, there are also serious disadvantages. One failing of the present idiomlist is its oversimplification of the structure of idioms. It does not readily provide for situations where an idiom sequence is interrupted, for example by an adverb. The question then has to be posed: How do we tag a sequence like *so as not to*? The CLAWS1 solution was:

so	CS
as	CS
not	XNOT
to	TO

– which failed to capture the similarity in structure with:

so	TO
as	TO''
to	TO''

The solution now advocated by the UCREL team is the introduction of a new tag, HH, which marks a pre-infinitive, i.e. precedes an infinitival *to*. This would yield tag-sequences like the following:

so	HH		so	HH
as	HH''		as	HH''
to	TO		not	XNOT
			to	TO

Another change which will shortly be implemented is the replacement of the familiar ditto-marks with a pair of numbers which indicate the relationship of the tag to the rest of the sequence. Thus IN21 is the first of two tags which combine to function as a preposition (IN), and IN22 is the second of two. Similarly, 31 indicates "first of three", 32 means "second of three", 44 means "last of four", etc. The examples above now become:

so	HH21		so	HH21
as	HH22		as	HH22
to	TO		not	XNOT
			to	TO

and

none	RB
the	RB''
less	RB''

becomes

none	RB31
the	RB32
less	RB33

This relatively simple change ensures that the first tag in a ditto-sequence is not confused with the same tag standing alone, and the second is not confused with the third or fourth. One practical effect of this modification will be to make ditto-tags easier to process at later stages such as parsing.

It is certain that IDIOMTAG has contributed greatly to the enhanced success rate of the LOB tagging suite. Yet the methods used provoke a serious theoretical question. The LOB tagging system is supposed to be uncontroversial, in order to maximize the usefulness of the tagged Corpus. However, it is more than likely that some researchers will find the "syntax versus orthography" arguments controversial in the extreme. On what syntactic grounds can it be asserted, for example, that *in front of* should be tagged:

in	IN
front	IN''
of	IN''

and not:

in	IN
front	NN
of	IN

– or that the *dining* in *dining room* should be tagged as a noun and not as an adjective or present participle? It must be remembered that the decisions made by IDIOMTAG will affect later stages, particularly the parser: tagging *in front of* with an IN ditto-tag will remove a whole prepositional phrase at parsing level. There is good reason, then, to ensure that consistency is maintained in the choice of idioms.

The imposition of such tagging decisions renders their inventors vulnerable to at least two accusations: first, that their list of idioms is arbitrary; and secondly, that they are allowing semantic constraints to influence their tagging criteria, despite claims by the UCREL team that its work is not concerned with semantics at this stage.

A practical facet of the same question arises from the program's dogged determination to tag all sequences in the idiomlist as idioms, no matter where they occur in the input text. On the somewhat rare occasions when a correct rendering of the sequence would tag the words "literally" rather than "idiomatically", the program is doomed to failure from the outset. Consider:

I	PP1A	I	PP1A
can	MD	can	MD
paint	VB	paint	VB
as	CC	as	QL
well	CC''	well	RB
as	CC''	as	CS
draw	VB	Mary	NP
.	.	.	.

IDIOMTAG in its present form is unable to cope with the second of these sentences, and tags *as well as Mary* with a CC ditto-tag. If we remove *as well as* from the idiomlist, the program will now tag the latter sentence correctly, but will leave the former wrongly tagged. Either option would be an unacceptable compromise, leaving work for the manual post-editor.

What is needed here is an algorithm for dealing with sequences which are genuinely ambiguous between idiom and non-idiom, such as *as well as, on to, up to, due to,* etc. IDIOMTAG will have to present its own interpretation of the string without overwriting the one it inherited from WORDTAG. The two choices will then be passed on to CHAINPROBS for disambiguation: a non-trivial problem in computational terms, since a means will have to be devised for assigning relative statistical probabilities to "chains" of differing lengths, for example:

I	PP1A	PP1A
can	MD	MD
paint	VB	VB
as	⎫	⎧ QL
well	⎬ CC	⎨ RB
as	⎭	⎩ CS
draw	VB	VB
.	.	.

(A ditto-tag is treated as a single tag for the purposes of calculating probabilities.)

In practice the task would be much more complex, since some of the words which are possible candidates for ditto-tagging are also ambiguous in their own right: *well* in the above example, if not tagged CC", could be RB (adverb), JJ (adjective), NN (noun) or UH (interjection).

There is further room for improvement in the format of the idiomlist, and the displaced tag would seem to be a suitable candidate for treatment. The existing program does not perform any checks on the tag which it is overwriting, and merely "assumes" that it matches the displaced tag as specified in the idiomlist. Some sequences are true "idioms" only when one or more of the words in the sequence appears in conjunction with a particular tag: this information could be beneficially utilized to locate the target phrases and to avoid doing any damage to the others.

The necessary information could be encoded in the idiomlist quite straightforwardly, by the use of (say) angle brackets instead of round brackets around the displaced tag to indicate that the program needed to check that the input text matched the idiom under consideration in tag as well as word. This procedure is already carried out for "wild tags" in square brackets, but in these cases only the *tag* is checked. What we are advocating here is a formalism which will permit tests on both the word *and* the tags which have been assigned to it.

However, for some phrases it is not sufficient to ascertain whether the desired tag is one of those possible for the word in question (which is all that the "wild tag" permits at present): it is necessary to know whether the desired tag is the *most likely* one. Again, as in the example discussed above, there is a need for intercommunication between IDIOMTAG and CHAINPROBS. Probably the only way to implement such a feature would be to run a second IDIOMTAG-like program *after* CHAINPROBS has completed its work. Such a program – termed the PREPARSER because of its position at the end of the tagging suite and prior to parsing – has been run successfully over the output from CLAWS1, resulting in considerable improvements.

A typical entry in the "preparse idiomlist" is:

in CS (IN), *that* CS'' <CS>

This causes the program to check the tagging of *that* before deciding whether or not the phrase constitutes an idiom: if *that* is tagged CS the resulting phrase is tagged CS CS'', but if tagged as anything else (DT, WP or QL, although in practice only DT is likely to follow *in*) the phrase is left alone, yielding the following correct results:

I	PP1A	the	ATI
told	VBD	situation	NN
him	PP3O	is	BEZ
that	CS	difficult	JJ
in	IN	in	CS
that	DT	that	CS''
case	NN	our	PP$
I	PP1A	time	NN
would	MD	is	BEZ
accept	VB	short	JJ

7. Conclusion

CLAWS2, then, might do well to incorporate a three-pass idiom processor: a new version of IDIOMTAG which makes a note of the phrases which it regards as idioms; a modified CHAINPROBS which, in addition to its previous tasks, uses probabilistic methods to decide whether the changes suggested by IDIOMTAG are reasonable, given their context; and finally a new module, the PREPARSER, which uses the tags selected by CHAINPROBS to locate further "idioms". Naturally the UCREL team will have to weigh up the advantages of enhanced tagging accuracy against the delay and inconvenience caused by the addition of extra code to the existing suite of programs.

One must not be unduly negative. Clearly, the 96–97% success rate of the LOB tagging suite speaks for itself; and to a considerable extent the end of accurate tagging must be permitted to justify the means of the occasional *ad hoc* rule. In any case much has been learnt from the problems and errors which arose from IDIOMTAG, and no doubt the next generation of IDIOMTAG, as part of CLAWS2, will incorporate many of the suggestions outlined in this chapter; although some tasks will provide work for the UCREL team for many months ahead.

Appendix – Examples of current idiomlist entries

[ATI], *next* AP, *but* IN, *one* CD1
a, little AP RB JJ@
according IN (VBG), *to* IN'' (IN)
all RB (RB), *right* RB'' (RB)
as QL, [JJ], *as* IN CS@
as CC (QL), *well* CC'' (RB), *as* CC'' (IN)
as QL, *well* RB, [VBN]
as RB (QL), *well* RB'' (RB)
at IN, *first* OD, [NN]
at IN, *times* NNS
because IN (CS), *of* IN'' (IN)
dining NN, *room* NN
either DTX, [ ], *or*
en IN, *masse* NN
ever RB (RB), *so* RB'' (QL)
for IN, *long* RB JJ%
human JJ, *being* NN
in IN (IN), *front* IN'' (NN), *of* IN'' (IN)
ipso RB (&FW), *facto* RB'' (&FW)
no RB, [RBR]
no CS (ATI), *matter* CS'' (NN), [WRB]
none RB (PN), *the* RB'' (AT), *less* RB'' (AP)
on IN (IN), *top* IN'' (NN), *of* IN'' (IN)
so TO (CS), *as* TO'' (CS), *to* TO'' (TO)
to RB, *and* CC, *fro* RB
under NPT (IN), *Secretary* NPT'' (NPT)
years NNS, *past* RI NN% IN% JJ%

CHAPTER 10

Dealing with ill-formed English text[†]

Eric Atwell and Stephen Elliott

1. What is ill-formed English?

Practical applications of natural-language computing generally involve analysing text which may contain imperfections such as typing errors. Many currently available word processing packages include a *spell* command or routine to deal with these errors, but this is generally resticted to string pattern matching rather than full linguistic analysis; as Berman (1982) notes, "... their usefulness must not be exaggerated. Most of the spelling systems are 'dumb spellers'. They simply match up every word in the document against words in the computerized dictionary and any word not recognized will be highlighted on the screen in some way."

Recently, more interest has been shown in the problem of dealing with ungrammatical (or semi-grammatical) English. A dictionary-matching system cannot detect errors in grammatically ill-formed sentences where each individual word is valid, as in

> *"You never lose the ability to paint once you have absorbed the first principles in art —
> practise* [sic] *is not as essential in painting as it is for instrument playing,"* she says.
> (C15 124–6)

or

> *'If you want to be a musician, you must practice* [sic] *so many hours a day'.*
> (D09 78–80)

[†] This chapter describes how the "constituent-likelihood" method of grammatical analysis, and specifically modified versions of CLAWS, can be used to detect errors in grammatically ill-formed English text. This approach was first proposed by Atwell (1983), and his research was subsequently supported by a research grant to Lancaster University by the International Computers Limited (ICL) University Grants Committee. In November 1984 Elliott took over the research post when Atwell moved from Lancaster to a Lectureship in the Artificial Intelligence Group of the Department of Computer Studies, Leeds University; Sections 1–12 deal with Atwell's work, and Section 13 describes Elliott's research progress up to the time of writing.

Without some "error-recovery strategy", a natural-language analysis system will simply fail when faced with such input. In his survey of the commercial applications of NL computing, Johnson (1985) notes that the problem of ill-formed input " ... is a serious one. If telegraphic style and other elliptical utterances are included, studies have shown that as much as 25% of queries to question-answering systems must be classed as ill-formed."

2.   Tagging ill-formed English text

One of the great advantages of the Constituent-Likelihood Automatic Word-tagging System (CLAWS) and the constituent-likelihood approach to grammatical analysis of text is that CLAWS will produce *some* analysis of any sentence, no matter how unusual the syntax; so clearly we can treat ill-formed input as a straightforward generalization of unrestricted natural language. However, ideally we would like to do more than simply produce a putative grammatical analysis of the text: in addition, constituent-likelihood analysis can also be used to *detect* and *flag* errors in the text. In fact, constituent-likelihood grammar, unlike other approaches to grammatical analysis, does not assume a clear distinction between grammatical and ill-formed sentences, merely gradations of "normality"; so first we must define exactly what counts as "unacceptable" to the system, in terms of some *threshold* level of normality. For other grammatical analysis systems, the definition of ill-formedness is in a sense built into the system: any sentences the system cannot analyse normally constitute ill-formed input. As Johnson (1985) points out, "they may not all strike a human user as defective, but an NLP system will have to be given a very restrictive sense of what is syntactically correct; ... any system, however comprehensive, will have limits to its capacity and therefore be likely to face sentences that it cannot analyse. From the system's point of view, of course, this situation is no different from facing real ill-formed input."

3.   Adapting CLAWS to detect errors in text

The systems for detecting grammatical errors mentioned above all attempt a full syntactic analysis of input text, but we have found that many errors can be detected simply by an adapted version of the CLAWS word-tagging system. The general technique is to look for "unusual" tag-pairs in the input text – often (but unfortunately not always) these mark some kind of syntactic infelicity, which may be due to an error. Other systems for dealing with ill-formed input require the researcher/designer to define in advance what constitutes ill-formedness, by listing each error-form to be dealt with explicitly; this means that any capability to deal with ill-formed input greatly increases processing requirements, and also that the "error-recovery routines" can cope only with errors falling into predefined categories. The modifications to CLAWS outlined below involve only minor increases in processing; and the resulting system is much more general, in that even unforeseen error-types may be diagnosed, so long as they involve unlikely tag co-occurrences.

There are a number of different techniques for discovering "unusual" tag-pairs; below we discuss a series of refinements of the basic technique.

4.   Generating cohorts for each word

The first technique to be described assumes that, if a sentence contains an error, the error is due to one or more words being mistyped, e.g. *practise* mistyped as *practice* (or *vice versa*). Of course, if the typing error results in a non-English "word" (e.g. *pratcise*) then the error could probably be detected by the "dumb spellers" discussed by Berman (1982); however, this is often not the case.

Research into spelling errors in typing (e.g. Damerau 1964, Peterson 1980; Pain 1981; Pollock 1982) has shown that the error-form and the intended word usually differ by only one or two characters; furthermore, it is possible to formulate a set of rules relating error-forms to the words probably intended. For example, Yannakoudakis and Fawthrop (1983a, 1983b) use such a rule-system to suggest corrections when input words are not found in the dictionary, but it could also be used for valid English words which are syntactically out of place, in order to find a set of words with similar spellings which might turn out to be grammatically more appropriate. This is the first step in diagnosing grammatical errors in this first algorithm: for each word in the input text, a cohort of similar words is generated, using a rule-system such as that of Yannakoudakis and Fawthrop. For example, if the sentence *I am very hit.* were input, the following cohorts would be generated:

I	am	very	hit .
	an	vary	hot
	a	veery	hut
			hat

(We have borrowed the term "cohort" from Marslen-Wilson (1985) with a slight modification of meaning.) Next, each member of a cohort is assigned a relative likelihood rating, taking into account relevant factors including:

(a)   the degree of similarity to the word actually typed (the word itself gets a weighting of 1 for this factor, and other words get lower weightings);

(b)   the syntactic constituent-likelihood bond between the tag(s) of each cohort member and the tag(s) of the words before and after;

(c)   the frequency of usage in general English (common words like *very* get a high weighting factor, rare words like *veery* get a much lower weighting);

(d)   if a cohort member occurs in a grammatical idiom or preferred collocation with surrounding words, then its relative weighting is increased (e.g. in the context *fish and ...* , *chips* gets a higher collocation weighting than *chops*);

(e)   domain-dependent lexical preferences should ideally be taken into account: for example, in an electronics manual *current* should get a higher domain weighting than *currant*.

All these factors are multiplied (using appropriate weightings) to yield a relative likelihood rating for each member of the cohort. The cohort-member with the highest rating is (probably) the intended word; if the word actually typed is different, an error can be diagnosed, and furthermore a correction can be offered to the user.

Unfortunately, this technique is computationally expensive: a cohort must first be computed for each word in the input (rather than just for non-English words requiring candidate corrections), which involves several look-ups in a large dictionary; and then a complex likelihood function must be evaluated for each cohort member. Furthermore, a major research effort is required to set up the initial system, to establish appropriate statistical measures for each of the relevant factors (in particular, measurements of collocational preferences and domain-specific preferences of words would involve the analysis of vast amounts of text – see for example Sinclair *et al.* 1970). Another problem is that in practice we cannot always rely on the initial assumption, viz. that grammatical incongruity is due to replacement errors, as in:

> *The evidence suggest* [sic] *that the fish are aware of the moving footrope before it reaches them.* (E06 87–8)

or:

> *As far as the practises* [sic] *and techniques of selling are concerned there are no 'secrets', no hidden mysteries.* (E35 135–6)

rather than omission errors, as in:

> *It may* [sic] *that once that was secured she was willing, and even eager to see her go.* (G27 52–3)

or insertion errors, as in:

> *Orsini's high-crowned hat with its jaunty plume blotted out the light; his his* [sic] *hand was on the door.* (K04 161–2)

As can be seen in these examples, omission and insertion errors may still give rise to grammatical incongruities which this technique can detect, but the correction suggested may be misleading: for example, with the insertion error above, the system is liable to suggest that the second '*his*' is replaced by another word (*hip?*) rather than deleted.

5.   Adding error-tags to the lexicon

Fortunately, it is possible to cut run-time processing requirements significantly without drastically reducing the power of the model. The technique described above would be very slow mainly because a cohort has to be generated (using rules such as those of Yannakoudakis and Fawthrop (1983a)) for each word during text-checking. Now, each input word also has to be assigned a set of grammatical tags, and for most words this is done by dictionary look-up (in fact, it may be desirable to do this for all words – see section 10 below); so cohort-generation at run-time could be avoided if each dictionary entry also contained the cohort for each word: cohorts would have to be generated once only for each word when the dictionary is first set up. This has the disadvantage of making each dictionary entry (and hence the whole dictionary) much larger. However, to measure the syntactic constituent-likelihood bond (the most important of the five factors listed above) of each cohort member, the system does not need to know the words themselves, but only their tags; in the example above (*I am very hit.*), an error can be diagnosed if the system works out that the tags of input word *hit* (NN, VB, VBD, and VBN) are all much less likely in the given context than JJ, the tag of a similar word (*hot*). So, a simpler alternative to the full cohort model would require each dictionary entry to hold (i) the word itself, (ii) the word's "own-tags", and (iii) the tags of any similar words (where these are different from the word's own-tags), which we shall call the "error-tags". For example:

WORD	OWN-TAG(S)	ERROR-TAG(S)
form	NN	IN£ RI£
hit	NN VB VBD VBN	JJ£
prophecy	NN	VB£

Note that error-tags are marked with £ to distinguish them from "own-tags".

If error-tags are stored in the dictionary, then full cohorts of possible corrections need only be generated when an error is diagnozed, which should occur only rarely (no system can be expected to cope with highly garbled English input). There is some loss in accuracy over the full cohort model: other factors (degree of similarity to actual input word, frequency of usage, idiomatic and collocational preferences, and domain-specific preferences) depend on the specific words in the cohort, and so cannot be taken fully into account (except that error-tags have a lower weighting than own-tags, which crudely reflects the first factor). However, it must be remembered that a statistical lexical analysis of even a fairly large corpus (such as the million-word LOB Corpus) could yield only very rough approximations for these other factors, and furthermore they are only minor factors in any overall relative likelihood formula, so probably the error-detection rate of this technique is not greatly impaired.

An important practical advantage of the error-tag-based technique is that it has been possible to implement a prototype system by some straightforward modifications to the CLAWS1 word-tagging system described in earlier chapters. The steps in error-detection using the modified CLAWS1 system are basically the same as for word-tagging, with minor additions:

(a)   The PREEDIT program puts each word on a separate line, as in the original CLAWS1.

(b)   WORDTAG assigns a set of own-tags and error-tags to each word, using a lexicon which includes error-tags; words not found in the lexicon are not passed on to default routines, but instead can be marked as invalid (errors) at this stage. IDIOMTAG is not used in the prototype.

(c)   CHAINPROBS chooses the "best" tag for each word; if an error-tag (marked £) is chosen, this indicates a probable error.

(d)   MARKERRORS, a modified version of LOBFORMAT, "rehorizontalizes" the text, and instead of writing a tag beneath each word, writes the message "ERROR?" beneath words which have been "error-tagged" (and writes a blank space beneath all other words).

```
my    farther  was very  crawl ,  he   bald   at me if I   dud    anything
      ERROR?          ERROR?   ERROR?          ERROR?
wrong , and sometimes he would   hot    and    bit    me , until I was so
                                 ERROR?        ERROR?
   week   and miserable that I wanted to   due ,    finally , won day, I decided
ERROR?                                     ERROR?
to    got    my won back on him :*' I'll    mike   him pay ; he will n't get
      ERROR?                                ERROR?
away with this !**' I stole a meat   clever ,   and I    maid   several   dense
                                     ERROR?              ERROR?           ERROR?
in his    hid    with it ! it must have hurt a    lit    !    son    *' the
          ERROR?                                  ERROR?  ERROR?
gruesome    tame   of Eroc Attwell **' appeared in all the papers – perhaps my
            ERROR?
friends would   learnt   to spell my name correctly at last !
                ERROR?
```

Figure 7   Sample output of MARKERRORS

Sample output from a trial run (using an imaginary text devised by Atwell) is shown in Figure 7 (from Atwell 1983). Tests were done using a small prototype lexicon; a great deal of work is required to build a full lexicon, since error-tags must be generated for each word. Another problem with this error-tag-based system is that it is still computationally expensive: each word now has error-tags as well as own-tags, so CHAINPROBS has to compare many more alternative tag-combinations. In any case, the artificiality of the text and the small size of the lexicon mean that the success of the algorithm is not realistically tested. Because of these factors, it seemed desirable to try an even simpler model which could be tested on realistic data.

6.   Measuring absolute likelihoods of tagpairs

In the error-tag-based model, an error is diagnosed if an error-tag is chosen as likelier in the given context than any of the word's own-tags. Since error-tags have a built-in downgrading bias against them (analogous to the downgrading factor for rare tags marked "@" or "%" – see p. 35 above), this should only happen when a word's own-tags all have very low absolute likelihoods in the given context. Therefore, it might be possible to do away with error-tags altogether, and simply flag a putative error whenever all the tags of a word in a given context have low absolute likelihoods (i.e even the best – likeliest – tag chosen by CHAINPROBS seems unlikely). The great practical advantage of this technique is that there is no longer any need for a special lexicon: the CLAWS tagging system can be used to choose the best tag for each word, the only modification required being in the final LOBFORMAT program which reformats the output.

To test the diagnostic power of absolute tag-co-occurrence likelihoods, LOBFORMAT was modified so that absolute likelihoods are included in the "verticalized" (one word per line) version of the tagged output text. Some sample output is shown in Figure 8; this is the start of the same (imaginary) text used in Figure 7 (but, since the output is in verticalized format to allow room for absolute likelihood markers, only the first 30 words have been shown). The asterisks and plus signs show the variations in best tag absolute likelihoods, measured in two alternative ways. Each record containing word, tag, and likelihood information now takes up two lines.

	PP$	my				28		*	
15					+				
	RBR	farther				28		*	(PEAK?)
13				+					
	BEDZ	was				27		*	
14					+				
	AP	very				27		*	
13				+					
	NN	crawl				25	*		
12			+						
	,	,				23	*		
11			+						
	PP3A	he				28		*	
17					+				
	JJ	bald				31			* (PEAK)
14				+					
	IN	at				26	*		
12			+						
	PP1O	me				25	*		
13				+					
	CS	if				24	*		
11			+						
	PP1A	I				28	*		

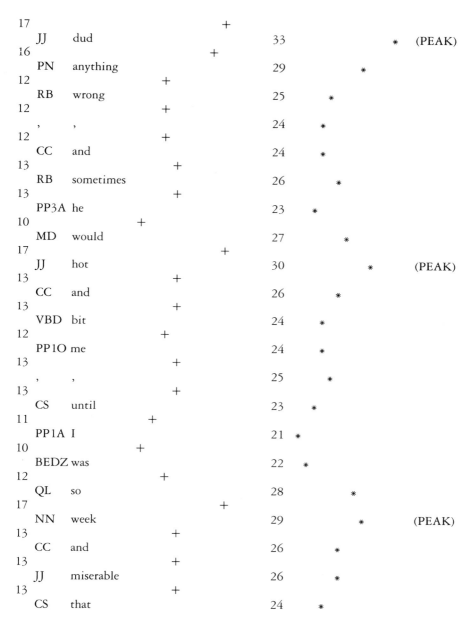

Figure 8 Modified output of CLAWS1, showing "unusualness" of each tagpair and tag-in-context. Peaks of unusualness can be used to diagnoze errors.

Every pair of lines contains:

(a) The tag chosen as likeliest in context by CHAINPROBS, e.g. RBR.

(b) The current word, e.g. *farther*.

(c)   An integer, e.g. 28, denoting the absolute likelihood of the current tag given the immediately preceding and following tags. (The "raw" absolute likelihoods are actually very small fractions, so they are scaled up to a more "palatable" number by taking the logarithm of the likelihood, converting this from negative to positive, and then rounding to the nearest whole number. Because of this scaling, note that high integers correspond to low probabilities − i.e. the integer is better thought of as an "unusualness" measure.)

(d)   An asterisk to depict tag-in-context likelihoods (c) graphically: the higher the number, the further right the asterisk.

The second line in each record (i.e. the lines between the alternate lines just described) contains an alternative absolute likelihood measure, namely the absolute likelihood of the co-occurrence of the previous and next tags; e.g. between PP$ and RBR line 2 contains 15 (scaled as before) to give us an integer "unusualness" grading. This is also accompanied by a corresponding graphical indicator, a plus sign; as with the asterisks, the greater the unusualness, the further right the plus sign.

The two alternative likelihood measures were printed out to see if either had greater diagnostic power, but it turns out that they "peak" at around the same points. This is in fact not so surprising since the tag-in-context likelihood (denoted by an asterisk) is simply the product of immediately previous and following tagpair bond probabilities (denoted by plus signs); since both measures are scaled logarithmically, the tag-in-context integer (e.g. 28) approximates to the sum of the previous and following tagpair integers (e.g. 15 + 13). The graph shows peaks in the unusualness measure around the words *bald*, *dud*, *hot*, and *week* (and to a lesser extent around *my farther*) in the figure, so clearly peaks can be taken as diagnostic of errors, once the question of what constitutes a "peak" has been defined computationally. One way to define peaks is in terms of thresholds: for example, we could say that every tag-in-context figure above (say) 28 constitutes a peak which should cause an error diagnostic to be printed (in a horizontal text, as in Figure7). Unfortunately, a cut-off at this level would mean some minor peaks would not be flagged, e.g. the local maximum around *my farther*, and, later on (not included in Figure 8), lesser peaks around *due* and *won*, do not rise above 28; however, if the threshold is lowered there is a danger of blurring the error flag, as often a sequence of words around an error would all get flagged (e.g. the whole sequence *I dud anything* in Figure 8 rates above 27).

Once an optimal threshold or other computational definition of peaks has been chosen, it is a simple matter to amend the LOBFORMAT program of CLAWS1 to produce output in the format of Figure 7, without tags or unusualness ratings but with putative errors flagged. This system can be run without modification to CLAWS1, even using the CLAWS1 lexicon and.suffixlist (see Ch. 3). However, even with an optimal measure of peaks, the success rate is unlikely to be as high as with the error-tag-based algorithm. To see why this should be the case, we should consider why one error in Figure 8, *crawl* (the fifth word down) does not have a noticeably high unusualness rating, and so will not be flagged, despite the fact that in Figure 7 the error-tag method has correctly flagged this as an error. The reason is that, in the error-tag-based system, CHAINPROBS can calculate that the best sequence of tags (including error-tags) for the word sequence .. *was very crawl* . is [BEDZ QL JJ .];

and since JJ is an error-tag, an error is flagged. However, in the absolute-likelihood-based model, CHAINPROBS no longer has the option of choosing JJ as the tag for *crawl*, and is forced to choose the best of the own-tags, namely NN; this in turn causes a mistagging of *very* as AP, since [AP NN] is likelier that [QL NN]. Furthermore, [AP NN] turns out not to be an exceptionally unusual tag co-occurrence. The point of all this is that, without error-tags, the system may mistag words immediately before or after error-words, and this mistagging may well distort the absolute likelihoods used for error diagnosis.

Nevertheless, this method has the practical advantage that the existing CLAWS lexicon and suffixlist can be used unchanged, so the prototype system can be used on any text, not just text with a restricted test vocabulary; therefore it might still be worthwhile to consider refinements which could increase the error-detection success rate.

7. Using "error likelihoods" of tagpairs

One possible refinement concerns the tagpair probability matrix used by CHAINPROBS. Although we stated above that the numbers in Figure 8 denoted the probabilities used by CHAINPROBS, in fact the revised version of LOBFORMAT run after CHAINPROBS does not get these numbers directly from CHAINPROBS: as this is an independent program taking the output of CHAINPROBS as its input, and CHAINPROBS does not include tagpair probabilities in its output, each tag-pair probability is looked up a second time in the matrix. This second look-up uses the same matrix as CHAINPROBS, but in fact this need not be the case: CHAINPROBS needs a matrix of likelihoods of tagpair co-occurrence, whereas the error detection mechanism needs a measure of likelihood that *this* tagpair is indicative of error. Such a measure is assumed above to be simply the "inverse" of tagpair co-occurrence likelihood; but it might be appropriate to use a quite different function. One way to build an alternative matrix would be to use a large "error corpus", a collection of texts containing ill-formed English, representative of the kind of text the error detection system is aimed at. This corpus would have to be automatically tagged using the (unmodified) CLAWS tagging system, and all errors in the text (manually) marked; we could then extract statistics for each co-occurring tagpair (t_1, t_2):

$Fv(t_1, t_2)$: frequency of the tagpair in valid text; and
$Fe(t_1, t_2)$: frequency of the tagpair in error-diagnostic positions.

These statistics would form the basis of the different tagpair matrix to be used by the error detector running after CHAINPROBS: the error-diagnostic likelihood Le for (t_1, t_2) in the matrix will be some function of $Fe(t_1, t_2)$ and $Fv(t_1, t_2)$. For example, if

$$Le = \frac{Fe + k_1}{Fe + Fv + k_2}$$

where k_1 and k_2 are suitably chosen constants, then a high value of Le (near unity) indicates that the tagpair is very rare in valid text and/or often occurs around errors, while a low value of Le (near zero) indicates that the tagpair occurs frequently in valid text (in may also occur around errors, but relatively far less frequently). Note that this may not be the optimal function defining Le in terms of Fe and Fv, but it is the simplest one to try first; similar error-diagnostic likelihood functions have been used successfully in computer vision in object recognition (see Ballard and Brown 1982; Boyle *et al.* 1986).

Unfortunately, although this may improve success rate in theory, the required statistics can only be gathered from a very large corpus of "error-ful" texts, requiring a large research effort. Research is currently in progress to collect and analyse an error corpus (see below).

8.   Replacing the tagpair probability matrix

As mentioned above, both the absolute-likelihood and error-likelihood based methods (sections 6 and 7) can use the current CLAWS system for analysis, with the error detection carried out in a separate final program, a modified version of LOBFORMAT which performs a second lookup in the tagpair probability matrix (in the error-likelihood model, a different tagpair probability matrix). Once an optimal second table has been decided upon, combined with an optimal threshold or other mechanism for deciding when to print out the putative error warning, the matrix of probabilities (real numbers) can be replaced with a matrix of booleans (TRUE if the tagpair should be flagged as a probable error, FALSE otherwise). This saves a lot of space (a full probability matrix contains $133 \times 133 = 17\ 689$ decimal numbers), and increases speed (comparisons with the threshold or analogous tests are no longer necessary). However, most of the processing time is taken up by earlier programs, particularly CHAINPROBS; so, until general performance improvements in CLAWS are achieved, substitution of booleans for probabilities will only be a modest step in the right direction.

9.   Related research

"Enabling technologies" is a currently-favoured term for tools and techniques which facilitate implementation of a system. Sections 5–8 above describe a number of alternative approaches or models for error detection in ill-formed input. We have also been tackling a number of related research tasks, investigating "enabling technologies" required for a practical implementation of an error detection system; these are discussed in the following sections.

10.   Building a full lexicon

As mentioned at the start of this chapter, several spelling-check programs are
currently available for checking that words in a text are valid English words, i.e.
match against a large wordlist; in the above sections we have concentrated on
detecting grammatical inconsistencies, on the assumption that non-English strings
can be detected by some other mechanism. In a practical system, this would involve
the user in first checking for non-words using a dictionary look-up program, and then
in checking for ill-formed English grammar using a second, separate program. This
may well be a reasonable approach, particularly for poor typists who produce a lot of
"typos" or non-words; and in fact this is the approach used by the only commercially
available system we know of which incorporates both a spelling-checker and a basic
style-checker: the Writer's Workbench system produced by AT&T Bell Laboratories
contains a number of separate programs including these two facilities, and users are
free to choose an appropriate combination of tools with which to analyse their text (see
Cherry *et al.* 1983, Cherry and Macdonald 1983, or Atwell 1986 for more details of
the Writer's Workbench collection of programs).

It might be argued that, since both spelling-checker and grammar-checker require
every text-word to be looked up in a lexicon (the first to check validity, the second to
find the word's part-of-speech tags), it would be more efficient to combine the two
processes. However, in principle the spelling-checker needs a full list of all valid
word-forms, whereas the grammar-checker needs only some mechanism for assigning
tags to any input word. A combination of a comparatively small lexicon with a default
suffixlist and other routines may suffice, as in the prototypes discussed above which
use the 7200-word CLAWS1 lexicon. (In practice spelling-checkers may also use a
default affix-list: *Unbeginnable* doesn't sound nice, but it might well occur somewhere.
Such neologisms can be catered for by a list of productive affixes to supplement the
lexicon. However, the list of valid "stems' is very large, so the argument still applies.)
Nevertheless, the reliance on default tagging routines for some words can reduce the
accuracy of word-tag assignment. A few words will be assigned incorrect tags, and,
perhaps more importantly, quite a few words will be "over-tagged": where a suffixlist
entry assigns two or more tags to a suffix, this means that the corresponding word
must have at least one of the tags, but not necessarily all of them. For example, the
word *mislead* is not in the CLAWS1 lexicon, and gets tagged according to the suffix
-ead [NN VB], when in fact it should only get one tag, VB (verb). This means that
no error will be diagnosed in, e.g., *A mislead man cannot find his way*, because NN will
apparently be available as one of *mislead*'s tags, and NN is acceptable in the given
context. So, a single comprehensive lexicon may be better after all to increase error
detection. This could be most easily derived from a machine-readable version of a
printed dictionary; but not all dictionaries are suitable, since detailed grammatical
codings are required. Two machine-readable dictionaries with a suitable grammatical
coding system analogous to the LOB tagset are the *Longman Dictionary of Contemporary
English* (*LDOCE* – Procter 1978), and the *Oxford Advanced Learner's Dictionary of
Current English* (*OALD* – Hornby and Cowie 1974). Atwell has written a program

which extracts words and grammatical codes from the *LDOCE* dictionary and converts the codes into their equivalent LOB tags (see also Alshawi *et al.* 1985); Mitton (1986) describes analogous research to extract wordlists with grammatical codes from the *OALD*.

11.   Revisions to the tagset

All the above implementations use the original LOB tagset described in Appendix B; but there are a number of reasons why a different tagset might be more appropriate for error-detection.

(a)   The aims of analysis are different, so the same tagset is not necessarily optimal for both applications. Specifically, in tagging the LOB Corpus, we aimed to give as detailed an analysis as possible, regardless of how long it took to compute (within reason); whereas for error detection in something like real time, we want to do the minimum analysis required to detect errors, so a much smaller tagset may suffice.

(b)   Experience of tagging the Corpus has suggested refinements and alterations to the LOB tagset on linguistic grounds (see, for example, Atwell 1982).

(c)   Comparative studies of the LOB tagset with the coding systems used in *LDOCE* and *OALD* have suggested some changes to the tagset; for example, *LDOCE* distinguishes singular common nouns which cannot be pluralized and plural common nouns which have no singular, so the code-to-tag conversion program mentioned above keeps this distinction, using the two new tags NNSING and NNSPLU respectively.

One approach to choosing suitable amendments to the tagset is to rely on intuitions about which tags are "discriminatory" in error-detection, but in practice this is very difficult since changing one tag has repercussions throughout the tagpair matrix. Some minor changes have been investigated, but no significant increase in error detection has yet resulted. An alternative approach is to try to build an alternative tagset from scratch. The CLAWS system is based on the assumption that the way humans intuitively assign tags to words could be approximated by a first order Markovian statistical model (see ch. 5); so a tagset that is defined purely in terms of such a model should yield even better results. To test this idea, Atwell designed a suite of programs called RUNNEWTAGSET to group the words in a large subsection of the LOB Corpus into word-classes on a purely Markovian statistical basis, without recourse to any linguistic intuitions about word-classes.

For each text word (token), RUNNEWTAGSET recorded the word immediately before (the left-context), and the word immediately following (the right-context). (Because processing was extremely slow, in practice left-contexts and right-contexts had to be dealt with in separate program runs.) Words appearing more than once in the text (i.e. types with many tokens) had associated with them a list of left-contexts and a list of right-contexts. The words (and associated contexts) were sorted into frequency order, and then, starting with the commonest words, all possible pairings of one word with another word (w₁, w₂) were compared: if the context-lists of w_1 were significantly similar to the context-lists of w_2, the two were deemed to belong to the same word-class, and the two words (and their context-lists) were merged. A threshold was used to test for "significant similarity"; initially, only words with very similar context-lists were merged, but then the threshold was lowered in stages, allowing less and less similar words to be merged at each stage.

RUNNEWTAGSET was tested on a sample of just over 200 000 words, about a fifth of the LOB Corpus. Unfortunately, this turned out to be far too small a sample for conclusive results: in a sample of this size, only 175 words occur 100 times or more, the minimum suggested by Sinclair *et al.* (1970) for statistical lexical collocation studies. However, this program run took several weeks (elapsed-time, not cpu-time) on an ICL 2960 mainframe computer, so it was impractical to try a much larger text sample. Figure 9 gives some results from this test run, showing which words were merged into classes at successively lowered thresholds; for example, at the initial threshold level of 0.8, *will, should, could, must, may,* and *might* were merged into a single word-class on the basis of their immediate lexical contexts.[†]

Even if the mammoth computing requirements could be met, this approach to automatic generation of a tagset or word-classification system is unlikely to be wholly successful because it tries to assign every word to one and only one word-class, whereas intuitively many words (including some very frequent words, e.g. *to, her, so, as*) can have more than one possible tag. We are investigating alternative strategies which allow for this, allowing words to belong to more than one class, but these appear to require even more computation. Despite the daunting problems, the possibility of automatic word-class generation is worth investigating because of the tremendous "payoff" if the search proves successful: see the concluding section below.

12.   Error corpus

To test out the error detector, and to optimize detection rates, we need a sample of test texts containing errors – an error corpus. All errors in these texts should be marked, so test runs can be evaluated automatically; not all errors manifest themselves in "error-forms", but at least the positions of insertion or omission errors can be marked. Furthermore, the errors can be classified according to the kind of processing required for detection. (In the following errors from the UCREL error corpus, the assumed correction is added in brackets after the error.) Four categories of error may be distinguished.

A: non-word error-forms, where the error can be found by simple dictionary-look-up; for example:

Hardie did not clal {call} himself a radical at all.

[†] A similar experiment to discover word-classes has been carried out on a corpus of about five million words by R. L. Mercer and others at the IBM Thomas J. Watson Research Center, New York. It is referred to in Jelinek (1986: 10, 33–46).

THRESHOLD = 0.80			
in	< for	end	< full
is	< was	end	< sense

THRESHOLD = 0.80

in < for
is < was
it < he
in < on
in < by
in < at
had < has
they < we
it < there
will < would
but < when
but < if
will < should
will < could
will < must
will < may
will < might
make < take
but < while
end < use
in < during
end < point
end < question
sense < number

THRESHOLD = 0.75

and < with
and < where
did < does
life < God
them < life
in < after
book < church
end < book
end < way
world < country
end < members
word < case
word < film
world < word
world < church

THRESHOLD = 0.70

and < as
it < this
in < from
are < were
it < she
one < some
him < me
but < then
world < government
but < though
make < get
go < come
make < find
end < part
end < most
course < war
year < week
and < since
Britain < Africa

end < full
end < sense

THRESHOLD = 0.65

in < and
it < I
will < can
they < you
him < her
world < people
world < time
him < us
him < Britain
but < because
but < *¹
is < >'s
first < same
world < day
but < yet
in < under
world < children
man < policy
world < right
used < left
used < given
home < mind
made < taken
made < found
made < used
one < many
world < council
going < possible
seems < went
seems < came
work < death
work < home
world < work
his < my
the < his
it < what
their < our
world < place
know < think
last < next
world < house
in < until
now < perhaps
world < public
done < seen
made < done
first < British
end < state
end < view
world < face
world < times
go < help
now < indeed

THRESHOLD = 0.60

the < a
world < end
the < their
that < which
him < them

that < all
in < or
. < ?
but < now
the < its
world < man
first < new
the < any
world < year
first < other
first < last
in < like
first < good
that < such
that < about
not < also
first < own
too < however
make < see
not < still
in < without
first < old
in < through
the < every
him < himself
fact < few
here < again
first < whole
first < young
world < days
fact < true
it < Jones
more < less
world < need
men < things
going < nothing
first < present
more < better
the < each
the < your
much < far
first < best
first < local
first < second
make < give
London < later
first < modern
world < power
make < become
that < having
that < least
but < whether

THRESHOLD = 0.55

in < but
in < that
be < make
, < ;
, < *−
world < fact
world < men
in < over
him < well

in < even
. < !
world < little
in < before
him < London
world < long
so < just
so < here
him < so
, < much
the < these
two < three
go < say
go < know
him < another
being < both
him < being
made < put
go < look
world < means
world < small
only < almost
not < only
. < :
first < very
him < themselves
made < called
never < ever
not < never
world < thought
two < four
him < something
more < rather
world < office
world < free

Figure 9 Test results of RUNNEWTAGSET

B: error-forms involving valid English words in an invalid grammatical context, the kind of error the CLAWS-based approach could be expected to detect. (These may be due to spelling or typing or grammatical mistakes by the typist, but this is irrelevant here: the classification is according to the type of processing required by the detection program.) For example:

> *They [Thy] kingdom come, thy will be done.*

C: error-forms which are valid English words, but in an abnormal grammatical/semantic context, which a CLAWS-type system would not detect, but which could be caught by a sophisticated parser; for example, breaking "long-distance" number agreement rules as in:

> *It is, however, reported that the tariff on textiles and cars imported from the Common Market are [is] to be reduced by 10 per cent.*

D: lexically and syntactically valid error-forms which would require "intelligent" semantic analysis for detection; for example:

> *She did not imagine that he would pay her a visit except in Frank's interest, and when she hurried into the room where her mother was trying in vain to learn the reason of his visit, her first words were of her fiancee [fiance].*

or:

> *Air is an elastic medium through which sand [sound] is transmitted.*

Collection and detailed analysis of texts for this error corpus is still in progress at the time of writing; but one important early impression is that different sources show widely different distributions of error-classes. For example, a sample of fifty errors from each of three different sources shows the following distribution:

(a) published (and hence manually proofread) text:
     A: 26   B: 14   C: 4   D: 6

(b) essays by 11- and 12-year-old children:
     A: 18   B: 19   C: 8   D: 5

(c) English written by non-native English speakers:
     A: 2   B: 24   C: 6   D: 18

This seems to indicate that a CLAWS-based grammar-checker would be particularly useful to non-native English speakers!

13.   Current work using the "absolute likelihood" method

The method of detecting errors by means of "absolute likelihoods", outlined in Section 6 above, is the basis of the method we are currently using in research at

Lancaster. In this section, we describe the progress that has been made so far.

As mentioned in section 12, to test thoroughly the error-detection algorithms we need a large collection of erroneous text. Considerable efforts have been made at Lancaster to collect such an "error corpus" containing errors of Type B above. At present we have errors from four sources:

(a) **ICL:**   International Computers Limited, who provided the research grant for the project, also provided a collection of word-processed documents from their Knowledge Engineering Group.

(b) **Oxford:**   From the Oxford Text Archive, we obtained a copy of the Gill Corpus, compiled by Dr Gill of the University of Warwick to test an automatic brailling machine.

(c) **LOB:**   The *Manual of Information* for the LOB Corpus (Johansson *et al.* 1978) lists all the errors found in the original texts. (Some of these were corrected in the machine-readable Corpus, and others were not.)

(d) **ITEC:**   In the summer of 1985, some trainees from the Information Technology Education Centre at Lancaster came to UCREL to gain experience with computers. A small proportion of their time was spent typing business-style documents into the computer.

By using errors from a variety of sources, we ensure that our programs will not be tuned to the mistakes of one particular typist.

These four sources have been carefully scanned for typing errors which form other English words (errors of Types B, C, and D above), and sentences containing such errors have been transferred to the error corpus. We now have a corpus of approximately 500 such errors. The whole corpus contains *c.* 13 500 words. Thus it is possible to see the context of each error, and the fact that entire sentences are stored also enables us to check how well the error-detection programs succeed not only in flagging errors, but in leaving correct text unflagged.

Within the error corpus, the comment tag **[ERROR!**] is used to identify each error for the human reader, but such tags are ignored by the CLAWS programs. By using a concordance program, such as the OCP (Oxford Concordance Program), we can produce a KWIC concordance listing of all the **[ERROR!**] flags. All the errors will then be readily identifiable in an "error concordance" listing as follows:

> *biographers add*   **[ERROR!**] *historians have been slow*
> *natural way of lie* **[ERROR!**] *which had accepted marriage*
> *and in which their* **[ERROR!**] *was not wise providence*
>   etc..

All the errors are readily identifiable since they occur immediately to the left of the error flag.

Such a concordance listing has another use. If we look at different "widths" of context on either side of an error, then it is possible to assess how obvious the error is. If a human reader cannot detect an error without a wide context, we cannot expect the program to find it. In fact, we decided to remove from the error-corpus all those errors which we believed to be impossible to detect by a CLAWS-based system, on the grounds that the error-form was of the same word category as the correction. These errors (belonging to Type D above) were collected together in one file, called "HARD".

Once we have a program which "scores" tag-pairs, the task is to determine the optimal threshold for identifying errors (cf. section 6 above). The problem with defining this threshold is that it has to cause as many errors as possible to be flagged while as few other words (non-errors) as possible are flagged. Currently we find that the two most successful thresholds are:

(a)   a sequence of two scores of at least 28;

(b)   a sequence of two scores, one of at least 28 and one of at least 29.

Both sets of figures refer to the score for a tag in the context of the preceding and following tags.

Once we have defined a threshold, we need to know how successful it is. The problem here is similar to that encountered in information retrieval, where the requirement is the extraction of a set of "target" documents from a large population of such documents. We need to calculate both the proportion of "target items" (i.e. errors) correctly retrieved (i.e. flagged), and the proportion of retrievals or flags which correctly identify errors. To evaluate how successful an information retrieval system is, then, two figures are needed: *recall* and *precision*. Recall is calculated as:

$$\frac{\text{Number of items correctly retrieved}}{\text{Number of items that should have been retrieved}}$$

Precision is calculated as:

$$\frac{\text{Number of items correctly retrieved}}{\text{Number of items actually retrieved}}$$

With these two independent measures, we have a simple indication of how successful any given threshold is at locating errors.

Below are two tables of results, using the two thresholds mentioned earlier (28–28 and 28–29). The column headings refer to the various error-corpus sources described above.

The low figure for the file of "hard" errors is to be expected, since these errors cannot (except through chance factors) be retrieved by a CLAWS-based error detector.

Threshold at 28–28

	Oxford	ICL	ITEC	LOB	(HARD)
No. of errors	296	40	6	78	(82)
No. of flags	518	64	6	165	(118)
No. of errors flagged	187	30	3	40	(7)
Recall	63.2%	75%	50%	51.3%	(8.5%)
Precision	36.1%	46.9%	50%	24.2%	(5.9%)

Threshold at 28–29

	Oxford	ICL	ITEC	LOB	(HARD)
No. of errors	296	40	6	78	(82)
No. of flags	362	46	2	110	(88)
No. of errors flagged	139	29	1	29	(4)
Recall	47%	72.5%	17%	37.2%	(4.9%)
Precision	38.4%	63%	50%	26.4%	(4.5%)

These results illustrate the trade-off between recall and precision: by raising the threshold it is possible to improve the precision score, but only at the expense of the recall score. Present results are reasonably promising, but we need to consider various refinements of the system in order to improve rates of error-detection in the future.

14.　Future prospects

Several strands of ongoing research are mentioned above: the alternative models for error-detection are still to be fully evaluated and compared. One aspect of the CLAWS system not discussed previously is its applicability to languages other than English. CLAWS does not require a formal description of the grammar of English in terms of rewrite rules, but rather is data-driven: the probabilistic "grammar" is automatically extracted from samples of tagged text, which may be tagged by human linguists using informal semi-intuitive principles. In principle, an analogous probabilistic grammar for another language, e.g. Dutch, could be extracted from a sample of tagged Dutch text; thus it is much more straightforward to adapt CLAWS to another language than to adapt a rewrite-rule based analysis system, where a new rewrite-rule grammar for the new language would have to be devised. Of course, Dutch equivalents of the lexicon, suffixlist, and idiomlist would also be required, but these would also be needed by any other analysis system. It follows that a constituent-likelihood-based system for dealing with ill-formed input could readily be converted to deal with a new language, whereas other systems, such as those discussed by Heidorn *et al.* (1983), Cherry *et al.* (1983), Cherry and Macdonald (1983), Charniak (1983), and Johnson (1985), are much more closely tied to English.

Even more exciting possibilities arise if we achieve success in the search for an automatic method for deriving a word classification system from raw text. If a general technique could be found, users could readily tailor the system to their own idiosyncratic grammatical style, simply by feeding in sample text to the "word-class extractor". If the technique turned out to work for other languages as well as English, then the error-detection system could be converted to other languages just as straightforwardly. However, Chomsky (1957) rejected the possibility of a discovery procedure for grammars: "I think that it is very questionable that this goal is attainable in any interesting way"; so we should not set our hopes too high.

CHAPTER 11

Automatic intonation assignment

Gerry Knowles and Lita Lawrence

1. Introduction

The project reported in this chapter[†] applies grammatical tagging to the problem of intonation assignment, and in this way brings together two formerly independent areas of research undertaken at Lancaster. We are working at the "linguistic" end of text-to-speech processing, and our eventual aim is to take a conventional written text as input, and convert it automatically into a detailed phonetic transcription, including intonation marking[‡]. This transcription is intended to be used as input to a speech synthesizer to produce high quality speech with natural-sounding rhythm and intonation.

Considerable importance is attached to the use of natural input, and the production of realistic output. Our input is therefore in principle any written English text which conforms to the normal orthographic conventions. It is tempting to simplify matters by using non-standard texts, e.g. instead of the normal:

> *An antiques dealer at no.128 reported seeing Dr Yates at about 4:15.*

it would be much easier to start with

> *An antiques-dealer at number a hundred and twenty-eight reported seeing Doctor Yates at about four-fifteen.*

For a project concentrating on the "sound-generating" end of text-to-speech work, using a simplified text (perhaps with regularized spellings) would be a reasonable short-cut; but it would defeat our present purpose. In any case the kind of pre-processing required for intonation assignment – the expansion of contractions and

---

[†] The project was supported in 1984–5 by the University of Lancaster Humanities Research Fund and by IBM (UK) Ltd, and subsequently by IBM (UK) Ltd. IBM have not only given financial support, but have actively participated in the project.

[‡] A spelling interpreter with letter-to-phoneme rules is currently being developed at Lancaster, but is not strictly part of the present project.

digits, and the recognition of compound nouns and lists, etc. – is required for text processing in general.

Our intended output is a transcription similar in kind to that which a phonetician might produce if asked to transcribe a text, marking intonation. However, whereas phoneticians have the skill of identifying patterns in existing spoken texts, they do not – *qua* phoneticians – have the creative skill of predicting how a written text might be effectively spoken aloud. It is not enough to imagine what speech might be like: we have all heard synthetic speech which tries to represent human speech but is apparently modelled on the performance of monsters from science fiction and horror movies! We therefore need good authentic models on which to base our intonation rules.

The finished transcription will contain all the textual information required for speech synthesis, including vowel and consonant phonemes, and the main variations in fundamental frequency (henceforth F_0). An actual speech synthesizer may need more detailed information, e.g. allophones, intensity, duration, and local variations in F_0. But these are predictable according to the general rules of English, and do not need to be specified for a particular text. They will consequently not be included in our transcription.

In accordance with our objectives, work on the project is divided into two parts:

(a) the collection of a suitable corpus of contemporary spoken English to provide models;

(b) the development of a set of rules for intonation assignment.

2.   The need for a corpus

There are two main approaches to the study of intonation: introspection, and the analysis of natural data.

The most common approach in recent years has been introspection. Much of what appears in books on intonation is based on the intuitive feelings of linguists who are also native speakers of English. But there is no guarantee whatever that linguists' intuitive feelings about intonation will mirror accurately what actually goes on in speech.

Linguists taking this approach study sentences which they have invented themselves, or which they have seen discussed in the literature. These inevitably reflect the traditional concerns of linguists, which may or may not be relevant to intonation. Invented sentences tend to be highly predictable, and constructed out of familiar ready-made chunks, e.g. *It was Max who persuaded Mary that Marcel Proust was eager to please.* The pooling of intuitive feelings about the possible intonation of such unreal sentences leads to the construction of theories about the intonation of an invented language closely related to English, but which is not English itself.

If sentences are invented to illustrate intonation patterns, they can be predicted to illustrate interesting phenomena, such as the rules concerning compound nouns, "given" and "new" information, or the conveying of illocutionary force. But interesting things occur relatively rarely in running texts. Real texts are substantially made up of phenomena which do not excite interest, such as the effect on intonation of the grammatical class of individual words. Intonation handbooks deal with interesting phenomena: but virtually nothing has been written on the intonation of ordinary unremarkable sentences.

Secondly, a study based on invented data leads to a common-sense description consistent with what one might intuitively expect to find in the intonation system. The study of real texts reveals patterns which one is unlikely to discover by introspection, and indeed some which run counter to common sense[†].

Introspection, however, does have an important role in work on intonation. Its great advantage is that one can isolate individual rules and patterns, and invent examples to illustrate them. In real texts, of course, rules and patterns do not generally occur in isolation, but interact in highly complex ways. It is not possible, just by looking at a text, to separate out these different patterns. The first step in analysis has to be an intuitive guess at what is going on. And having identified a rule, it is much easier to explain it by inventing a new example than by referring to the original data.

The objection to the introspective method is not to the introspection itself, but to the unacceptability of the data commonly used. Given natural data, introspection is the only practical method of separating out interacting patterns.

In our methodology, introspection is not seen to be opposed to the use of natural data, but complementary to it. On the one hand, it is self-evident that, if we wish to assign natural intonation patterns to written texts, we need to obtain our rules from the close study of appropriate natural data. Much of the work involves the interaction of several different patterns, and this can only be studied in real data. On the other hand, in the absence of any automatic procedure for analysing the data, we have to identify the component patterns by imagining the effect of changing words, or adding or deleting words. This application of introspection to natural data is very different from the currently fashionable method of pondering the introspections of other linguists. It is absolutely essential to start with a corpus of appropriate texts.

A corpus of contemporary spoken English

Our aim is to produce a representative corpus of contemporary spoken English, which will be used as a database to test the intonation assignment program, and to provide models suitable for speech synthesis.

[†] This point is dealt with at length in Knowles (in preparation), 'The automatic accentuation of English texts'.

Corpus material

The corpus will be composed of samples of contemporary British English. It is desirable in any corpus to include samples of a large variety of different styles, in order to ensure that the corpus is truly representative. However, there are restrictions on the material which can be included:

(a) **Quality of recording** The material must be of sufficiently good recorded quality for at least part of it to be analysed instrumentally, e.g. to extract F_0. This means that recordings must be made under studio – or near-studio – conditions. There must be no background music or other ambient noise.

(b) **Quality of text** To start with, we need to work on good models of English intonation. In practice this means using prepared monologues produced by skilled speakers. Material which contains informal conversational speech with its attendant problems of interrupted sentences, unintelligible speech and hesitations has to be excluded.

  The study of conversation is extremely interesting in its own right. But prepared monologue is a more suitable model for synthetic speech than extempore chatter. Secondly, conversational intonation is highly complex, and it would seem sensible to start work on texts which are intonationally simpler. The results of our project are likely to be of considerable value in conversation analysis, but the corpus itself will not.

(c) **Accent and dialect** In view of the problems associated with non-standard dialects and strong regional accents, we are selecting only texts in standard British English spoken with Received Pronunciation. There are important sociolinguistic variables in intonation, and they are understood just well enough for us to know that they would cause serious problems.

  Despite these restrictions, it is hoped that the corpus will reflect several varieties of spoken British English. The main source of the material to date has been BBC radio broadcasts[†] and recorded lectures from, for example, the productions of the Open University. The recordings selected have the advantage of consisting mainly of prepared, rehearsed readings of texts, and are therefore more formal than spontaneous speech. For example, the BBC programmes "From our own correspondent", "News", and "Money Box" are amongst those we have sampled. Although Radio 4 has provided most of the programmes we have used, news broadcasts from Radios 2 and 3 are included to reflect different styles of presentation. It was also considered useful to include some small samples of highly stylized spoken English, such as that used in the narration of children's stories, or in the delivery of a sermon, but such texts will not be used in the initial testing of the intonation assignment program. The identification of what features distinguish one style of English from another is not easily definable, but the corpus will be divided into categories reflecting different registers, e.g.:

[†] Broadcast material is of course copyright, and is used in the corpus by permission of the copyright holders.

(a) news

(b) religion

(c) reportage

(d) story-telling (children's stories)

(e) educational (e.g. lectures)

(f) story-telling (adults' stories)

Preparation of the corpus

The target size is 100 000 words. This is much smaller than most written corpora, but each text will exist in several different versions, the production of which is a time-consuming operation:

(a) spoken recording

(b) written transcription (unpunctuated)

(c) orthographic transcription

(d) prosodic transcription

(e) grammatically tagged version

It is rarely possible to obtain a transcription of the spoken recording, and so we have to produce a written version ourselves. At the beginning of the project we simply listened to the recordings and wrote the text down as we saw fit. However, this laid us open to the charge that intonational cues in the spoken recordings were influencing the placement of punctuation marks, and that this method would result in circularity if we subsequently used the punctuated text to recover the intonation patterns. Since the study of the relationship between the orthographic and prosodic transcriptions is central to our project, it is essential that prosodic information should not influence in any way the production of the orthographic version, and *vice versa*. A different method has now been adopted:

(a)   A written version of the spoken recording is made without punctuation, but otherwise conforming to standard orthographic practice. Certain conventions have been adopted to maintain consistency and to ensure that the texts conform to an acceptable standard for "natural" written English. For example, titular forms are abbreviated if they are normally found so in an ordinary text (*Mr*, *Dr*, etc.); and digits are retained in addresses, dates and times, as they would usually be.

(b)   This text is punctuated by "volunteers" who have not heard the original recording, and who are not directly involved in the project. As far as possible, consistency is maintained by using an explicit set of punctuation guidelines[†].

(c)   The punctuated text is used as input to the intonation assignment program.

(d)   The phoneticians making a prosodic transcription of the recording use the unpunctuated text.

[†] Drawn up by Geoffrey Leech.

It should be mentioned that this method is not entirely free of problems. Whereas there are relatively few genuine ambiguities in spoken English (assuming that utterances are considered in the original context in which they are produced), there may be quite a number of ambiguities in a written text, especially if it is not punctuated. For example, the distinction between restrictive and non-restrictive relative clauses is usually marked by intonation in speech and by punctuation in writing: someone punctuating a text without access to the spoken original may misinterpret the text, and mispunctuate it accordingly. However, this proves in practice to be a minor problem, compared to the problem of circularity.

The prosodic transcription

We are using the prosodic transcription as a "target" model for intonation assignment, by identifying systematic correspondences between intonation and orthography.

Phonetic transcription is among the traditional skills of the phonetician. Superficially, the phonetician is trained to convert auditory information into visual information. In practice, only part of the total information is extracted, and this depends on the system of notation adopted. Secondly, what phoneticians actually extract may not be quite what they claim to extract. It is by no means uncommon for terms – e.g. "stress" – to be defined in one way and used in quite another. It is essential, therefore, to check the validity and reliability of the transcriptions.

The transcription is done by two phoneticians, one at Lancaster (Gerry Knowles) and one at IBM (UK) Scientific Centre (Briony Williams). They work on different texts, or on different parts of the same text, but in each case there is a short section which is transcribed by both. For this section a plot of F_0 is also prepared by IBM. In general, there is substantial agreement on the movement of pitch, although the relationship of perceived pitch to F_0 – even when both transcribers agree – is not always clear. There is much less agreement on the interpretation of pitch movements in terms of the conventional British "tones", and on the placement of minor tone-group boundaries.

We are using a modified version of O'Connor and Arnold's notation (O'Connor and Arnold 1973). This was chosen because it carries the minimum of theoretical overheads, and because it is closely related to an interlinear graph of the pitch movement (the "tadpole" notation). But there is no objective way of getting from the pitch movement to the tone-marks: one has to make a subjective assessment of the significance of minor pitch jumps, of the slope of pitch movement, and of the lengthening or shortening of syllables. This problem does not arise in studies of invented data, because "classroom" intonation patterns are perfectly clear.

It may be that our notation system is leading us to listen for the wrong things in the pitch movement: we certainly need to reconsider the assumed units of intonation. Leaving aside the problems for our corpus, our experience does raise a query over published transcriptions of natural data which have not been adequately checked, or on which different transcribers claim to agree exactly, or for which some notation is claimed to have proved ideal.

The grammatically tagged version

As the first stage in the grammatical analysis, we are using the LOB suite of tagging programs, since these are already available at Lancaster, and involve little manual post-editing. The results achieved on a sample text (96.8% correct tag assignments) are comparable to those achieved on the LOB Corpus. However, the set of tags used in the tagging programs was designed to be used on written texts, and although in general the difference between spoken and written English may be regarded as negligible in this respect, there are some instances where the tagset is not entirely suitable for spoken texts. The problem is most obvious with respect to the tags assigned to the "grammatical" words in the text – *up*, *which*, *of*, etc. – which might occur more frequently in an idiomatic context in a spoken text than a written text, or which might require a more specific tag for our purposes than the one assigned.

One example of the latter concerns the word *which*, which may only be assigned the tag WDT (wh-determiner) by the tagging programs, and is correctly tagged when it appears in the following context:

Which book does he want?

But in the following case, *which* is a relative pronoun:

the book which he wants ..

It is important to distinguish these two functions of *which*, as they are accented differently: the determiner is usually accented, and the relative pronoun – when not preceded by a preposition or in certain other contexts – unaccented. A "relative pronoun" tag must therefore be among the possible tags for this word. Experiments involving the addition of an extra tag to an entry in the lexicon indicate that the desired tag may be selected and the word correctly disambiguated without any amendments to the tagging programs themselves.

On the other hand, some tags are too specific for our purposes, particularly those representing classes of nouns. Of the 133 tags in the LOB tagset, 29 represent varieties of nouns, e.g. NN represents singular common noun, and NR singular adverbial noun. We have found some of these distinctions unnecessary, and prefer in this instance to keep the noun information to a minimum by referring only to the first character of the tag: this indicates the overall class of the word, which is sufficient. However, information which appears redundant may be very useful elsewhere: the recognition of plurality in nouns is irrelevant for intonation assignment, but is important for a spelling interpreter, e.g. final *s* in *gas* is pronounced /s/, while in *ideas* it is the plural marker and pronounced /z/.

The results we have to date indicate that the grammatical analysis provided by the LOB tagging programs is of great value to our project. With minor amendments to the tagset, the programs originally designed for written texts can be adapted to deal with spoken texts.

3.   Rules for intonation assignment

Assigning intonation to texts

We started the project with a prior understanding of some disparate parts of the intonation system, including patterns associated with compounds, apposition, co-ordinate lists, "given" and "new" information, parallelism, etc. The problem is that these structures are all rather difficult to identify automatically, and their presence in a sentence modifies the intonation pattern that would otherwise occur. It is necessary to start with the default pattern that occurs in the absence of special structures. In an attempt to predict this we made a number of working assumptions:

(a)   The first stage in assigning intonation to a sentence is to divide it into tone-groups.

(b)   This division depends on the internal structure of the sentence (and largely on its syntactic structure).

(c)   Intonation is assigned from left to right.

These assumptions were not formulated explicitly in advance: it became clear, in the course of research, first that we had made such assumptions, and secondly that they were fundamentally wrong. In fact, before the project started, another false assumption had been identified and rejected:

(d)   In each tone-group, the important words have to be identified, and given an accent.

Assumptions (a)–(c) follow from the way linguists are trained to think of the grammar of sentences, and may have nothing to do with the nature of intonation. In fact, the idea that it is necessary to parse the whole sentence is psychologically unrealistic anyway. We can start to produce a sentence before planning its ending, and, when we read a text aloud, we often start a sentence before we have scanned to the end. We can even fit an intonation pattern to ungrammatical and nonsensical strings. We certainly need grammatical information, but not up to the level of the complete sentence. It was a stroke of good fortune, therefore, that there happened to be no parser available for the analysis of the corpus when we started the project, and we were forced to do without one.

In the case of assumption (d), it is generally taken for granted and without comment in the literature on stress and accent that the speaker stresses important items in the sentence. In contrast, all our accentuation rules suppress accents, and this seems to be producing the correct results. Instead of looking for words to accent, we identify candidates for deaccentuation. Where our algorithms fail, it is found that the speaker has carried out a rule that is either optional or not yet built into the program. There is no reason to doubt the fundamental approach in which the accent pattern is determined by deaccentuation rules.

Bottom-up tone-grouping

Our first attempt at tone-grouping was top-down. Tone groups often begin with a "leading" grammatical word, such as a preposition, a determiner or a conjunction: by recognizing such words one can divide a sentence into prosodically relevant word groups. The problem is that these groups are often rather smaller than conventional minor tone-groups, so that one has to have a second set of bottom-up rules merging small groups into bigger ones. This is an inverted "Duke of York" procedure: surely it is better to work just one way, either up or down.

The second attempt worked consistently bottom-up, and began to put together some obvious well-known facts and familiar rules, e.g.:

(a) clitic attachment

(b) grammatical collocations

(c) high-level groups

Weak grammatical words attach themselves as clitics to lexical words, e.g. *the man, to walk,* and in doing so lose the accent they would have if pronounced in isolation. This is the first level of grouping above the word. The next level groups words of particular grammatical classes, e.g. adjective + noun (*old man*) or verb + adverb (*walked slowly*). At the top level there are no grammatical restrictions, and e.g. *the man walked slowly* could be run together as a single tone group.

Accent count

In addition to grammatical criteria, speakers use some measure of the size of items to be grouped together in tone groups. We originally counted accented syllables, but found we got equally good results by counting accented words (so that e.g. a word like *TElePHOnic*, with two accents, has a value of 1).

In a group of words with a maximum count of two, e.g. *old man, twenty eight,* the last accent takes the intonational nucleus, and, if there is more than one accent, the first takes the onset.

Longer groups are sometimes run together, in which case one of the potential accents is suppressed. The rules for this have not yet been fully worked out, but they seem to depend on grammatical class, and on whether the longer group comes first or second. Here are some rules for conflating two groups with a total of three accents:

For a group with one accent followed by a group with two, a grammatical word ending the first group or beginning the second loses its accent, e.g.:

> *aBOUT* + *FORty FIVE* becomes *a[bout] FORty FIVE*
> *she LOOKED* + *aBOUT FORty* becomes *she LOOKED a[bout] FORty*

The syllable in lower case and enclosed in square brackets is the one that loses its accent.

If a group with two accents is followed by a group with one, the potential nucleus of the first group is suppressed:

> *TWEnty EIGHT* + *DAYS* becomes *TWEnty [eight] DAYS*

Phrases subject to this rule are sometimes hyphenated in writing, e.g. *twenty-eight.* There are many compound adjectives in this category, e.g. *RED-HAIRED* but *a RED-[haired] SCOTSman.*

Right-to-left grouping

We speak and read sentences from left to right, and parsers tend to work in the same direction; but it does not follow that we plan sentences from left to right. Another possibility is that we set up some intermediate target within the sentence and plan backwards in anticipation of that target.

This must be so for intonation assignment. We have found in practice that the formation of word groups has to proceed from right to left. Accordingly, when processing a text, we read it in from left to right up to a punctuation mark, and then process that chunk from right to left. This seems to imitate, albeit crudely, what a fluent human reader does when scanning ahead going through a text.

4. Conclusion

Corpus and computer change fundamentally the nature of research in linguistics. The need to solve a problem which is not of one's own choosing leads to the discarding of cherished orthodox views in favour of new ideas based squarely on the structure of the language as it really is. In this way it is possible to replace received opinion with hard knowledge. In this paper we have more than once had to question ideas which are currently received in linguistics. However, no matter how many linguists accept an idea, there is no real value in it if it merely reflects the prevailing fashion.

Apart from the many matters of detail, our work so far points to two important conclusions. First, the assumption that one can account for English intonation by just sitting and thinking about it is not to be taken seriously. It is only by closely studying a corpus of natural data that one can begin to understand the problems, let alone find algorithms to solve them.

Secondly, the assumption that one needs to parse a sentence before doing any interesting linguistic processing is almost certainly false. If speakers and readers deal with much smaller groups of words, then a full parse may actually be irrelevant[†]. The onus is not on us to explain why we are doing without a parser: the onus is on grammarians who insist on a parser to explain – with reference to authentic data – exactly why they need it.

[†] It is assumed here that "parsing" is a matter of drawing constituent structure trees. A very different view of parsing presented by R. A. Hudson (1984), based on dependency trees, may prove fruitful for intonation assignment. Unfortunately, we became aware of this work too late to take it into account in the preparation of this paper.

CHAPTER 12

Towards a distributional lexicon

Andrew Beale

1. Introduction

The "distributional lexicon" was conceived as a long-term goal of the UCREL project, and, at the time of going to press, the suite of programs for constructing it still has to be finalized.[†] Preliminary versions of programs have been written, and an extensive set of lemmatization rules has been prepared. This chapter will therefore provide a description of the work completed to date. In addition, we will give some indication of the possible applications of the distributional lexicon as we envisage it, once further work has been done. Eventually, the distributional lexicon will be made available to the academic community.

Lexicography, of course, has a long tradition, but the advent of microchip technology has not only improved the data processing facilities available to the lexicographer, it has introduced new research possibilities. There is currently much research into applications of the lexical and grammatical information contained in machine-readable dictionaries, such as the *Longman Dictionary of Contemporary English* (Procter 1978), the *Oxford Advanced Learner's Dictionary of Current English* (Hornby and Cowie 1974) and *Webster's Seventh New Collegiate Dictionary* (1963). Applications include parsing of natural language (e.g. Alshawi, Boguraev and Briscoe 1985), automatic semantic analysis (Chodorow and Byrd 1985), and style checking or "text critiquing" of word-processed text (MacDonald 1983).

Frequency analysis of English-language corpora (Carroll *et al* 1971; Francis and Kučera 1982) has uses, for instance, in grading lexical items for language teaching (Engels *et al* 1981), in comparing the vocabulary usage of American and British English (Hofland and Johansson 1982), and in automatic spelling-checking (Ch. 10 in this volume). Computer corpora, if large enough, can provide the lexicographer with authentic examples of keywords in context to illustrate the use of a word (see the *Collins COBUILD English Dictionary*, 1987).

[†] A distributional lexicon of the LOB Corpus has now been completed. [Editors' note, May 1987.]

2. Overview

The LOB distributional lexicon will be a database of frequencies of combinations of words and tags extracted from the post-edited version of the tagged LOB Corpus. Figure 10 outlines the major stages involved in producing the distributional lexicon.

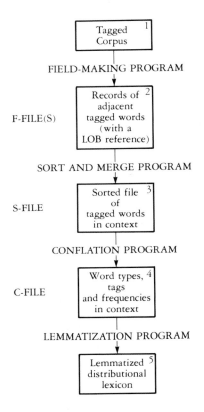

Figure 10   The production of a distributional lexicon

3. Field making, sorting and conflation

A field-making program copies each tagged word in the horizontalized version of the post-edited tagged corpus and produces a file of fixed-format records containing fields for adjacent running words and their tags (an "F-file"). The output of the field-making program is essentially an unsorted tagged concordance. This file is then sorted so that identical word-forms in the Corpus (word tokens of the same type) occur together, and distinct word-forms (or word types) follow each other in alphabetical order. F-files will be sorted and merged using two different key specifications to show the left and right lexical combinations of any keyword, until the whole Corpus has been processed.

After sorting, a program conflates identical grammatical words (words with the same spelling and the same tag), and produces frequency counts for each grammatical word. The output file from the conflation program ("C-file") therefore contains a list of primary, secondary and n-ary entries, indented according to proximity to the primary sort field. Right-sorted combinations are arranged as follows:

> Keyword, tag, frequency
> > 1st right adjacent word, tag, frequency
> > .
> > .
>
> > .. *n*th right adjacent word, tag, frequency
> > .
> > .
> > .
> > .
> .
> .

(Dots indicate an unspecified number of rows or columns.)
Left-sorted combinations are arranged similarly in a "mirror image" data-structure.

4. Significant combinations

The most straightforward, and perhaps the crudest, way of discarding the many lexical combinations that occur so infrequently that they do not merit being held in the distributional lexicon at all, is to delete all entries in the C-file that occur only once, or below some arbitrarily constant frequency; the conflation program has a "threshold" constant that prevents any entries below a fixed frequency from being written to the data-structure above. This does not account for the proportionate likelihood of a word or tag occurring before or after a keyword, which is dependent on the frequency of the keyword, and, in due course, once a large enough file of n-ary entries has been accumulated, we envisage writing a procedure to compute the proportionate likelihood of adjacent words, which would provide a better means of discarding infrequently occurring lexical combinations.

There are two conflicting problems associated with this. The first is the need to have as large as possible a corpus of tagged texts to give reliable lexical combinations for the many content words that are considered common English lexis but which, nevertheless, occur infrequently in any random sample of text. The second problem is the enormous magnitude of the distributional files that need to be created in order to give a reasonable indication of significant combinations of a sizeable range of English lexis. Our prototype distributional lexicon will be based on the million tagged words of the LOB Corpus, but this will not be large enough to produce significant figures for many combinations of words, because a large proportion of words in the LOB Corpus – or any comparable corpus of natural language – are word types that occur only once.

An interim solution is to produce a data-structure of all the grammatical keywords in the Corpus (approximately 65 000), sorted into alphabetical order, each keyword giving access to left or right neighbouring tags. This would reduce the amount of data to be held, and, at the same time, it would provide a representative index of the different syntactic environments of common English words together with their relative frequencies.

5.   Lemmatization

Linguistically and computationally, one of the most interesting tasks in the development of the distributional lexicon to date has been devising rules for automatic lemmatization. We intend to implement a lemmatization program that will assign so-called inflexional or morpho-syntactic variants to lexical classes and sum together the frequencies of the member word-forms of each morpho-syntactic paradigm. This program will be run once the data-structure of keywords in context, outlined in section 3, has been finalized. The remainder of this chapter will be about lemmatization.

Dictionaries usually present information about morpho-syntactic variants or members of the same lexical class, such as *write, writes, wrote, writing, written*, under a single headword or entry word, generally known as a lexeme. The lexeme is represented as a typographically marked base form, the singular form of a noun for instance, or the stem of a verb. Morpho-syntactic variants are included as subentries or "run-ons" under this headword, by showing any suffixes to be appended to the headword, or by citing the whole variant, if it is a "strong" or irregular form. An automatic procedure that accepts tagged text as input and outputs a list of alphabetically sorted headwords with sublists of inflexional variants is known as a lemmatization procedure.

There are regularities in inflexional patterns which suggest basic rules for an automatic suffix-stripping routine as a first approximation to a comprehensive lemmatization procedure. For instance, by removing final *-s* or *-ed* or *-ing* from many verb forms, and by removing *-s* from regular plural nouns, the regular verb and noun lexemes may be obtained. But clearly, irregularity in both morphology and orthography creates numerous exceptions to such rules, and designing a leakproof automatic lemmatization procedure is by no means a trivial programming task.

Lists of untagged graphic word types arranged alphabetically and in order of frequency are available in both printed and machine-readable form (Hofland and Johansson 1982; Kučera and Francis 1967; and others); and the sorting of any machine-readable text into a list of word types with associated frequencies is now a well-established data-processing task (see, for example, the Oxford Concordance Program: Hockey and Marriott 1980). But for a database of the kind that we envisage, a word listing procedure that does not account for word-class membership suffers two major drawbacks:

(a) Words of the same form belonging to distinct word classes, such as the noun and verb forms of *abuse, blow, conduct, house*, and *watch*, appear as single entries.

(b) Paradigms of morpho-syntactic variants such as *take, takes, took, taken, taking* are not grouped together in any grammatically consistent order, but instead occur in alphabetical sequence.

If an untagged list of phonological rather than orthographic word types were listed, it would be homophones rather than homographs that would be conflated: *meet ~ meat, I ~ eye, night ~ knight, him ~ hymn, pane ~ pain*, etc. would occur as single entries, whereas the different phonological forms of homographs such as *abuse, conduct, record*, etc. would be entered as distinct phonological types. This shows that the grammatical status of a word form is not dependent on the medium of realization, and the conflation of grammatical words according to medium – whether of spoken or written forms – should not be reflected in the presentation of grammatical statistics.

The tagged LOB Corpus provides the grammatical information required to disambiguate homonyms of the kind listed in (a). Homonym disambiguation can be achieved by using tagged text as input and by writing a word-listing procedure that creates more than one separate entry for word forms with more than one tag. In this way, separate entries for the nouns and verbs as in (a) above are produced. A listing of words associated with distinct tags is known as a list of *grammatical words* (Francis and Kučera 1982: 3).

A lemmatized word list (see Francis and Kučera 1982) is an alphabetical sequence of lexemes, each with a secondary list of morpho-syntactic variants. For instance, the noun lemma represented by the lexeme PLAY includes the sublist of grammatical words *play* NN, *plays* NNS, *play's* NN$, *plays'* NNS$; and the verb lemma represented by the lexeme PLAY includes the sublist *play* VB, *plays* VBZ, *played* VBD, *played* VBN, *playing* VBG. (For details of tags see Appendix B.) Any spelling variants, such as *playin'* VBG, are also included in the relevant lemma.

Some of the morpho-syntactic variants are duplicated in the sublist of grammatical words included in each lemma. For instance, *played* occurs twice in the previous example where *took* VBD and *taken* VBN would be distinct variants under the entry word TAKE. Wherever there is morpho-syntactic variation of forms belonging to a major word-class, there must be subcategorization, but morpho-syntactic variation can, of course, be irregular: some forms exhibit no variation – plural-only nouns, for instance, like *cattle* and *police*, or "zero" inflecting nouns, like *sheep*; while other forms, such as strong verbs, exhibit irregular suffixation or suppletion. These irregularities have to be captured in some way by the lemmatization routine or else the irregular forms must be post-edited.

We intend to implement a lemmatization program by using a set of suffix-stripping rules (see the Appendix to this chapter) and an exceptions wordlist. The suffix-stripping routine will be, in essence, a double look-up procedure: an attempt will be made to find one rule for both the tag and the suffix (in the string-theoretical sense) of each grammatical word in the distributional lexicon to be lemmatized. If the input grammatical word matches more than one suffix rule, then it is the first and most specific rule in the ordered list for the relevant tag that is invoked: an input form will invoke, at most, only one suffix-stripping rule.

By way of illustration, the general rule for lemmatization of words tagged VBG is rule 28:

$$-ing \rightarrow -$$

This rule removes the *-ing* suffix from the stem and leaves the remainder of the form unchanged. If the *-ing* suffix of the input form is preceded by a consonant, a vowel, and a consonant, then the more specific rule 27:

$$(-)CVCing \rightarrow (-)CVCe$$

is invoked, replacing *-ing* by *-e*. But if the input word form ends in *-ening*, then rule 13:

$$-ening \rightarrow -en$$

(which is more specific still) is invoked.

Word forms that cannot be lemmatized by removal or modification of word-final characters in this way will be looked up in an exceptions wordlist (see Table 3). Two data files will therefore be used: the exceptions wordlist will be searched first, and if the input word form is not in the wordlist, then the suffix list will be searched.

6.   Testing the lemmatization rules

We drew up a provisional list of suffix stripping rules that would apply to words with a given tag. These rules were then modified, extended or deleted by referring to reverse-order lists of word forms belonging to the relevant grammatical classes.

An editing routine was used to extract all occurrences of word tokens in the Corpus matching a specified criterion. All words with the tags VBZ, VBD, VBN, and VBG were extracted to obtain the different verb forms. Similarly, all words with a tag ending in S were extracted to obtain plural forms, and all occurrences of words containing apostrophes were extracted to obtain genitive forms. Reverse-order lists of the word types belonging to these distinct classes were then created so that the suffixes of all the appropriate word forms in the Corpus could be compared with the suffix rules.

The default rule for lemmatization of VBZ forms is a rule that removes the final *-s* and leaves the rest of the form unchanged. But in checking through the reverse-order lists, it was evident that forms ending in *-ches* and *-shes* require another suffix-stripping rule deleting the *e* preceding the *s*. Many other more detailed refinements could be made by reference to the reverse order lists. As well as showing suffix rules that might not be obtained by linguistic intuition, the reverse-order lists also showed forms in the Corpus that are so exceptional that they cannot be incorporated into the suffix-stripping routine. For instance, *ached* is an idiosyncratic exception to the VBD suffix-stripping rules. Similarly, most VBD forms ending in *-sted* have a lexeme ending in *-st* (*blasted, lasted, roasted, contrasted, infested* ...), but this is not true of *basted, pasted, tasted,* and *wasted,* which have to be cited as whole-word exceptions.

In some cases, the decision about whether to include a suffix-stripping rule was made by comparing the number of occurrences of words that would be exceptions if the rule was included to the number of words that would be exceptions if the rule was excluded. For instance, word forms ending *-nged* or *-nging* have lexemes ending *-ng* or *-nge* according to whether the <ng> represents a "hard" /ŋ/ or a "soft" /ndʒ/ sound (*banged, singing, belonging ~ changed, arranging, challenged*). There were 53 "hard" examples and 224 "soft" examples of word tokens (13 "hard" and 24 "soft" word types) in the reverse-order lists of past tense forms and past participle forms. Hence a rule of the kind:

$$-nged \rightarrow -ng$$

was deemed inappropriate. The default rule for all forms ending in *-ged* was left as:

$$-ged \rightarrow -ge$$

and forms like *banged* and *belonged* were cited as whole word exceptions in the exceptions word list.

But the situation was different for VBG words ending *-nging* where the "hard" /ŋ/ outnumbered the "soft" /ndʒ/ 160 to 59 as tokens (and 15 to 9 as word types). On the basis of these figures, it was decided to include the rule:

$$-nging \rightarrow -ng$$

for words like *banging, flinging, bringing, belonging,* and to cite words like *changing, exchanging,* and *challenging* in the exceptions word list.

The difference between the *-nging* and *-nged* frequencies is due to the irregular English morphology of forms like *sing, singing, sang, sung* which admit a regular *-ing* form but have irregular past forms.

After searching through the reverse-order lists of all the relevant word types in the Corpus, we estimated that there were roughly 818 grammatical word types which are exceptions to the 79 existing suffix-stripping or suffix-modifying rules, excluding personal pronouns and forms of the verbs BE, HAVE, and DO which have their own distinct tags; these common exceptional forms will be lemmatized either by including additional exceptional rules or by manual post-editing.

7. Towards automatic text critiquing

Once all the stages outlined in section 2 have been completed, trials will begin on using the distributional lexicon for automatic text critiquing. An automatic text critiquing system provides an analysis of the predictable features of input English grammar and lexis. The information contained in the distributional lexicon could be used for style checking in a manner similar to the spelling checker described in Chapter 10. Once a sufficiently sizeable database of lexical entries and tags has been accumulated, input text could be analysed, and deviant combinations flagged. The system would be useful for quality control of the output from a machine translation system, by assigning probability weightings to alternative translations, for instance.

The existing million word-tokens of the LOB Corpus could only provide a rough-and-ready text critiquing system, but the suite of tagging programs has been modified to accept input text without the special coding and pre-editing requirements of the original LOB Corpus formating program (as described in Chapter 8). The distributional lexicon could therefore be augmented as more information becomes available. Given the increasing speed and storage capabilities of electronic data processing, and the cumulative nature of computer corpus research, it seems entirely appropriate, at this point, to speculate that a text critiquing system based on co-occurrence preferences of English texts will become a feasible natural language tool in the foreseeable future.

Appendix[†]

Table 1 of this appendix is a list of suffix-stripping rules for automatic lemmatization of the word forms in the tagged LOB Corpus. The suffix rules for verb forms apply to individual input tags, whereas the rules for plural and genitive forms apply to groups of tags labelled with so-called "cover symbols". The cover symbol *$ is used for tags ending in -$, which represent genitive variants of different subclasses of nouns, pronouns, determiners, post-determiners, adverbs, cardinal and ordinal numbers. Similarly, *S is used for tags ending in -S which represent plural forms. The full set of individual tags for each of the three cover symbols used in this appendix is given in Table 2. Suffix rules for cover symbols are intended to apply only to the word tags specified in Table 2: CS (which happens to end in -S but means "subordinating conjunction) is not contained in *S, and, for the purposes of lemmatization, *$ and *S$ are disjoint. (Note that these "cover symbols", while similar to those described in Chapter 6, are not co-terminous with them.)

In some cases, an extra condition is stipulated which must be true if a particular rule is to be invoked. For instance, rule VBZ(3) is only invoked if more than one (unspecified) letter precedes the specified word ending. Extra conditions are given in

† I would like to acknowledge the help of Dr. C. D. Paice in the compilation of this Appendix.

brackets immediately following the rule to which they apply. P represents the number of letters preceding a suffix that are required if the rule is to be invoked; C represents "consonant", i.e. any alphabetic character, including *y*, but excluding the class *a, e, i, o, u*, which is represented by V. The general grammatical descriptions, or "lemma tags", output for each input word tag are based on the categorizations given in Francis and Kučera (1982). All examples are taken from the LOB Corpus.

Table 3 presents a selection of words that are exceptions to the suffix-stripping rules for automatic lemmatization. (The full list of exceptions is too unwieldy to be included in this Appendix.) Numbers in brackets indicate the suffix rule which applies incorrectly (or fails to apply when it should) to the exceptional word form.

Table 1

Rule number	Word ending	Lexical ending	Examples
-- VBZ $\Rightarrow$ verb ---			
1	-ches→	-ch	*reaches, catches* → REACH, CATCH.
2	-shes→	-sh	*flashes, publishes* → FLASH, PUBLISH.
3	-ies→	-y	(P > 1) *studies, qualifies* → STUDY, QUALIFY (but not *dies, lies, ties, vies*).
4	-sses →	-ss	*passes, crosses* → PASS, CROSS.
5	-xes →	-x	*relaxes, taxes* → RELAX, TAX.
6	-s →	-	*reads, makes* → READ, MAKE.
--- VBD $\Rightarrow$ verb ---			
1	-ead →	-ead	*lead, (mis)read, spread* → LEAD, READ, SPREAD.
2	-ied →	-y	(P > 1) *fancied, embodied, identified* → FANCY, EMBODY, IDENTIFY (not *died, lied, tied, vied*).
3	-Ved →	- Ve	*(dis)agreed, died, tiptoed, ensued* → AGREE, DIE, TIPTOE, ENSUE.
4	-ffed →	-ff	*staffed, sniffed, scoffed, handcuffed* → STAFF, SNIFF, SCOFF, HANDCUFF.
5	-lled →	-ll	(P < 4) *called, stalled, spelled* → CALL, STALL, SPELL (not *initialled* etc).
6	-ssed →	-ss	*passed, witnessed, kissed* → PASS, WITNESS, KISS.
7	-C_1C_2ed →	- C_1	($C_1 = C_2$) *rubbed, embedded, hugged, travelled, slapped, transferred, regretted* → RUB, EMBED, HUG, TRAVEL, SLAP, TRANSFER, REGRET.
8	-ced →	-ce	*placed, pieced, advanced* → PLACE, PIECE, ADVANCE.
9	-ged →	-ge	*managed, acknowledged, besieged, changed* → MANAGE, ACKNOWLEDGE, BESIEGE, CHANGE.

10	-Vthed →	-Vthe	*bathed, breathed, clothed* → BATHE, BREATHE, CLOTHE.
11	(-)VVled →	(-)VVl	*sailed, concealed, revealed, wheeled, oiled, hauled* → SAIL, CONCEAL, REVEAL, WHEEL, OIL, HAUL.
12	-rled →	-rl	*swirled, curled* → SWIRL, CURL.
13	-wled →	-wl	*crawled, sprawled, howled* → CRAWL, SPRAWL, HOWL.
14	-led →	-le	*enabled, giggled, compiled, ruled, puzzled* → ENABLE, GIGGLE, COMPILE, RULE, PUZZLE.
15	-ened →	-en	*reddened, widened, strengthened, awakened, opened* → REDDEN, WIDEN, STRENGTHEN, AWAKEN, OPEN.
16	-oned →	-on	*abandoned, fashioned, commissioned, stationed, mentioned* → ABANDON, FASHION, COMMISSION, STATION, MENTION.
17	-ered →	-er	*considered, squandered, ordered, cheered, bothered* → CONSIDER, SQUANDER, ORDER, CHEER, BOTHER.
18	-sed →	-se	*released, summarised, sensed, reversed, used, housed* → RELEASE, SUMMARISE, SENSE, REVERSE, USE, HOUSE.
19	-iated →	-iate	*appreciated, associated, appropriated, vitiated, negotiated* → APPRECIATE, ASSOCIATE, APPROPRIATE, VITIATE, NEGOTIATE.
20	-ited →	-it	*inhabited, inhibited, exhibited* → INHABIT, INHIBIT, EXHIBIT.
21	-ved →	-ve	*saved, achieved, moved, observed* → SAVE, ACHIEVE, MOVE, OBSERVE.
22	-wed →	-w	*reviewed, flowed* → REVIEW, FLOW.
23	-xed →	-x	*relaxed, mixed* → RELAX, MIX.
24	-yed →	-y	*played, obeyed, destroyed* → PLAY, OBEY, DESTROY.
25	-zed →	-ze	*gazed, squeezed, recognized* → GAZE, SQUEEZE, RECOGNIZE.
26	-uVCed →	-uVCe	*squared, persuaded, enquired, graduated, quoted* → SQUARE, PERSUADE, ENQUIRE, GRADUATE, QUOTE.
27	(-)CVCed →	(-)CVCe	*ascribed, preceded, welcomed, chimed, noted* → ASCRIBE, PRECEDE, WELCOME, CHIME, NOTE.
28	-ed →	-	*screamed, climbed, yielded* → SCREAM, CLIMB, YIELD.
29	-aid →	-ay	*(over)laid, paid, said* → LAY, PAY, SAY.

-- VBN ⇒ verb --
(as VBD + the following)

30	-iven →	-ve	*(for)given, driven, striven* → GIVE, DRIVE, STRIVE.
31	-wn →	-w	*(with)drawn, hewn, shown, known, thrown* → DRAW, HEW, SHOW, KNOW, THROW.

```
------------------------------------------ VBG  ⇒  verb -----------------------------------------
```

1	-ffing →	-ff	*sniffing, stuffing* → SNIFF, STUFF.
2	-lling →	-ll	(P < 4) *calling, selling* → CALL, SELL.
3	-ssing →	-ss	*dressing, discussing* → DRESS, DISCUSS.
4	$-C_1C_2$ing →	$-C_1$	($C_1 = C_2$) *bobbing, shedding, chugging, compelling, swimming, spinning, overlapping, conferring, chatting* → BOB, SHED, CHUG, COMPEL, SWIM, SPIN, OVERLAP, CONFER, CHAT.
5	-cing →	-ce	*voicing, dancing, influencing* → VOICE, DANCE, INFLUENCE.
6	-nging →	-ng	*hanging, clinging, bringing, singing* → HANG, CLING, BRING, SING.
7	-ging →	-ge	*engaging, judging, urging, deluging* → ENGAGE, JUDGE, URGE, DELUGE.
8	-Vthing →	-the	*(sun)bathing, breathing, loathing* → BATHE, BREATHE, LOATHE.
9	-rling →	-rl	*snarling, whirling* → SNARL, WHIRL.
10	-wling →	-wl	*bowling, howling* → BOWL, HOWL.
11	(-)VVling →	(-)VVl	*concealing, failing, boiling, fooling* → CONCEAL, FAIL, BOIL, FOOL.
12	-ling →	-le	*assembling, circling, fiddling, reconciling, wrestling* → ASSEMBLE, CIRCLE, FIDDLE, RECONCILE, WRESTLE.
13	-ening →	-en	*broadening, widening, lengthening, darkening* → BROADEN, WIDEN, LENGTHEN, DARKEN.
14	-oning →	-on	*abandoning, rationing, functioning, mentioning, poisoning* → ABANDON, RATION, FUNCTION, MENTION, POISON.
15	-ering →	-er	*offering, lingering, hammering, sneering* → OFFER, LINGER, HAMMER, SNEER.
16	-sing →	-se	*easing, purchasing, realising, pulsing, exposing* → EASE, PURCHASE, REALISE, PULSE, EXPOSE.
17	-iating →	-iate	*appreciating, associating, negotiating* → APPRECIATE, ASSOCIATE, NEGOTIATE.
18	-iting →	-it	*inhabiting, prohibiting, exhibiting* → INHABIT, PROHIBIT, EXHIBIT.
19	-uing →	-ue	*rescuing, arguing, continuing, issuing* → RESCUE, ARGUE, CONTINUE, ISSUE.
20	-ving →	-ve	*leaving, saving, receiving, arriving, starving* → LEAVE, SAVE, RECEIVE, ARRIVE, STARVE.
21	-wing →	-w	*(with)drawing, (inter)viewing, growing* → DRAW, VIEW, GROW.
22	-xing →	-x	*coaxing, boxing* → COAX, BOX.
23	-ying →	-ie	(P = 1) *dying, lying, tying* → DIE, LIE, TIE.
24	-ying →	-y	(P > 1) *(re)paying, certifying* → PAY, CERTIFY.
25	-zing →	-ze	*gazing, squeezing, organizing* → GAZE, SQUEEZE, ORGANIZE.
26	-uVCing →	-uVCe	*persuading, guiding, squaring, acquiring, insinuating, quoting* → PERSUADE, GUIDE, SQUARE, ACQUIRE, INSINUATE, QUOTE.

| 27 | (-)CVCing → | (-)CVCe | *masquerading, wading, preceding, (jack-)knifing, assuming, indicating* → MASQUERADE, WADE, PRECEDE, KNIFE, ASSUME, INDICATE. |
| 28 | -ing → | - | *labouring, eating, sweating, floating, fighting* → LABOUR, EAT, SWEAT, FLOAT, FIGHT. |

-- *S (⇒ see Table 2) --

1	(-)men →	(-)man	*chairmen, herdsmen, Scotsmen, Aldermen* → CHAIRMAN, HERDSMAN, SCOTSMAN, ALDERMAN.
2	-ches →	-ch	*branches, marches, Churches* → BRANCH, MARCH, CHURCH.
3	-shes →	-sh	*ashes, wishes* → ASH, WISH.
4	-ies →	-y	(P > 1) *delicacies, tragedies, Burgundies, Universities, eighteen-twenties* → DELICACY, TRAGEDY, BURGUNDY, UNIVERSITY, EIGHTEEN-TWENTY (not *lies, pies, ties*).
5	-sses →	-ss	*basses, successes, Misses* → BASS, SUCCESS, MISS.
6	-xes →	-x	*Fairfaxes, boxes* → FAIRFAX, BOX.
7	-'s →	-	*1930's, 6's, R101's, B's, M.P.'s, so-and-so's, Jones's* → 1930, 6, R101, B, M.P., SO-AND-SO, JONES.
8	-s →	-	*ideas, lbs, hundreds, Lords, Palaces, ones, Greeks, others, Sundays, Kennedys* → IDEA, LB, HUNDRED, LORD, PALACE, ONE, GREEK, OTHER, SUNDAY, KENNEDY.

-- *$ (⇒ see Table 2) --

| 1 | -s' → | -s | *Lucas', Charles', Ellis', Chambers'* → LUCAS, CHARLES, ELLIS, CHAMBERS. |
| 2 | -'s → | - | *Sylvia's, one's, else's, Church's, Turk's, son's, witness's, tonight's, another's, City's* → SYLVIA, ONE, ELSE, CHURCH, TURK, SON, WITNESS, TONIGHT, ANOTHER, CITY. |

-- *S$ (⇒ see Table 2) --

1	-ches' →	-ch	*witches'* → WITCH.
2	-ies' →	-y	(P > 1) *ladies', libraries', Universities'* → LADY, LIBRARY, UNIVERSITY.
3	-s' →	-	*Americans', Caxtons', others', Speakers'* → AMERICAN, CAXTON, OTHER, SPEAKER.
4	(-)men's →	(-)man	*foremen's, women's, sportsmen's* → FOREMAN, WOMAN, SPORTSMAN.

Table 2

Cover Symbol	Word Tag	Lemma Tag
*S =	APS	→ post-det.
	CDS	→ card. num.
	CD1S	→ card. num./noun
	NNPS	→ cap. noun
	NNS	→ noun
	NNUS	→ meas. noun
	NPLS	→ loc. noun
	NPS	→ prop. noun
	NPTS	→ titl. noun
	NRS	→ adv. noun
*$ =	AP$	→ post-det.
	CD$	→ card. num.
	CD1$	→ card. num./noun
	DT$	→ det.
	NN$	→ noun
	NNP$	→ cap. noun
	NNU$	→ meas. noun
	NP$	→ prop. noun
	NPL$	→ loc. noun
	NPT$	→ titl. noun
	NR$	→ adv. noun
	OD$	→ ord. num.
	PN$	→ nom. pro.
	RB$	→ adverb
*S$=	APS$	→ post-det.
	NNPS$	→ cap. noun
	NNS$	→ noun
	NNUS$	→ meas. noun
	NPLS$	→ loc. noun
	NPS$	→ prop. noun
	NPTS$	→ titl. noun
	NRS$	→ adv. noun

Table 3

VBZ ⇒ verb

(3) *belies.*

(6) *kicks-off, teacheth, dieth, maketh, smelleth, tilleth, cometh, containeth, runneth, witnesseth, sitteth, giveth, reneweth, saith, goes, foregoes, undergoes, echoes, focuses, buzzes.*

VBD or VBN ⇒ verb

(3) *subpoenaed, echoed, re-echoed, haloed, wooed, vetoed, kayoed.*

(5 or 7) *recalled, dialled, installed, refilled, remilled.*

Note: *appalled, enthralled, fulfilled, distilled, instilled, enrolled* will end in *-l* after suffix stripping while *-ll* is a possible spelling variant (cf. similar *-lling* forms).

(6) *biassed, canvassed, focussed.*
(7) *ebbed, added, egged, (programmed), erred, burred, purred, (netted), silhouetted, gazetted, boycotted, (whizzed).*
(9) *banged, ganged, twanged, longed, belonged, prolonged, thronged, bunged.*
(10) *bequeathed, smoothed, frothed, betrothed, mouthed.*
(11) *beguiled.*
(14) *(led), misled, bled, fled.*
(15) *contravened, convened, intervened.*
(16) *condoned, honed, phoned, telephoned, postponed, droned, toned, intoned, stoned.*
(17) *interfered, adhered, persevered.*
(18) *biased, focused.*
(20) *cited, recited, excited, ignited, united, reunited, sited, invited.*
(22) *(wed), awed, overawed, owed.*
(23) *axed.*
(24) *dyed, eyed.*
(27) *blossomed, accustomed, developed, redeveloped, enveloped, galloped, tailored, mirrored, censored, sponsored, monitored, motored, murmured, combated, budgeted, fidgeted, ricocheted, bracketed, rocketed, blanketed, marketed, carpeted, interpreted, misinterpreted, closeted, riveted.*

.
.
.

Sources of material

Roger Garside

1. Corpora

The untagged Brown Corpus of written American English and the untagged and tagged LOB (Lancaster-Oslo/Bergen) Corpus of written British English which are described in this book are available in various formats *for academic research purposes only* from:

> International Computer Archive of Modern English (ICAME),
> The Norwegian Computing Centre for the Humanities,
> P.O. Box 53,
> N-5014 Bergen-University,
> Norway

Information about the texts used, the encoding systems for orthographic information, and the tags assigned is available for the three corpus versions respectively in Francis and Kučera (1964), Johansson *et al.* (1978), and Johansson (1986b). ICAME also makes available the London–Lund Corpus of British spoken English, and various KWIC concordances for the corpora on microfiche. It publishes a periodical, *ICAME Journal*, on developments in corpus linguistics. For further information, write to the above address.

2. Software

The only software currently available is the CLAWS1 tagging system described in Chapters 3 and 4. This suite of programs is written in Pascal and is available in its original version for the ICL 2900 series running the VME operating system, in a version (courtesy Tom Horton and Eric Wilson, Department of Computer Science, University of Edinburgh) for DEC VAX computers running the VMS operating system, and in a Unix version currently running on a Sun workstation. The modules currently available, either separately or together, are:

(a)   PREEDIT: This program takes an input running text in the format of the LOB Corpus (see pp. 21–40 of Johansson *et al*. 1978) and converts it into a format more suitable for further processing by the remaining programs in the suite.

(b)   WORDTAG: This program, described in detail in Chapter 3, assigns a set of one or more candidate tags to each word in a text, at this stage not using information about the context of a word. The program makes use of two files of data, which may be of interest in their own right: a lexicon SORTEDWORDLIST2 of 7200 words and their associated tags, and a suffixlist SUFFIXLIST2 of 720 word-endings and their associated tags.

(c)   IDIOMTAG: This program, described in detail in Chapter 9, searches a text for various patterns of words and tags, in order to adjust the tags assigned by the WORDTAG program. The program makes use of a file IDIOMLIST of patterns and actions to take if they are recognized.

(d)   CHAINPROBS: This program, described in detail in Chapter 4, makes use of contextual information about tag sequences in order to disambiguate the words of a text. It makes use of a matrix LOBSUCCRES3 of tagpair probabilities, and a list ORDER2PROBS of tag-triples and their scaling factors.

(e)   LOBFORMAT: This is a reformating program which can act on manual post-editing information if present, and can generate either a "vertical" or a "rehorizontalized" (running text) version (or both) of a text processed by the rest of the CLAWS1 suite.

There are a number of subsidiary files (CHARCODINGS, INPUTOUTPUT, TAGCONVERT, TAGTYPE, TAGINIT) which are incorporated in the above programs at compile-time; the last two encapsulate the "LOB" tagset used by CLAWS1, as described in Appendix B. There is also a file DOCLIST which gives further information about the suite of programs.

These programs and data files are available *for academic research purposes only* (a) as source listings for study, or (b) in machine-readable source form *on a tape supplied by the requester*. Currently the programs can be supplied only in 1600bpi ANSI format as produced by the DEC VMS "copy" command, or in 1600bpi Unix "tar" format. Further details are available from:

> Unit for Computer Research on the English Language (UCREL),
> Bowland College,
> University of Lancaster,
> Bailrigg,
> Lancaster LA1 4YT
> Telephone (0524) 65201 extension 325, 4120, or 4131

Warning: UCREL does not have the resources to make available these programs in a supported form. They are made available as they were constructed during the course of the research described earlier in the book, with minimal documentation, and they are supplied in the expectation that those who obtained them will be prepared to put in a certain amount of effort to get them running on their system.

Alternative grammatical coding systems

Geoffrey Sampson

This appendix offers a brief comparative survey of the various systems of classifying and tagging English words used by different groups working with the LOB and Brown Corpora. By now quite a complex range of alternative conventions have been evolved.

The earliest set of wordtags were those used by workers on the Brown Corpus (see Francis 1980; Francis and Kučera 1982). Most other tagsets in current use have been evolved directly or indirectly from the Brown tagset. The Brown tagset includes 87 simple wordtags, but the number of available codings is larger than this because a minority of words are given compound tags. The tagged Brown Corpus uses 179 different (simple and compound) wordtags, and further compounds are in principle possible.

The simple wordtags stand either for classes of grammatically-similar words (e.g. NN for singular common noun) or for individual words which are grammatically unique (e.g. DOZ for *does*, with its special auxiliary function); six of the 87 tags stand for punctuation marks.

Compounding is used in the Brown system for two purposes. First, words including enclitics are given pairs of tags representing the uncontracted words from which they derive:

> *won't* MD∗   cf. *will not*   MD∗
> *he's* PPS+BEZ   cf. *he is*   PPS BEZ

The Germanic genitive (apostrophe-s) suffix is regarded as an enclitic when it occurs with stems other than nouns and pronouns, as in *Alexander the Great's*: since *Great* is tagged JJ (adjective), *Great's* is tagged JJ$, but JJ$ is not counted as one of the 87 simple tags. The second type of compounding involves the tags FW- (foreign word), -HL (word in headline), -NC (cited word), -TL (word in title, e.g. of a book); these four tags are never used independently as simple tags, but are affixed to the ordinary tag for words to which they apply. Thus a large number of combinations are possible. To quote an extreme case, the word *des* occurring in a French book title is tagged FW-IN+AT-TL, since *des* meaning "of the" represents a portmanteau of preposition (IN) and article (AT), and it is a foreign word and occurs in a title.

The groups in Britain and Norway who worked on the LOB Corpus decided not to use compound wordtags; but they defined a number of additional simple tags in order to mark grammatical distinctions ignored by the Brown system. For most of the period during which research on automatic analysis of the LOB Corpus has been carried out, the tagset used has been one comprising 132 wordtags. (If one includes the "sentence-initial marker" which is inserted at the beginning of each sentence in the LOB Corpus, this figure becomes 133; but the sentence-initial marker is not counted as a wordtag here, since it corresponds to no item occurring in ordinary written English.) Since this tagset has been used jointly by both British and Norwegian researchers, it is appropriately named the "LOB tagset". (Recently two minor variants of the LOB tagset have been evolved, which will be referred to by the affiliation of their developers as the "Oslo" and "Leeds" tagsets.)

The LOB tagset avoids compound tags for words which include enclitics by treating enclitics as separate words: thus *won't* appears in the LOB Corpus as *will >n't* and is tagged MD XNOT. The Germanic genitive suffix is not split off in this way; any word including this suffix is assigned a tag ending in the character $, and all such tags are listed in the tagset like any other tag. Words are not given special tags because they occur in headlines or titles. (In the "vertical" format of the Corpus, the record for a word playing one of these roles is flagged accordingly, but the flag does not appear in the wordtag field.) Most cited words are given their normal tag, and in the few cases where this is inappropriate they are assigned NC as a complete tag. Foreign words are either tagged as English words (if they are used as such in the text) or else given the tag &FW irrespective of their grammatical status in their own language.

Most of the extra tags in the LOB tagset were introduced to handle the following: capitalized words which derive from, but are not themselves, proper names (e.g. *Londoner*); person and number in the system of personal pronouns; and "grammatical idioms" (cf. Ch. 9), i.e. sequences of two or more orthographic words which function grammatically as units, such as *each other* which is effectively a reflexive pronoun. Brown tags *each other* with the tags that the respective words would receive in other contexts: DT AP. LOB instead uses the ditto sign to mark the unity of the sequence and tags PPLS PPLS'' (where PPLS is the tag for plural reflexive pronoun). These "sequence tags" are not listed separately in the tables below. (In the "Leeds" variant of the LOB scheme, ditto marks are replaced by numerical codes: *each other* becomes PPLS21 PPLS22.) Also, each punctuation mark is treated as a one-member word-class in the LOB system, whereas the Brown tagset groups several punctuation marks together as equivalent and ignores some others.

In preparing the tagged version of the LOB Corpus for publication, the Norwegian research group found it convenient to add four extra tags in order to distinguish relative from interrogative pronouns. Thus the "Oslo tagset" used for the published tagged Corpus (Johansson 1986b) has 136 members. On the other hand, when the UCREL group began to move on from the problem of automatic word-tagging to the larger problem of parsing, they found it necessary to introduce a few new wordtags for words having a special role with respect to higher levels of grammatical structure.

Thus, in the LOB tagset the word *for* is tagged IN like any other preposition; but the UCREL clause categories include a type of clause, coded Tf (*for-to* clause), which is introduced by this and no other preposition, so the "Leeds" tagset assigns it a special wordtag INF. As well as a few cases like this, the Leeds system also adds to the LOB tagset a "ghost" wordtag HH which is used only to derive sequence tags for infinitive-introducing phrases such as *so as*, *in order* – such sequences are tagged HH21 HH22, but no single word is tagged HH. Counting HH, the Leeds tagset comprises 137 tags.

However, the Leeds tagset was intended only as a temporary stopgap. In the longer term it seemed desirable to develop a larger tagset having two virtues lacking in all the sets discussed so far. First, the new tagset ought to come much closer to the ideal of providing distinct codings for all classes of words having distinct grammatical behaviour. The Leeds tagset gave *for* a special tag because there is an entire grammatical category which is defined by reference to this particular word; but none of the tagsets quoted so far take note, for instance, of the fact that a noun denoting a period of time will often head a phrase functioning adverbially (*Last night we discussed ...*), or that a noun denoting an organization can occur in the singular with a plural verb (*The committee have resolved ...*). In the new "Lancaster" tagset, special classes of words such as these are given distinct tags of their own. Secondly, for purposes of automatic processing it is unfortunate that none of the tagsets discussed so far is very systematic in the way that tags are built up from individual characters; the tags are designed to have mnemonic value for humans but not to be easily handled computationally. For instance, the words *have* and *do* are in most respects verbs like any other, though they also have auxiliary functions not shared by the generality of verbs tagged VB; but their tags HV, DO are entirely different from VB. Conversely, the tag DO resembles the tag DT, but DT stands for a class of words (determiners) quite different from *do*. In the Lancaster tagset, the characters in a wordtag are systematically arranged to reflect increasing differentiation from left to right: thus *do*, *have*, and (say) *eat* are tagged respectively VD0, VH0, VV0 – the first character shows that all are verbs, the next character distinguishes "special case" verbs from ordinary verbs (which repeat the preceding letter), and 0 explicitly codes for base (uninflected) form.

At the time of writing the Lancaster tagset remains open to the possibility of minor revisions. The specification of it in the table which follows is based on a draft of 1985, which provided a total of 166 tags. However, the difference between 166 and 132 understates the extent to which the Lancaster tagset makes finer distinctions than LOB. One difference between the two systems is that the Lancaster tagset treats all cases of the Germanic genitive suffix as an enclitic comparable to >*n't* or >'*ll*. Thus the Lancaster tagset needs only one wordtag, $, where LOB needs a special tag ending in the $ symbol for each type of word capable of taking the genitive suffix. If the Lancaster tagset amalgamated genitive markers with stem tags as LOB does, its membership would rise to 200 or more. Furthermore the Lancaster tagset abandons the LOB system of special tags for capitalized words; instead, typographical features are indicated by a set of diacritical marks (not specified here) representing properties such as "word-initial capital", "all capitals". Again, if these distinctions were taken into account in listing the Lancaster tags the number of them would become much larger still.

Each tagset discussed so far descends ultimately from the Brown tagset. But there is also another coding system (the "Gothenburg" system) which was developed independently by Alvar Ellegård in connexion with his grammatical research on the Brown Corpus (Ellegård 1978). Ellegård directed a project under which 64 of the 500 texts in the Brown Corpus, i.e. about 128 000 words, were manually parsed (Ellegård's "treebank" is thus considerably larger than the UCREL database discussed in Chapter 7); and for this purpose he defined his own parsing scheme, which includes a set of wordtags. The Gothenburg tags combine letters representing stem-type with letters representing inflexions (e.g. *themselves* is RLS, where R stands for "personal pronoun", L for "reflexive", and S for "plural"); Ellegård lists the individual letters rather than the permissible combinations, so that it is not a trivial task to count the number of possible wordtags in his system, but there appear to be about sixty. (One factor keeping this number low by comparison with Brown and its descendants is that Ellegård's system ignores all punctuation marks.)

Most of the research reported in this book uses the LOB tagset or the only slightly different Leeds variant. However, other corpus-related publications have used either the Brown tags (in the case of work on the Brown Corpus) or the Oslo tags (in the case of the tagged version of the LOB Corpus and the KWIC concordance to it). The up-to-date version of the UCREL wordtagging system, CLAWS2, has been designed to yield tags from the Lancaster set (so that wordtags quoted in Chapter 8 are taken from this set); and ultimately it seems clear that the Lancaster tagset will be preferable to the earlier alternatives. However, so much experience and research material has by now been developed using the older tagsets that they are likely to remain in use for some time to come.

Apart from the various sets of wordtags used by researchers working with the Brown and LOB Corpora, several other coding systems exist for computer-oriented grammatical classification of words of written English. The systems used by the TOSCA project led by Jan Aarts at Nijmegen (see e.g. Aarts and van den Heuvel 1984) and the ASCOT project led by Willem Meijs at Amsterdam (e.g. Akkerman *et al.* 1985), and the system incorporated in Roger Mitton's computerized version of the *Oxford Advanced Learner's Dictionary of Current English* (Mitton 1986), are worthy of mention here but cannot be discussed in detail.

One other tagging system which does deserve extended illustration, however, is that developed by the group led by Jan Svartvik at Lund for tagging the London–Lund Corpus of Spoken English (see e.g. Svartvik and Eeg-Olofsson 1982). This is a highly-differentiated scheme, comparable to the Lancaster system with respect to number of tags distinguished; but it manifests characteristic differences from all of the tagsets discussed so far, reflecting distinctive characteristics of spoken as opposed to written language. Since orthographic word-boundaries have no relevance to speech, the Lund scheme quite frequently treats as single units sequences which are written as two or more words; some of these (e.g. *for example*) are treated as "idioms" in the LOB or Lancaster systems, but many (e.g. *I'm sorry, any of*) are not. More significantly, where the schemes discussed earlier all include a single, low-frequency category of "interjections", the Lund system distinguishes many types of "discourse item": greetings (*goodbye*), "softeners" (*I mean*), expletives (*fuck off*), "hesitators" (*now*), and various others. On the other hand the Lund system makes relatively few distinctions among types of noun. (Naturally it totally ignores punctuation.)

Lund wordtags are hierarchically structured, consisting of a capital representing main grammatical category (A = adverb, B = determiner-or-pronoun, etc.), a second capital or digit representing subcategory (AB = wh-type adverb, B2 = predeterminer), and three lower-case letters chosen mnemonically to stand for a sub-subcategory or a grammatically-unique item (thus B2deg = degree predeterminer, e.g. *quite*). Tags for inflected forms include an inflexion code separated from the code for the root by a plus-sign; words including enclitics receive tags constructed from the tags of the two words involved, linked by an asterisk. Thus *there's* is coded as AXei*VB+3.

The Lund tagset is explicitly regarded by its creators as permanently open to revision, depending on the uses to which it is put in practice. Our table represents the version current at June 1986, which included 197 tags.

Ideally it would be desirable to supplement this survey of alternative word-tagging conventions with a comparison of the different parsing schemes used by various research projects concerned with the computational analysis of English. Apart from the UCREL scheme described in Chapter 7, other important parsing schemes would include at least the one incorporated in Alvar Ellegård's database already referred to (a scheme which is in some ways more informative than the UCREL scheme – for instance, it includes codes for the functions as well as the forms of grammatical constituents), and the scheme used by Jan Aarts's TOSCA project. Unfortunately, published statements of these schemes give much less detail than is available for the UCREL parsing scheme; and Ellegård's scheme in particular is extremely different in kind from the UCREL scheme, having affinities with dependency analysis (whereas the UCREL parsing scheme is a pure constituent-structure system). These considerations make it impractical to include a point-by-point comparison of the various parsing schemes here.

The first of the two tables that follow incorporates the Brown, LOB, Leeds, Oslo, Gothenburg, and Lancaster tags in a single listing. In this table, wordtags from each tagset are printed bold. The tags set flush with the left margin are those of the Brown tagset (including four tags for genitive-inflected words that are regarded as compound tags within the Brown system but are treated as standard tags within the LOB tagset). An indented column of tags headed by the name of a tagset indicates that this group of tags between them roughly partition the class of words covered by the unindented (or less-indented) tag above the column. (The symbols "Br", "Go", "La", "Ls", "Os" abbreviate Brown, Gothenburg, Lancaster, Leeds, Oslo.) A sequence of two or more tags on the same line indicates that the classes of words covered by the tags within their respective tagsets are broadly the same. The abbreviation "w.i.c." means "word-initial capital".

Except where otherwise indicated, LOB tags are the same as Brown tags, and Leeds and Oslo tags are the same as LOB tags. The Gothenburg and Lancaster systems, however, include only those tags which are explicitly specified in the table. The published statement of the Gothenburg system is not sufficiently detailed to allow equivalents for tags in other systems to be determined with certainty in all cases; some of the Gothenburg tags, for instance the tag Q, seem to cover a wide range of word types, and only those equivalences which are reliable have been included here.

It should be stressed that this table can be no more than a general guide to the definitions of the various wordtags. The format can conveniently indicate only cases where groups of tags in one tagset partition the words covered by single tags in another tagset; in fact, particularly with the Lancaster tagset vis-à-vis its predecessors, words are often reallocated between tags in much more complex patterns. Even where tags are shown as equivalent, this means only that "core" examples coincide; it would be quite impossible here to identify all the ways in which boundaries between tags diverge from tagset to tagset. A full specification of the rules for applying any one of these tagsets amounts to quite a lengthy document. (Stig Johansson and the present writer plan in the near future to publish a comprehensive definition in book form of the UCREL parsing scheme, covering both hypertags and wordtags.)

The Lund tagset for spoken English is allotted a separate table of its own, since its coverage is somewhat different from that of tagsets for written English, and it contains considerable internal structure which would be concealed if its individual tags were separately inserted into the main table. We are grateful to Jan Svartvik for preparing the table of Lund tags.

Wordtags for Written English

Br
. sentence closer: . ; ? !
   LOB, La
   . full stop
   ; semi-colon
   ? question mark
   ! exclamation mark
(left bracket (round or square) ⎫
) right bracket (round or square) ⎪
, comma   ⎬ same in La
: colon   ⎭
-- LOB *- La - dash
inverted commas, ellipsis mark, formulae not tagged in Brown
   LOB, La
   ... ellipsis
   &FO formula
   LOB
   *' open inverted commas

Br

   **' close inverted commas

     La lumps open and close inverted commas together as **''**

genitive inflexion **>'s >'** tagged separately only in La, as **$**

* LOB XNOT Go G La **XX** *not,* **>***n't*

ABL pre-qualifier: *quite, rather*

ABN La **DB** pre-quantifier: *half, all*

ABX pre-quantifier and double conjunction: *both*

   La

   LE leading co-ordinator: *both* before *and*

   DB2 plural before-determiner: *both* without *and*

AP Go **Q** post-determiner: *many, much, next, former, other*

   La

   ATA after-article: *other, only*

   DA after-determiner capable of pronominal function and neutral for number: *such,*
     former, same

   DA1 singular after-determiner: *little, much*

   DA2 plural after-determiner: *few, several, many*

   DA2R comparative plural after-determiner: *fewer*

   DA2T superlative plural after-determiner: *fewest*

   DAR comparative neutral after-determiner: *more, less*

   DAT superlative neutral after-determiner: *most, least*

AP$ possessive post-determiner: *other's*

AT article: *the, a, every, no*

   Go

   T definite article: *the*

   F indefinite article: *a*

   Q quantifier: *every*

   LOB La

   AT **AT1** singular article: *a, every*

   ATI **AT** neutral article: *the, no*

BE La **VBO** *be*

   Go

   B indicative *be*

   BM imperative *be*

   BB subjunctive *be*

BED La **VBDR** *were*

   Go

   BD indicative *were*

   BDB subjunctive *were*

BEDZ Go **BD** La **VBDZ** *was*

BEG Go **BG** La **VBG** *being*

BEM Go **B** La **VBM** *am,* **>***'m*

BEN Go **BN** La **VBN** *been*

BER Go **B** La **VBR** *are,* **>***'re*

BEZ Go **B** La **VBZ** *is,* **>***'s*

Br
CC Go **Y** co-ordinating conjunction: *and, but, or, yet*
   La
   CC general co-ordinating conjunction
   CCB *but*
   CF semi-co-ordinating conjunction: *so, then, yet*
CD Go **L** cardinal numeral: *two, 6, hundred, 2.34*
   LOB
   CD general cardinal
      La
      MC cardinal: *two, 6, 2.34*
      NNO numeral noun, neutral for number agreement: *dozen, hundred*
   CD1 La **MC1** *one, 1*
   CD-CD La **MC-MC** hyphenated number: *42–3, 1770–1827*
CS Go **Z** subordinating conjunction: *if, although, as, because*
   Ls
   CS subordinating conjunction other than *as*
         La
         CS general subordinating conjunction
         CSH *the* introducing comparative clauses
         CSN *than* as conjunction
         CST *that* as conjunction
         CSW *whether* as conjunction
   CSA **CSA** *as* as conjunction
DO La **VDO** *do*
   Go
   D indicative *do*
   DM imperative *do*
DOD Go **DD** La **VDD** *did*
DOZ Go **D** La **VDZ** *does*
   (Go **D** . . . tags are for *do* as auxiliary only)
DT Go **E** La **DD1** singular determiner: *this, that, another*
DT$ possessive singular determiner: *another's*
DTI Go **Q** La **DD** neutral determiner capable of pronominal function: *any, some*
DTS Go **ES** La **DD2** plural determiner: *these, those*
DTX determiner and double conjunction: *either, neither*
   La
   LE leading co-ordinator: *either* before *or*
   DD1 singular determiner: *either* without *or*
EX Go **X** La **EX** existential *there*
FW- LOB, La **&FW** foreign word
pre-infinitive not tagged in Brown, LOB
   Ls
   HH pre-infinitive: *so as, in order*
      La
      BCS before-conjunction: *in order, even* before *that/if*
      BTO before-infinitive: *in order, so as* before *to*

Br

-HL word in headline (tagged only in Brown)

HV Go **H** La **VHO** *have*

HVD Go **HD** La **VHD** *had*, >'*d* (preterite)

HVG Go **HG** La **VHG** *having*

HVN Go **HN** La **VHN** *had* (past participle)

HVZ Go **H** La **VHZ** *has*, >'*s*

    (Go **H** . . . tags are for *have* as auxiliary only)

IN Go **P** preposition

  Ls

  IN general preposition

        La

        II general preposition

        ICS preposition-conjunction of time: *after, before, since, until*

  INF   **IF** *for* as preposition

  INO   **IO** *of*

  INW   **IW** *with, without*

JJ Go **J** adjective

  LOB

  JJ general adjective

        La

        JJ general adjective

        JA predicative adjective: *tantamount, afraid, asleep*

        JK adjective catenative: *able* in *be able to, willing* in *be willing to*

  JJB   **JB** attributive adjective: *utter, late, model* in *a model prisoner, 15-nation* in *the 15-nation NATO council*

        JNP adjective with w.i.c.: *Welsh, Keynesian*

JJS LOB **JJB** semantically superlative adjective: *main, chief, top, uppermost*

  La

  JB attributive adjective: *main, chief, top*

  JBT attributive superlative adjective: *utmost, topmost*

JJR Go **JR** comparative adjective: *older, better, stronger, upper*

  La

  JJR general comparative adjective: *older, better, stronger*

  JBR attributive comparative adjective: *upper, outer*

JJT Go **JT** La **JJT** morphologically superlative adjective: *oldest, best, strongest*

MD modal auxiliary: *can, may, would, ought*

  Go

  M present modal auxiliary: *can, may*

  MD preterite modal auxiliary: *might, would*

  La

  VM modal auxiliary: *can, may, would*

  VMK modal catenative: *ought, used*

-NC LOB **NC** cited word

  La tags cited words as normal words, except that **NC2** is used for plural cited words, as in *too many ifs and buts*

Br

NN Go **N** singular common noun: *book, girl, sheep, headquarters* governing *is*

LOB

  NN singular common noun: *book, girl, sheep*

  NNP singular common noun with w.i.c.: *Londoner, Luddite*

    La (tags covering LOB **NN+NNP**)

    NN common noun neutral for number: *sheep, cod, headquarters*

    NN1 singular common noun: *book, girl*

    NNJ organization noun neutral for number: *Company, Co., group*

    NNT1 singular temporal noun: *day, week, year*

    NNU1 singular unit of measurement: *inch, kilo*

NNU La **NNU** abbreviated unit of measurement neutral for number: *in., kg*

NPL singular locative noun with w.i.c.: *Island, Street*

    La

  NNL locative noun neutral for number: *Is.*

  NNL1 singular locative noun: *island, Street*

NPT singular titular noun with w.i.c.: *Bishop, Mrs*

    La

  NNS1 singular titular noun: *Mrs, President, Rev.*

  NNSA1 following abbrev. singular titular noun: *M.A.*

  NNSB preceding abbrev. titular noun: *Rt. Hon.*

  NNSB1 preceding abbrev. singular titular noun: *Prof.*

  ZZ letter of the alphabet, as in *it fitted to a T, if x is greater than y*

    La

  ZZ1 singular letter of the alphabet

  ZZ2 plural letter of the alphabet

NN$ Go **NX** possessive singular noun: *girl's*

LOB

  NN$ general possessive singular noun

  NNP$ possessive singular common noun with w.i.c.: *Institution's*

  CD$ possessive cardinal: *two's complement*

  CD1$ *one's*

  NNU$ possessive abbreviated neutral unit of measurement: *cwt's*

  NPL$ possessive singular locative noun with w.i.c.: *Island's*

  NPT$ possessive singular titular noun with w.i.c.: *Mayor's*

  OD$ possessive ordinal: *sixth's*

  La does not use unitary tags for apostrophe-s words, but uses **NN1$** for singular possessive nouns not containing apostrophe, e.g. *domini* in *anno domini*

NNS Go **NS** plural common noun: *books, girls, sheep, Associates, headquarters* governing *are*

LOB

  NNS plural common noun: *books, girls, sheep*

  NNPS plural common noun with w.i.c.: *Englishmen*

    La (tags covering LOB **NNS+NNPS**)

    NN2 plural common noun: *books, girls*

    NNJ2 plural organization noun: *groups, councils, unions*

    NNT2 plural temporal noun: *days, weeks, years*

Br

APS plural post-determiner: *others*

CDS plural cardinal: *threes, 3s, hundreds*

> La

> MC2 plural cardinal number: *threes, 3s*

> MF fraction neutral for number: *two-thirds*

> NNO2 plural numeral noun: *hundreds, millions*

CD1S *ones*

NNUS La NNU2 plural unit of measurement: *ins., feet*

NNLS La NNL2 plural locative noun with w.i.c.: *Islands*

NPTS plural titular noun with w.i.c.: *Presidents, Messrs*

> La

> NNS2 plural titular noun: *Presidents*

> NNSB2 preceding abbrev. plural titular noun: *Messrs*

NNS$ Go NSX possessive plural noun: *girls', children's*

LOB

NNS$ possessive plural noun

APS$ possessive plural post-determiner: *others'*

NNPS$ possessive plural common noun with w.i.c.: *Associates'*

NNUS$ possessive abbrev. plural unit of measurement: *c.c.s'*

NPLS$ possessive plural locative noun with w.i.c.: *Islands'*

NPTS$ possessive plural titular noun with w.i.c.: *Presidents'*

NRS$ possessive plural adverbial noun: *Sundays'*

NP Go C singular proper noun: *London, Naismith, October, Andes*

> La

> NP proper noun neutral for number: *Indies, Andes*

> NP1 singular proper noun: *London, Frederick, Naismith*

> NPM1 singular month noun: *October*

NP$ Go CX possessive singular proper noun: *Juliet's*

NPS Go CS plural proper noun: *Naismiths, Americas, Octobers*

> La

> NP2 plural proper noun: *Naismiths, Americas*

> NPM2 plural month noun: *Octobers*

NPS$ Go CSX possessive plural proper noun: *Naismiths'*

NR adverbial noun: *home, west, tomorrow, Sunday*

> La

> ND noun of direction: *west*

> NPD1 singular weekday noun: *Sunday*

> RT nominal adverb of time: *tomorrow*

NR$ possessive adverbial noun: *tomorrow's*

NRS plural adverbial noun: *Sundays, yesterdays*

> La NPD2 plural weekday noun: *Sundays*

OD Go K La MD ordinal numeral: *second, 2nd*

PN Go Q nominal pronoun: *anybody, everyone, nothing, none*

> La

> PN neutral nominal pronoun: *none*

> PN1 singular nominal pronoun: *anybody, everyone, nothing, one* as pronoun

Br

PN$ Go **QX** possessive nominal pronoun: *everybody's*

PP$** La **APP$ possessive personal pronoun: *my, your, our*

   Go

   RX singular possessive personal pronoun: *my*

   RSX plural possessive personal pronoun: *our*

PP$$** La **PP$ second possessive personal pronoun: *mine, yours, ours*

PPL Go **RL** singular reflexive personal pronoun: *myself, herself*

   La

   PNX1 reflexive indefinite pronoun: *oneself*

   PPX1 singular reflexive personal pronoun: *yourself, itself*

PPLS Go **RLS** La **PPX2** plural reflexive personal pronoun: *ourselves, themselves*

PPO objective personal pronoun: *me, us, him; it, you* in non-subject position

PPS 3rd singular nominative pronoun: *he, she; it* in subject position

PPSS other nominative pronoun: *I, we, they, you* in subject position

   Go classifies Brown **PPO+PPS+PPSS** words in terms of number only:

   R *I, me, you, he, him, she, her, it*

   RS *we, us, they, them*

   LOB and its descendants reclassify Brown **PPO+PPS+PPSS** words in terms of
      morphology rather than syntax:

LOB	La	
PP3A	**PPHS1**	*he, she*
PP3	**PPH1**	*it*
PP1O	**PPIO1**	*me*
PP1OS	**PPIO2**	*us*
PP3O	**PPHO1**	*him, her*
PP3OS	**PPHO2**	*them*
PP2	**PPY**	*you*
PP1A	**PPIS1**	*I*
PP1AS	**PPIS2**	*we*
PP3AS	**PPHS2**	*they*

QL La **RG** degree adverb: *very, so, too*

QLP La **RGA** post-adjectival/adverbial degree adverb: *enough, indeed*

RB Go **A** adverb: *quickly, well, understandably,* etc., *else, along* as adverb

   LOB

   RB general adverb

     La

    RR general adverb

    RA adverb after nominal head: *else, galore*

    REX apposition-introducer: *namely, e.g.*

    RL locative adverb: *alongside, forward*

   RI adverb, homograph of preposition: *before, along, by*

RB$ adverb with possessive suffix: *else's*

RBR Go **AR** comparative adverb: *better, longer, more*

   La

   RGR comparative degree adverb: *more, less*

   RRR comparative general adverb: *better, longer*

Br
RBT Go **AT** superlative adverb: *best, longest, most*
  La
  RGT superlative degree adverb: *most, least*
  RRT superlative general adverb: *best, longest*
RN nominal adverb: *here, there, now, then*
  La
  RL locative adverb: *here, there*
  RT nominal adverb of time: *now, then*
RP prepositional adverb which is also particle: *across, off, up, about*
  La
  RP prepositional adverb which is also particle
  RPK prepositional adverb catenative: *about* in *be about to*
-TL word in title (tagged only in Brown)
TO Go **U** La **TO** infinitive *to*
UH Go **I** La **UH** interjection: *hello, no*
VB La **VV0** verb, base form: *eat, request*
  Go
  V indicative verb
  VM imperative verb
VBD Go **VD** La **VVD** verb, preterite: *ate, requested*
VBG Go **VG** present participle: *eating, requesting*
  La
  VVG present participle
  VVGK present participle catenative: *going* in *be going to*
  VDG *doing*
VBN Go **VN** past participle: *eaten, requested*
  La
  VVN past participle
  VVNK past participle catenative: *bound* in *be bound to*
  VDN *done*
VBZ Go **V** La **VVZ** 3rd singular form of verb: *eats, requests*
WDT *wh-* determiner: *what, which, whatsoever, whichever*
  Os
  WDT interrogative *wh-* determiner: *what, whatever*, interrogative *which*
  WDTR relative *wh-* determiner: *which*
  La
  DDQ *wh-* determiner without *-ever*: *what, which*
  DDQV *wh-ever* determiner: *whatsoever, whichever*
WP$ possessive *wh-* pronoun: *whose*
  Os
  WP$ interrogative *whose*
  WP$R relative *whose*
  La
  DDQ$ possessive *wh-* determiner: *whose*
  PNQV$ *whosever*

Br

WPO objective *wh-* pronoun: *whom*; *who, which, that* in non-subject position

WPS nominative *wh-* pronoun: *who, whoever, which, that* in subject position

  LOB and its descendants reclassify **WPO+WPS** by morphological rather than syntactic criteria:

  WPA nominative *wh-* pronoun: *whosoever*

  WP *wh-* pronoun neutral for case: *who, that* as relative pronoun

    Os

    WP interrogative *wh-* pronoun neutral for case: *who, whoever*

    WPR relative *wh-* pronoun neutral for case: *that, who*

    La

    PNQS *wh-* pronoun without *-ever*: *who, that*

    PNQVS *wh-ever* pronoun: *whoever*

  WPO objective *wh-* pronoun: *whom, whomsoever*

    Os

    WPO interrogative objective *wh-* pronoun: *whom, whomsoever*

    WPOR relative objective *wh-* pronoun: *whom*

    La

    PNQO objective *wh-* pronoun without *-ever*: *whom*

    PNQVO objective *wh-ever* pronoun: *whomever*

WQL *wh-* degree adverb: *how, however*, in *how green, however well*

  La

  RGQ *wh-* degree adverb without *-ever*: *how*

  RGQV *wh-ever* degree adverb: *however*

WRB non-degree *wh-* adverb: *when, how* in *how did it work*

  LOB lumps **WQL** and **WRB** together as **WRB**

    La

    RRQ non-degree *wh-* adverb without *-ever*: *where, when, why, how*

    RRQV non-degree *wh-ever* adverb: *wherever, whenever, however*

  Go lumps all Brown **W…** tags together as **W**

Lund wordtags for spoken English

TAG	CAT	SUBCAT	SUBSUB or ITEM	EXAMPLE
AApro	adverb	adjunct	process	*correctly*
AAspa	adverb	adjunct	space	*outdoors*
AAtim	adverb	adjunct	time	*often*
ABman	adverb	wh-type	manner	*how*
ABrea	adverb	wh-type	reason	*why*
ABspa	adverb	wh-type	space	*where*
ABspa*VB+3	adverb	wh-type+s-form	space	*where's*
ABtim	adverb	wh-type	time	*when*
ACapp	adverb	conjunct	appositional	*for example*
ACcon	adverb	conjunct	contrastive	*by contrast*
ACinf	adverb	conjunct	inferential	*otherwise*
AClis	adverb	conjunct	listing	*in addition*
ACres	adverb	conjunct	resultive	*consequently*
ACsum	adverb	conjunct	summative	*all in all*
ACtra	adverb	conjunct	transitional	*by the way*
ADcnt	adverb	disjunct	content	*probably*
ADsty	adverb	disjunct	style	*personally*
AEels	adverb	postmodifier	*else*	
ANnot	adverb	negative	*not*	
AQapp	adverb	discourse item	appositional	*I'm sorry*
AQexp	adverb	discourse item	expletive	*fuck off*
AQgre	adverb	discourse item	greeting	*goodbye*
AQhes	adverb	discourse item	hesitator	*now*
AQneg	adverb	discourse item	negative	*no*
AQord	adverb	discourse item	order	*give over*
AQpol	adverb	discourse item	politeness	*please*
AQpos	adverb	discourse item	positive	*yes, [m]*
AQres	adverb	discourse item	response	*I see*
AQsof	adverb	discourse item	softener	*I mean*
AQtha	adverb	discourse item	thanks	*thank you*
AQwel	adverb	discourse item	*well*	
ASemp	adverb	subjunct	emphasizer	*actually*
ASfoc	adverb	subjunct	focusing	*mainly*
ASint	adverb	subjunct	intensifier	*a bit*
AXexi	adverb	existential	*there*	
AXexi*VB+3	adverb	existential	*there's*	
AXexi*VM+8	adverb	existential	*there'll*	
AXexi*VM+9	adverb	existential	*there'd*	
Blass	determiner	*of*-quantifier	assertive	*some of*
Blcar	determiner	*of*-quantifier	cardinal	*one of*

Blmul	determiner	*of*-quantifier	multal	*more of*
Blneg	determiner	*of*-quantifier	negative	*little of*
Blnon	determiner	*of*-quantifier	non-assertive	*any of*
Blpau	determiner	*of*-quantifier	paucal	*few of*
Blqua	determiner	*of*-quantifier	quantitative	*a bit of*
Bluni	determiner	*of*-quantifier	universal	*all of*
B2deg	determiner	predeterminer	degree	*quite*
B2mul	determiner	predeterminer	multal	*once*
B2pau	determiner	predeterminer	paucal	*less*
B2qua	determiner	predeterminer	quantitative	*double*
B2uni	determiner	predeterminer	universal	*all*
B3ass	determiner	central	assertive	*some*
B3def	determiner	central	definite	*the*
B3deg	determiner	central	degree	*what*
B3dem	determiner	central	demonstrative	*that*
B3ind	determiner	central	indefinite	*a, an*
B3itr	determiner	central	interrogative	*whatever*
B3mul	determiner	central	multal	*much*
B3neg	determiner	central	negative	*neither*
B3non	determiner	central	non-assertive	*any*
B3pos	determiner	central	possessive	*your*
B3qua	determiner	central	quantitative	*enough*
B3uni	determiner	central	universal	*each*
B3wh-	determiner	central	wh-type	*whichever*
B4gor	determiner	postdeterminer	general ordinal	*additional*
B4mul	determiner	postdeterminer	multal	*many*
B4neg	determiner	postdeterminer	negative	*little*
B4oth	determiner	postdeterminer	*other*-type	*another*
B3pau	determiner	postdeterminer	paucal	*few*
B4qua	determiner	postdeterminer	quantitative	*several*
BHass	pronoun	head	assertive	*some*
BHdem	pronoun	head	demonstrative	*that*
BHdem*VB+3	pronoun	head	demonstrative	*that's*
BHdem*VM+8	pronoun	head	demonstrative	*that'll*
BHgen	pronoun	head	general	*one*
BHitr	pronoun	head	interrogative	*what*
BHitr*VB+3	pronoun	head	interrogative	*who's*
BHmul	pronoun	head	multal	*many*
BHneg	pronoun	head	negative	*no one*
BHneu	pronoun	head	personal *it*	
BHneu*VB+3	pronoun	head	personal *it's*	
BHneu*VM+8	pronoun	head	personal *it'll*	
BHneu*VM+9	pronoun	head	personal *it'd*	
BHnon	pronoun	head	non-assertive	*any*
BHobj	pronoun	head	personal: obj	*me*

BHoth	pronoun	head	*other*-type	*another*
BHpau	pronoun	head	paucal	*few*
BHper	pronoun	head	personal *you*	
BHper*VB+4	pronoun	head	personal *you're*	
BHper*VH+0	pronoun	head	personal *you've*	
BHper*VM+8	pronoun	head	personal *you'll*	
BHper*VM+9	pronoun	head	personal *you'd*	
BHpos	pronoun	head	possessive	*hers*
BHqua	pronoun	head	quantitative	*enough*
BHref	pronoun	head	reflexive	*herself*
BHrep	pronoun	head	replacive	*one*
BHsub	pronoun	head	personal:subj	*I*
BHsub*VB+1	pronoun	head	personal+*'m*	*I'm*
BHsub*VB+3	pronoun	head	personal+*'s*	*he's*
BHsub*VB+4	pronoun	head	personal+*'re*	*they're*
BHsub*VH+0	pronoun	head	personal+*'ve*	*I've*
BHsub*VM+8	pronoun	head	personal+*'ll*	*I'll*
BHsub*VM+9	pronoun	head	personal+*'d*	*I'd*
BHuni	pronoun	head	universal	*all*
CAcoo	conjunction	co-ordinator	*and*	
CBcoo	conjunction	co-ordinator	*but*	
CCcon	conjunction	subordinator	condition etc.	*although*
CCexc	conjunction	subordinator	exception	*except*
CCpre	conjunction	subordinator	preference	*rather than*
CCpro	conjunction	subordinator	proportion	*as*
CCpur	conjunction	subordinator	purpose	*lest*
CCrea	conjunction	subordinator	reason	*as*
CCres	conjunction	subordinator	result	*in order that*
CCspa	conjunction	subordinator	space, place	*as far as*
CCtim	conjunction	subordinator	time	*according as*
CDnom	conjunction	subordinator	*that*	
CRcoo	conjunction	co-ordinator	*or*	
FAcar	numeral	cardinal		*eight, 8*
FBord	numeral	ordinal		*eighth, 8th*
FCnom	numeral	nominal	unmarked	*hundred, 100*
FDnom	numeral	nominal	currency etc	*£1000*
GAwhi	pronoun	relative	*which*	
GAwho	pronoun	relative	*who*	
GAwho*VB+3	pronoun	relative	*who+s*	
GAwho*VH+0	pronoun	relative	*who+'ve*	
GAwho*VM+9	pronoun	relative	*who+'d*	
GBwhm	pronoun	relative	*whom*	
GCwha	pronoun	relative	*what*	
GCwha*VB+3	pronoun	relative	*what+'s*	
GDtha	pronoun	relative	*that*	

GDtha*VB+3	pronoun	relative		*that*+'s
GDtha*VM+8	pronoun	relative		*that*+'ll
GDtha*VM+9	pronoun	relative		*that*+'d
GEwhs	pronoun	relative		genitive *whose*
JA	adjective	unmarked		*big*
JA+R	adjective	comparative		*bigger*
JA+T	adjective	superlative		*biggest*
JH	adjective as	NPhead		(the) *rich*
JL	adjective	language		(in) *Dutch*
JN	adjective	nationality		*Dutch* (books)
NC	noun	common	unmarked	*Church*
NC+2	noun	common	plural	*academics*
NC+Z	noun	common	genitive	*hill's*
NP	noun	proper	unmarked	(an) *Indian*
NP+2	noun	proper	plural	(the) *Indians*
NP+Z	noun	proper	genitive	*Churchill's*
NX	nominal	abbreviation		*BBC*
PA	preposition			*into*
TO	inf marker		*to*	
VA+0	verb	main	base	*add*
VA+0DN	verb	main	base/past/ppl	*broadcast*
VA+0N	verb	main	base/ppl form	*become*
VA+3	verb	main	s-form	*becomes*
VA+D	verb	main	past form	*became*
VA+DN	verb	main	past/ppl form	*added*
VA+G	verb	main	ing-form	*adding*
VA+N	verb	main	ppl form	*taken*
VB+0	verb	form of BE	*be*	
VB+1	verb	form of BE	*am*	
VB+3	verb	form of BE	*is*	
VB+3*ANnot	verb	form of BE	*isn't*	
VB+4	verb	form of BE	*are*	
VB+4*ANnot	verb	form of BE	*aren't*	
VB+5	verb	form of BE	*was*	
VB+5*ANnot	verb	form of BE	*wasn't*	
VB+6	verb	form of BE	*were*	
VB+6*ANnot	verb	form of BE	*weren't*	
VB+G	verb	form of BE	*being*	
VB+N	verb	form of BE	*been*	
VD+0	verb	form of DO	*do*	
VD+0*ANnot	verb	form of DO	*don't*	
VD+0*BHper	verb	form of DO	*d'you*	
VD+3	verb	form of DO	*does*	
VD+3*ANnot	verb	form of DO	*doesn't*	
VD+D	verb	form of DO	*did*	

VD+D*ANnot	verb	form of DO	*didn't*
VD+G	verb	form of DO	*doing*
VD+N	verb	form of DO	*done*
VH+0	verb	form of HAVE	*have*
VH+0*ANnot	verb	form of HAVE	*haven't*
VH+3	verb	form of HAVE	*has*
VH+3*ANnot	verb	form of HAVE	*hasn't*
VH+D	verb	form of HAVE	*had*
VH+D*ANnot	verb	form of HAVE	*hadn't*
VH+G	verb	form of modal	*having*
VM+0*ANnot	verb	form of modal	*mustn't*
VM+8*BHobj	verb	form of modal	*let's*
VM+8	verb	form of modal	*can*
VM+8*ANnot	verb	form of modal	*can't*
VM+9	verb	form of modal	*could*
VM+9*ANnot	verb	form of modal	*couldn't*
VM+9*VH+0	verb	form of modal	*should've*

VMidi	verb	modal	idiom	*had better*
VMmar	verb	modal	marginal	*dare to*
VXcat	verb	catenative		*appear to*
VXsem	verb	semi-auxiliary		(be) *able to*
XX	misc	foreign words		*en route*

References

Abbreviations:
ACL   Association for Computational Linguistics
ALLC   Association for Literary and Linguistic Computing
ICAME   International Computer Archive of Modern English
IEEE   Institute of Electrical and Electronic Engineers

Aarts, J. and T. van den Heuvel (1984)   'Linguistic and computational aspects of corpus research', in Aarts and Meijs (1984), 83–94.

Aarts, J. and W. Meijs (eds) (1984)   *Corpus linguistics: recent developments in the use of computer corpora in English language research*. Amsterdam: Rodopi.

Ackley, D. H., G. E. Hinton, and T. J. Sejnowski (1985)   'A learning algorithm for Boltzmann machines', *Cognitive Science* 9, 147–69.

Ades, T. (1981),   'Time for a purge', *Cognition* 10, 7–15.

Akkerman, E., P. Masereeuw, and W. Meijs (1985)   *Designing a computerized lexicon for linguistic purposes: ASCOT Report No. 1.* Amsterdam: Rodopi.

Alshawi, H., B. Boguraev, and E. Briscoe (1985),   'Towards a dictionary support environment for real time parsing', *Proceedings of the Second European ACL Conference*, 171–8.

Atwell, E. S. (1981)   *LOB Corpus tagging project: manual pre-edit handbook*. Departments of Computer Studies and Linguistics, University of Lancaster (unpublished).

Atwell, E. S. (1982)   *LOB Corpus tagging project: manual postedit handbook (a minigrammar of LOB Corpus English, examining the types of error commonly made during automatic (computational) analysis of ordinary written English)*. Departments of Computer Studies and Linguistics, University of Lancaster (unpublished).

Atwell, E. S. (1983)   'Constituent-likelihood grammar', *ICAME News* 7, 34–67.

Atwell, E. S. (1986)   'Beyond the micro: advanced software for research and teaching from computer science and artificial intelligence', in Leech and Candlin (1986), 167–83.

Atwell, E. S., G. N. Leech, and R. G. Garside (1984) 'Analysis of the LOB Corpus: progress and prospects', in Aarts and Meijs (1984), 41–52.

Bahl, L. R., F. Jelinek, and R. L. Mercer (1983) 'A maximum likelihood approach to continuous speech recognition', *IEEE Transactions on Pattern Analysis and Machine Intelligence* Vol. PAM1–5 (Mar. 1983), 179–90.

Baker, J. K. (1979) 'Trainable grammars for speech recognition', in D. H. Klatt and J. J. Wolf (eds), *Speech communication papers for the 97th meeting of the Acoustic Society of America*, 547–50.

Ballard, D. and C. Brown (1982) *Computer vision*. Prentice-Hall.

Bergenholtz, H. and B. Schaeder (eds) (1979) *Empirische Textwissenschaft: Aufbau und Auswertung von Text-Corpora*. Königstein: Scriptor.

Berman, C. (1982) 'A system to watch all your Ps and Qs', *Computing* 2nd Sept. 1982, 22–3.

Boyle, R., P. Dew, and R. Thomas (1986) *Computer vision: a first course.* Blackwell.

Carroll, J. B. (1971) 'Statistical analysis of the corpus', in Carroll *et al.* (1971) xxi–xli.

Carroll, J. B., P. Davies, and B. Richman (eds) (1971) *Word frequency book.* American Heritage.

Charniak, E. (1983) 'A parser with something for everyone', in King (1983), 117–50.

Cherry, L., M. Fox, L. Frase, P. Gingrich, S.Keenan, and N. Macdonald (1983) 'Computer aids for text analysis', *Bell Laboratories Records* May/June 1983, 10–16.

Cherry, L. and N. Macdonald (1983) 'The Writer's Workbench software', *Byte* Oct. 1983, 241–8.

Chodorow, M. S. and R. J. Byrd (1985) 'Extracting semantic hierarchies from a large on-line dictionary', *Proceedings of the 23rd ACL Conference*, 299–304.

Chomsky, N. (1957) *Syntactic structures*. Mouton.

Cole, R. A. (ed) (1980) *Perception and production of fluent speech*. Erlbaum.

Collins COBUILD English Language Dictionary (1987). Collins.

Cravero, M., L. Fissore, R. Pieraccini, and C. Scagliola (1984) 'Syntax driven recognition of connected words by Markov models', in *Proceedings, 1984 IEEE International Conference on Acoustics, Speech and Signal Processing.*

Damerau, F. (1964) 'A technique for computer detection and correction of spelling errors', *Communications of the Association for Computing Machinery* 7, 171–6.

Derouault, A.-M. and B. Mérialdo (1984) 'Language modeling at the syntactic level, in *Proceedings of the Seventh International Conference on Pattern Recognition.*

Eeg-Olofsson M. and J. Svartvik (1984) 'Four-level tagging of spoken English', in Aarts and Meijs (1984), 53–64.

Ellegård, A. (1978)   *The syntactic structure of English texts: a computer-based study of four kinds of text in the Brown University Corpus.* Gothenburg Studies in English, 43.

Engels, L. K., B. Van Beckhoven, T. Leenders, and I. Brasseur (1981)   *Leuven English teaching vocabulary-list.* Leuven: Acco.

Erman, L. D. and V. R. Lesser (1980)   'The Hearsay-II speech understanding system: a tutorial', in Lea (1980), 361–81.

Fallside, F. and W. A. Woods (eds) (1985)   *Computer speech processing.* Prentice-Hall International.

Fodor, J. A., T. G. Bever, and M. F. Garrett (1974)   *The psychology of language.* McGraw-Hill.

Francis, W. N. (1979)   'Problems of assembling and computerizing large corpora', in Bergenholtz and Schaeder (1979), 110–23.

Francis, W N. (1980)   'A tagged corpus – problems and prospects', in S. Greenbaum, G. Leech, and J. Svartvik (eds) *Studies in English Linguistics – for Randolph Quirk.* Longman, 192–209.

Francis, W N. and H. Kučera (1964; revised 1971 and 1979)   *Manual of information to accompany a standard corpus of present-day edited American English, for use with digital computers.* Providence, R. I.: Department of Linguistics, Brown University.

Francis, W. N. and H. Kučera (1982)   *Frequency analysis of English usage: lexicon and grammar.* Houghton Mifflin.

Frazier, L. (1985) 'Syntactic complexity', in D. R. Dowty, L. Karttunen, and A. M. Zwicky (eds)   *Natural language parsing: psychological, computational, and theoretical perspectives.* Cambridge University Press, 129–89.

Fujisaki, T. (1984)   'A stochastic approach to sentence parsing', in *Proceedings of the 10th International Conference on Computational Linguistics and the 22nd Annual Meeting of the ACL,* 16–19.

Geens, D., L. K. Engels, and W. Martin (1975)   *Leuven Drama Corpus and frequency list.* Institute for Applied Linguistics, Catholic University of Leuven.

Greene, B. B. and G. M. Rubin (1971)   *Automatic grammatical tagging of English.* Providence, R. I.: Department of Linguistics, Brown University.

Heidorn, G. E., K. Jensen, L. A. Miller, R. J. Byrd, and M. S. Chodorow (1982)   'The EPISTLE text-critiquing system', *IBM Systems Journal* 21.3, 305–26.

Hockey, S. and I. Marriott (1980)   *The Oxford Concordance Program, Version 1.0, user's manual.* Oxford University Computing Service.

Hofland, K. and S. Johansson (1982)   *Word frequencies in British and American English.* Bergen: Norwegian Computing Centre for the Humanities; London: Longman.

Hornby, A. S. with A. P. Cowie (eds) (1974)   *Oxford Advanced Learner's Dictionary of Current English.* 3rd edition. Oxford University Press.

Householder, F. W. (1952) Review of Z. S. Harris, 'Methods in structural linguistics', *International Journal of American Linguistics* 18, 260–8.

Hudson, R. A. (1984) *Word grammar*. Blackwell.

Jelinek, F. (1986) 'Self-organized language modeling for speech recognition', Continuous Speech Recognition Group, IBM Thomas J. Watson Research Center (unpublished).

Jensen, K. and G. E. Heidorn (1982) 'The fitted parse: 100% parsing capability in a syntactic grammar of English'. Computer Science Research Report RC9729 (#42958), IBM Research Division (San José).

Johansson, S. (ed) (1982) *Computer corpora in English language research*. Bergen: Norwegian Computing Centre for the Humanities.

Johansson, S. (1986a) 'ICAME Bibliography', *ICAME News* 10, 62–79.

Johansson, S. (1986b) *The tagged LOB Corpus: users' manual*. Bergen: Norwegian Computing Centre for the Humanities.

Johansson, S., G. N. Leech, and H. Goodluck (1978) *Manual of information to accompany the Lancaster–Oslo/Bergen Corpus of British English, for use with digital computers*. Department of English, University of Oslo.

Johansson, S. and M.-C. Jahr (1982) 'Grammatical tagging of the LOB Corpus: predicting word class from word endings', in Johansson (1982), 118–46.

Johnson, T. (1985) *Natural language computing: the commercial applications*. London: Ovum.

King, M. (ed) (1983) *Parsing natural language*. Academic Press.

King, M. (ed) (1986) *Machine translation: the state of the art*. Edinburgh University Press.

Kirkpatrick, S., C. D. Gelatt, and M. P. Vecchi (1983) 'Optimization by simulated annealing', *Science* 220, 671–80.

Knowles, G. (in preparation) 'The automatic accentuation of English texts.'

Kučera, H. (1985) 'The analysis of the English verbal group', paper presented to the *ICAME sixth international conference on English language research on computerised corpora, Lund* (unpublished).

Kučera, H. and W. N. Francis (1967) *Computational analysis of present-day American English*. Providence, R. I.: Brown University Press.

Kuhn, T. S. (1962) *The structure of scientific revolutions*. (2nd edition enlarged, 1970.) Chicago University Press.

Lawrence, Lita J. (1984) 'Tagging errors in the LOB Corpus', B. A. project report, Dept. of Computer Studies, Lancaster University.

Lea, W. A. (ed) (1980) *Trends in speech recognition*. Prentice-Hall.

Leech, G. and C. N. Candlin (eds) (1986) *Computers in English language teaching and research*. Longman.

Leech, G., R. Garside, and E. S. Atwell (1983a) 'The automatic grammatical tagging of the LOB Corpus' *ICAME News* 7, 13–33.

Leech, G., R. Garside, and E. S. Atwell (1983b)   'Recent developments in the use of computer corpora in English language research', *Transactions of the Philological Society*, 23–40.

Lowerre, B. and R. Reddy (1980)   'The Harpy speech understanding system', in Lea (1980), 340–60.

Macdonald, N. H. (1983)   'The UNIX Writer's Workbench software: rationale and design', *Bell Systems Technical Journal* 62.6, 1891–1908.

Marshall, I. (1983)   'Choice of grammatical word-class without global syntactic analysis: tagging words in the LOB Corpus', *Computers and the Humanities* 17, 139–50.

Marslen-Wilson, W. D. (1985)   'Aspects of human speech understanding', in Fallside and Woods (1985), 383–404.

Meijs, W. (ed) (1987)   *Corpus Linguistics and beyond: Proceedings of the Seventh International Conference on English Language Research on Computerized Corpora.* Amsterdam: Rodopi.

Mitton, R. (1986)   *A description of the files CUV0ALD.DAT and CUV2.DAT*, available from the Oxford Text Archive, Oxford University Computing Centre.

de Mori, R. (1983)   *Computer models of speech using fuzzy algorithms*. Plenum Press.

Newell, A. N. (1980)   'Harpy, production systems, and human cognition', in Cole (1980).

O'Connor, J. D., and G. F. Arnold (1973)   *Intonation of colloquial English*. Longman.

Oxford University Computing Service (1983)   *Text Archive*. Document available from O.U.C.S., 13 Banbury Road, Oxford OX2 6NN.

Pain, H. (1981)   'A computer aid for spelling error classification in remedial teaching', in Tagg, D. (ed) *Computers in education: proceedings of the IFIP 3rd World conference on computers in education*. North-Holland.

Peterson, J. (1980)   'Computer programs for detecting and correcting spelling errors', *Communications of the Association for Computing Machinery* 23, 12, 676–87.

Pierce, J. R. (1969)   'Whither speech recognition?' *Journal of the Acoustical Society of America* 46, 1049–51.

Pollock, J. (1982)   'Spelling error detection and correction by computer: some notes and a bibliography', *Journal of Documentation* 38.4, 282–91.

Procter, P. (ed-in-chief) (1978)   *Longman Dictionary of Contemporary English*. Longman.

Quirk, R. (1960)   'Towards a description of English usage', *Transactions of the Philological Society*, 40–61.

Quirk, R. and J. Svartvik (1979)   'A corpus of modern English', in Bergenholtz and Schaeder (1979), 204–18.

Renouf, A. (1984) 'Corpus development at Birmingham University', in Aarts and Meijs (1984), 3–39.

Sager, N. (1981) *Natural language information processing.* Addison-Wesley.

Sampson, G. R. (1986a) 'A stochastic approach to parsing', in *Proceedings of the 11th International Conference on Computational Linguistics* (*COLING '86*), Bonn, 151–5.

Sampson, G. R. (1986b) 'MT: a nonconformist's view of the state of the art', in King (1986).

Sampson, G. R. (1987) 'Evidence against the "grammatical"/"ungrammatical" distinction', in Meijs (1987), 219–26.

Sampson, G. R. (forthcoming) 'Simulated annealing as a parsing technique'. To appear in N. Sharkey, ed., *Advances in cognition II.* Ablex.

Sapir, E. (1921) *Language.* Harcourt, Brace & World.

Selman, B. (1985) 'Rule-based processing in a connectionist system for natural language understanding'. *Technical Report CSRI-168*, Computer Systems Research Institute, University of Toronto.

Sinclair, J. (1982) 'Reflections on computer corpora in English language research', in Johansson (1982), 1–6.

Sinclair, J. (1986) 'Basic computer processing of long texts', in Leech and Candlin (1986), 184–203.

Sinclair, J., S. Jones, and R. Daley (1970) *English lexical studies.* Report to OSTI on project C/LP/08. Department of English, University of Birmingham.

Smith, A. R., J. N. Deneberg, T. B. Slack, C. C. Tan, and R. E. Wohlford (1985) 'Application of a sequential pattern learning system to connected speech recognition', in *Proceedings, 1985 IEEE International Conference on Acoustics, Speech and Signal Processing.*

Sparck Jones, K. and Y. A. Wilks (eds) (1983) *Automatic natural language parsing.* Ellis Horwood.

Steedman, M. (1983) 'Natural and unnatural language processing', in Sparck Jones and Wilks (1983), 132–40.

Suppes, P. (1970) 'Probabilistic grammars for natural languages', *Synthese* 22, 95–116.

Svartvik, J. and M. Eeg-Olofsson (1982) 'Tagging the London-Lund Corpus of Spoken English', in Johansson (1982), 85–109.

Svartvik, J., M. Eeg-Olofsson, O. Forsheden, B. Oreström, and C. Thavenius (1982) *Survey of Spoken English: report on research 1975–81.* Lund Studies in English, 63. Lund: CWK Gleerup.

Svartvik, J. and R. Quirk (1980) *A corpus of English conversation.* Lund Studies in English 56. Lund: CWK Gleerup.

Thouin, B. (1982) 'The METEO system', in V. Lawson (ed) (1982) *Practical experience of machine translation*, Amsterdam: North Holland, 39–44.

Webster's Seventh New Collegiate Dictionary (1963). G. & C. Merriam.

Weischedel, R. M. and N. K. Sondheimer (1983) 'Meta-rules as a basis for processing ill-formed output', *American Journal of Computational Linguistics* **9**, 161–77.

Wells, R. S. (1947) 'Immediate constituents', *Language* **23**, 81–117.

Winograd, T. (1983) *Language as a cognitive process, Vol. 1: Syntax.* Addison-Wesley.

Woods, W. A. (1977) 'Lunar rocks in natural English: exploration in natural language question answering', in A. Zampolli (ed) *Linguistic structures processing.* North-Holland.

Yannakoudakis, E. J. and D. Fawthrop (1983a) 'The rules of spelling errors', *Information Processing and Management* **19**.2, 87–99.

Yannakoudakis, E. J. and D. Fawthrop (1983b) 'An intelligent spelling error detector', *Information Processing and Management* **19**.2, 101–108.

Index

Note: bold characters indicate main entries.

abbreviations, **xi–xiii**, 11, 23, 33, 34, 36, 97, 99, 100, 102, 104–8
absolute rules, 22
accent, 147
acoustic analysis, 11
acoustic signals, 29
acronyms, xiii
additive probability *see under* probabilities
AI *see* artifical intelligence
ambiguity, 21, 26, 27, 39, 43, 48, 51, 53, 56, 99, 106, 112, 117, 144
Amsterdam, University of, 10, 168
a priori, 29
applied language studies, 1
ARPA (Advanced Research Projects Agency) Speech Understanding Project, 29
artificial intelligence (AI), xiii, 1–3, 16, 22, 24, 26, 120n
augmented transition networks (ATNs), 18–19
authentic language, 16, 18, 22–23, 25, 26, 28, 82, 87, 92, 94, 149
automatic language-processing, 20, 28

Baker's algorithm, 62–63
behaviourism, 2
Bergen, University of, x, 9, 30, 36, 40
Birmingham Collection of English Text, 6
Birmingham, University of, 24, 27
Boltzmann machines, 24
bond, constituent-likelihood, 122, 124
bonding, degree of, 61
brackets, 68, 69, 73; *see also* hyperbrackets
Brown, University of, 8–9
Brown Corpus, vii, x, xiii, 4–10, 30, 32, 35, 39, 42, 45, 53, 90, 110, 163, 165, 168
Brown tagging system, 30–31, 34, 58, 70

capitalization, 34, 97, **101–2**, 106
Carnegie-Mellon University, vii, 29
case-law, 90–94
CHAINPROBS, 33, 35, **39–41**, 42, 45, **47–53, 55–56**, 57, 62, 66, 103, 107, 110–12, 117–18, 125–26, 128–30, 164
character sets, xii, 98, 104
Chomsky, N., 24–25, 62, 138
Chomsky normal form, 62
CLAWS, viii, x, xiii, 20, 26, 27, 30–31, 33, 34, 42, 44, 47, 48, 59, 60–62, 66–67, 94, 97, 108, 120n, 121–22, 126, 129–30, 135–38
CLAWS1, xiii, 9, 10, 30–31, 34, 40, 49, 53, 55, 56, 66–68, 97, 99–103, 105, 106, 110, 111, 114, 115, 118, 124, 125, 128, 131, 163–64
CLAWS2, viii, xiii, 10, 30, 34, 40, 97, **103–9**, 118
clitics, 147; *see also* enclitics *and* contracted forms
co-ordination, 80, 86, 89
cognitive approach, 23–24, 26–29
cognitive psychology, 2, 16
cognitive science, 1
cohort, 122–24
collocation, 15, 27, 123, 133, 147
combinatorial explosion, 64
commercial contexts, 5, 23–24
competence *see* linguistic competence
competence/performance distinction, 27–28
compound coding symbols, 98, 99
compound tags, 165–66, 169
computational linguistics (CL), xiii, 1, 11, 16–18, 20, 23–24, 27–29, 44, 60, 96

computer corpora, vii, 5
computer science, 1
concordance, xiii, 9, 150, 163, 168
constituent structure, 57, 92
constituent-likelihood, 22, 26, 64, 120n,
    121, 138
constituent-likelihood grammar, 21, **57–65**,
    66, 121; *see also* probabilistic grammar
context frame rules, 43–44, 45, 110
contracted forms, 31, 34, 67, 100, 105,
    106, 139; *see also* enclitics
corpus of spoken English, ix, 140
corpus-based approach, 1–4, 6, 10–11, 14
correlative construction, 94
cover symbols, 70–71, 74, 77, 80, 156

data-driven techniques, 24
databanks, 15
databases *see* linguistic databases *and*
    treebank
daughter sequences, 21–22
declarative language, 23
deductive logic, 16
dependency, long-distance, 62
designator symbols, 98, 104
dictionary, 15, 34, 35, 59, 123, 124, 133,
    149, 152
disambiguation, 8–10, 13, 33, 39, 40,
    42–43, 45–46, 48, 53–56, 60, 71,
    110, 117, 153
distributional lexicon, ix, 14–15, **149–62**
ditto-tag, 31, 40, 53, 68, 111, **112–13**,
    114, 116, 117
domain of discourse, 3, 16
domain-dependent preferences, 123
dynamic programming, 62

ellipsis, xii
empirical approach, 4, **21–24**, 26
enclitics, xii, 83, 101, 106, 111, 165–67;
    see also contracted forms
endocentric constructions, 86
English grammar, 25, 27–28, 85
English language, 1, 3
error corpus, 129, **133–35**, 136
error detection, ix, x, **120–38**
error-tags, 124–29
errors
    spelling, ix, 13, 135
    tagging, 41, 51, 53–55, 59, 111
    typing, 120, 135

evaluation procedure, 12
evolutionary model, 10
extra-linguistic considerations, 26

feedback, 10, 12, 94
figure of merit, 74–76
finite-state grammar, 62
Francis, W.N., vii, x, 4, 7, 8, 9, 149,
    153, 157, 163, 165
frequencies, 2, 22, 150
    relative, 20–21
    word-frequency lists, 8–9
frequency analysis of corpora, 149
full stop, 11, 97–100, 102, 105–8
function words, 35, 64

Generalized Phrase-Structure Grammar
    (GPSG), 18, 19
generative grammars, 18–20, 25, 57
generative linguistics, 87
genitive forms, 101, 166
genitive markers, 37, 106, 165–67, 169
genitive phrases, 80
Gill corpus, 136
"God's truth", 95, 96
"grammatical"/"ungrammatical" distinction,
    22, 121
grammatical analysis, 6, 11, 145; *see also*
    parsing
grammatical categories, 88–90
grammatical class, 30; *see also* word class
grammatical database *see* treebank
grammatical deviance, 20
grammatical rules, 17–19
grammatical tagging, 8–9; *see also* tagging
    system *and* word-tagging
grammatical word, 153

HARPY, 29
headword, 152
heuristics, 23, 29, 54, 64, **79–80**
high-level languages, 23
higher-level constituents, **60–61**, 63
homographs, 8–9, 31, 153
homophones, 153
"horizontal" version, xi, 31, 41, 150
human processing of language, 2, 16–17,
    25–28
hyperbrackets, 61–64; *see also* brackets
hypertags, 60, 63, 68, 77, 88, 95
hyphens, 36, 38

IBM (UK) Ltd, 139n
IBM (UK) Scientific Centre, Winchester, x, 144
IBM Thomas J. Watson Research Center, New York, vii, 6, 133n
ICAME, viin, 5n, 163
ICL, x, 120n, 133, 136, 163
idiomlist, 59, 113–14, 115–17, 119, 138
  preparse idiomlist, 118
idiom-tagging, 33
idioms, grammatical, 123; *see also* LOB idioms
IDIOMTAG, 33, 35, 39–40, 49, 52, 53, 56, 66, 68, 111–14, 116–18, 125, 164
ill-formed input, 120–38
immediate constituent (IC), xiii, 25, 77, 90
inference-based approach, 2
inflexion, 152, 168
information retrieval, 137
information technology (IT), xiii, 18, 87
intelligence, 17, 29; *see also* artificial intelligence (AI)
intonation, 139–48
introspection, 14, 140–41
iterative process, 35

Journal of the Acoustical Society of America, 29

knowledge of language, 15
knowledge-based approach, 2
knowledge-resources, 12
Kučera, H., vii, x, 4, 8, 9, 58, 149, 153, 157, 163, 165
KWIC (Key Word In Context) *see* concordance

Lancaster, University of, vii, 5, 9, 22, 30, 36, 41, 66, 81, 136, 139, 145
language-production, 25
language-recognition, 25–26
Leeds, University of, vii, 22, 120n
left-branching structures, 25
lemma, 8, 153
lemmatization, 149, 152–55
lemmatized concordance, 9
lemmatized word frequency list, 9
Leuven Drama Corpus, 6
levels of analysis, 9, 12

lexeme, 8, 152, 153, 155
lexicographic research, 6, 8, 149
lexicon, 13, 14, 35–38, 52, 58, 59, 77, 102, 104–8, 110, 111, 124, 125, 128, 129, 131, 138, 164
lexicon of tagpairs, **68–70**, 79
likelihood, 21, 35, 39
  absolute, 126–30, 135–38
  relative, 57–59, 122, 124
linguistic competence, **27–28**, 29, 96
linguistic databases, 14–15; *see also* treebank
linguistic theories, 24, 44
Lisp, 23
LOB Corpus, vii-xii, **5–10**, 17–19, 24, 30, 31, 34, 35, 40–45, 51, 55, 56, 59, 67, 72, 76, 81, 83, 97, 99, 110, 124, 132, 145, 150, 152, 153, 156, 157, 163–66
LOB idioms, viii, **110–19**, 168
LOB references, xi, 31, 32
LOBFORMAT, 33, 40, 48, 125, 126, 128–30, 164
logic-based approaches, 27
logic-based models, 29
logical inferencing, 17
London–Lund Corpus, 6, 111, 168
Longman Dictionary of Contemporary English (LDOCE), 131–32, 149
LUNAR, 3, 18–19
Lund, University of, 10, 168–69

machine translation, xiii, 4, 14, 24
machine-readable corpora, 2, **4–6**, 8
machine-readable dictionaries, 131–32
mainframe computers, 5
man–machine interface, 4
manual intervention, 34, 35, 97, 101
marker symbols, 98–100, 104
MARKERRORS, 125
Markov models, **59–60**, 61–63, 132
matrix of tag-pair transition probabilities, 21, 39, 41, **45–46**, 49, 53–56, 110, 129, 130, 132, 164
METAL, 24
mnemonic significance, 30
model of computer text comprehension, 11
model of human cognition, 26
model of human language-processing, 22
Montreal, University of, 24
morphological analysis, 11, 37
morphological irregularity, 8, 152
morpho-syntactic variants, 152

mother-daughter relationship, 21–22,
  62–63, 77, 83
motor skills (robotics), 2

natural language front ends, 4
natural language generation, 13
natural language processing, vii, **2–4**, 9,
  13–15, 17, 18, 96
neologisms, 35, 131
Nijmegen, University of, 10, 168
NL *see* natural language
non-probabilistic techniques, 16, 21
non-terminal/terminal ratios, 83, 83n
normalisation, 76
Norwegian Computing Centre for the
  Humanities, Bergen, 5, 5n, 163
numerals, 36

optical character recognition (OCR), 4, 5,
  104
orthographic ambiguities, 97, 109
orthographic analysis, 11, 97
orthographic irregularity, 152
orthographic units, 31, 36, 40, 104, 111,
  163
orthographic variation, 107
orthographic word, 21, 166
Oslo, University of, x, 5, 9, 30, 36, 40
*Oxford Advanced Learner's Dictionary of Current
  English* (OALD), 131–32, 149, 168
Oxford Concordance Program, 136, 153
Oxford Text Archive, 6, 136

parse-tree, 21, 22, 60, 63, 64, 68, 76, 83,
  88
parsing, 6, 9–12, 18, 19, 26, 60, 146,
  148, 149
  automatic, 18, 30, 44, 82, 83, 86, 89,
    90, 94
  manual, 19, 76, 77, **82–84**
  probabilistic, **21–23**, 60–62, **66–81**
parsing scheme, viii, 63, 81, **82–96**
partial parse, 69, 76
Pascal, xii, 23, 163
performance *see* competence/performance
  distinction
phonetic transcription, 139–40, 144
phrase-structure grammar, 25
pitch movement, 144

post-editing, 30, 33, 35, 39, **40–41**, 42,
  48, 56, 102, 103, 109, 117
pragmatic analysis, 12
precision, 137–38
pre-editing, 30, **31–35**, 36, **99–101**,
  102–4, **105–6**, 107, 109
predictions, 2, 3, 10, 13, 14, 25, 45, 56
predictive power, 61
PREEDIT, **33–35**, 125, 164
prefixes, 38
PREPARSER, 118
probabilistic disambiguation *see*
  disambiguation
probabilistic grammar, 12, 62–63, **76–79**,
  138; *see also* constituent-likelihood
  grammar
probabilistic models, 16
probabilistic systems, 15, 26
probabilistic techniques, vii–ix, 2–3, 9,
  23–27, 29
probabilities
  additive, 47–51, 56
  conditional, 53, 56
  relative, 59, 73, 108
probability weightings, 59, 107, 111
production strategies, 25
productions, 14, 21, 22, 62, 77
programming language, 23
Prolog, 23
proper names [= proper nouns], 30, 36,
  100–2, 105, 107, 108, 166
prosodic features, 14
prosodic transcription, 144
psychological plausibility, 22
psychological realism, 26
psychological theory, 29
punctuation, xii, 9n, 14, 23, 33–4, 45,
  74, 83, 99, 100, 104–6, 108, 143,
  144, 166

quantitative methods, 2, 3; *see also*
  statistical methods *and* probabilistic
  techniques
question-and-answer systems, 4, 18, 121

rarity marker, 35, 46–47, 49
recall, 137–38
recordings, 143
registers, 142–43
relative likelihood function, 58, 60
reverse-order lists, 154–55

rewrite rules, 58, 65, 87
right-branching structures, 25
RUNNEWTAGSET, 132–33, 134

sampling, of texts, 7
Sapir, E., 19, 27, 93
scaling factor, 49, 54–55, 164
search space, 63–64
semantic analysis, 9, 11, 12, 149
semantic component, 60
semantics, 12, 26, 27, 60, 116
sense resolution, 11
sensory perception, 2
sentence-boundaries, 99, 105, 108
simulated annealing, x, 22, 64, 64n
singular branching, 88
speech analysis, 29
speech processing, 11
speech recognition, 4, 11, 62
speech research, 28, 29
speech synthesis, ix, x, 14, 139–40
speech-understanding systems, 29
spelling checker, 13, 14, 131, 149
spelling corrector, 13
spelling errors *see under* **errors**
spelling variants, 153
statistical methods, 16, 21, 24–25, 29,
      44–45; *see also* quantitative methods
      and probabilistic techniques
statistics, collection of, 77–78, 82
stochastic concepts, 22
stress, 14, 144, 146
style checker, 131, 149
stylistic acceptability, 4, 14
subcategorization, 61, 76, 78, 89
suffix rules, 157–161
suffix-stripping, 37, 152, 154, 155
suffixlist, 36–38, 59, 102, 107, 108, 128,
      129, 131, 138, 164
Suppes, P., 25
Survey of English Usage, 6
syntactic analysis, 9–12; *see also* parsing
syntactic recognition, 12
syntactic unit, 33, 35, 39
SYSTRAN, 24

T-tag assignment, 23, 68–72, 79–81
T-tag lexicon, 71–73
tag disambiguation *see* disambiguation
tag pairs, 110, 111, 121, 122, 126, 128,
      129, 130; *see also* matrix of tag-pair
      transition probabilities

tag selection, 42–56
tag triples, 54–55, 56, 111
tag-assignment, 33, 35, 52, 54, 102, 110,
      131
tag-transition frequencies, 21; *see also* matrix
      of tag-pair transition probabilities
tagging system, 31–33, 58, 67; *see also*
      grammatical tagging *and* word tagging
TAGGIT, 9, 10, 32–3, 34, 35, 42–45, 110,
      111
tagset, 9, 30, 31, 67, 70, 77, 106, 131,
      132, 145, **165–183**
   automatic generation of, 132–33
TAUM-METEO, 24
taxonomy, 94
text critiquing, ix, 4, 13, 15, 86, 149,
      156
text evaluation, 15
text synthesis, 13–14
text-to-speech synthesis, 4, 14, **139–148**
threshold, 47, 51, 56, 64, 121, 128, 130,
      133, 134, 137, 138, 151
tone group boundaries, 144
tone grouping, 146–47
top-down, 29
transformational grammars, 25–26
transition probabilities *see* matrix of tag-pair
      transition probabilities
translation, 16; *see also* machine translation
tree closing, 63–64, 73–76
tree evaluation function, 23, 63
tree shape, 86–87
tree-likelihood estimates, 22
treebank, 76–79, **82–84**, 90, 93, 168
triples *see* tag triples
type-token distribution, 58–59; *see also*
      word-types *and* word-tokens
typesetting, computerized, 6
typographic information, xi–xii, 33–34,
      103, 167
typographical shifts, xii, 17–18, 33, 98,
      101, 104

UCREL, vii–xiii, 14, 16, 20, 57, 60, 62,
      63, 86, 110, 111, 115, 116, 118,
      133, 149, 164, 166–69
unbounded movement rules, 87
ungrammatical sentences, 45, 54, 120; *see*
      also ill-formed input
unrestricted language, viii, 9, 16, 35–36,
      41, 65, 82, 121
upper case/lower case distinction, 34, 107,
      108; *see also* typographical shifts

"vertical" version, xi, 31, 99, 100, 102, 106–8, 111, 126, 166
verticalizing, 31–34, 105
vision, 2, 3
vocabulary, 31–2

weightings *see* probability weightings
well-formed/ill-formed dichotomy, 19–20, 23
wild tags, 114, 117
wildcards, 114

word class, 9, 13, 15
word processing, 6
word-initial capital (w.i.c.), xiii, 11, 34, 36, 38, 101, 102, 109, 168, 169
word-tagging, 10, 21, 30, 57, 60–62; *see also* grammatical tagging
word-tags *see* tagset
word-tokens, 8, 13, 58–59, 150, 154
word-types, 9, 14, 34, 58–59, 150–53
WORDTAG, 31, 33, **35–37**, 39, 40, 42 45–47, 49, 52, 61, 66, 102–6, 108, 110–14, 117, 125, 164